The *Readable* Delaware General Corporation Law

2020-2021 with Visilaw Markings

Lynn M. LoPucki

Diana—
Thanks for your great work in producing this edition
Lynn LoPucki

Key to VisiLaw Markings

Marking	Name	Description
■	Sentence	The mark indicates the end of a sentence that is not also the end of a paragraph.
Primary sentence structure		
❮text❯	Primary exception	The marks frame an exception to the remainder of the sentence.
If text **[then]**	Primary if-then	The marks indicate the primary if-then structure of the sentence, thus dividing the sentence into separately analyzable parts.
and	Primary conjunction	The marks identify a conjunction that indicates the relationship between the major clauses in a sentence or between subsections in a sentence.
Text	Skeletal sentence	Underlining indicates the main structure of independent and dependent clauses in the primary sentence structure. Highlighting is of the subject, verb, direct object, and adjectives, and adverbs that directly modify any of them. If there are more than one subjects, verbs, or direct objects, marking may be of one or all.
Secondary sentence structure		
◂text▸	Secondary exception	The marks frame an exception to some applications of the remainder of the sentence.
<u>If</u> text <u>then</u>	Secondary if-then	The marks indicate an if-then structure that divides only a particular clause or subsection of a sentence.
and	Secondary conjunction	The marks identify a conjunction that indicates second-level relationships between listed items or clauses that are not parts of the primary sentence structure. Tertiary conjunctions are not marked.
(text**)**	Cohesive phrase	The marks frame a group of words that should be read and considered as a unit.
	Custom markings	Readers may use colored pens and highlighters to make additional markings.

The *Readable* Delaware General Corporation Law

2020-2021 with VisiLaw Markings

Lynn M. LoPucki

© 2020 Lynn M. LoPucki

VisiLaw is a registered trademark of Lynn M. LoPucki

Table of Contents

Acknowledgments xi

Preface xiii

Introduction to the VisiLaw Marking System 1

Subchapter I. Formation

§ 101. Incorporators; how corporation formed; purposes. 9
§ 102. Contents of certificate of incorporation. 9
§ 103. Execution, acknowledgment, filing, recording and effective date of original certificate of incorporation and other instruments; exceptions. 15
§ 104. Certificate of incorporation; definition. 19
§ 105. Certificate of incorporation and other certificates; evidence. 20
§ 106. Commencement of corporate existence. 20
§ 107. Powers of incorporators. 20
§ 108. Organization meeting of incorporators or directors named in certificate of incorporation. 20
§ 109. Bylaws. 21
§ 110. Emergency bylaws and other powers in emergency. 22
§ 111. Jurisdiction to interpret, apply, enforce or determine the validity of corporate instruments and provisions of this title. 23
§ 112. Access to proxy solicitation materials. 24
§ 113. Proxy expense reimbursement. 25
§ 114. Application of chapter to nonstock corporations. 25
§ 115 Forum selection provisions. 26
§ 116. Document Form, Signature and Delivery. 26

Subchapter II. Powers 28

§ 121. General powers. 28
§ 122. Specific powers. 28
§ 123. Powers respecting securities of other corporations or entities. 30
§ 124. Effect of lack of corporate capacity or power; ultra vires. 30
§ 125. Conferring academic or honorary degrees. 30
§ 126. Banking power denied. 32
§ 127. Private foundation; powers and duties. 32

Subchapter III. Registered Office and Registered Agent 32

§ 131. Registered office in State; principal office or place of business in State 32
§ 132. Registered agent in State; resident agent. 32
§ 133. Change of location of registered office; change of registered agent. 36
§ 134. Change of address or name of registered agent. 36
§ 135. Resignation of registered agent coupled with appointment of successor. 37
§ 136. Resignation of registered agent not coupled with appointment of successor. 37

Table of Contents

Subchapter IV. Directors and Officers...38

- § 141. Board of directors; powers; number, qualifications, terms and quorum; committees; classes of directors; nonstock corporations; reliance upon books; action without meeting; removal..38
- § 142. Officers; titles, duties, selection, term; failure to elect; vacancies. 42
- § 143. Loans to employees and officers; guaranty of obligations of employees and officers. 42
- § 144. Interested directors; quorum. 43
- § 145. Indemnification of officers, directors, employees and agents; insurance...............43
- § 146. Submission of matters for stockholder vote...46

Subchapter V. Stock and Dividends 46

- § 151. Classes and series of stock; redemption; rights...46
- § 152. Issuance of stock; lawful consideration; fully paid stock....................................49
- § 153. Consideration for stock...50
- § 154. Determination of amount of capital; capital, surplus and net assets defined..........50
- § 155. Fractions of shares. 51
- § 156. Partly paid shares...51
- § 157. Rights and options respecting stock..51
- § 158. Stock certificates; uncertificated shares...52
- § 159. Shares of stock; personal property, transfer and taxation. 52
- § 160. Corporation's powers respecting ownership, voting, etc., of its own stock; rights of stock called for redemption..53
- § 161. Issuance of additional stock; when and by whom...54
- § 162. Liability of stockholder or subscriber for stock not paid in full............................54
- § 163. Payment for stock not paid in full..54
- § 164. Failure to pay for stock; remedies..55
- § 165. Revocability of preincorporation subscriptions. 55
- § 166. Formalities required of stock subscriptions. 55
- § 167. Lost, stolen or destroyed stock certificates; issuance of new certificate or uncertificated shares..55
- § 168. Judicial proceedings to compel issuance of new certificate or uncertificated shares. 56
- § 169. Situs of ownership of stock...56
- § 170. Dividends; payment; wasting asset corporations. 56
- § 171. Special purpose reserves...57
- § 172. Liability of directors and committee members as to dividends or stock redemption. 57
- § 173. Declaration and payment of dividends..58
- § 174. Liability of directors for unlawful payment of dividend or unlawful stock purchase or redemption; exoneration from liability; contribution among directors; subrogation...58

Subchapter VI. Stock Transfers..58

- § 201. Transfer of stock, stock certificates and uncertificated stock..............................58
- § 202. Restrictions on transfer and ownership of securities..59
- § 203. Business combinations with interested stockholders. 60
- § 204. Ratification of defective corporate acts and stock. 65
- § 205. Proceedings regarding validity of defective corporate acts and stock...................72

Subchapter VII. Meetings, Elections, Voting and Notice 74

- § 211. Meetings of stockholders..74
- § 212. Voting rights of stockholders; proxies; limitations...75
- § 213. Fixing date for determination of stockholders of record.....................................76
- § 214. Cumulative voting. 77
- § 215. Voting rights of members of nonstock corporations; quorum; proxies..................78

Table of Contents

§ 216. Quorum and required vote for stock corporations..79
§ 217. Voting rights of fiduciaries, pledgors and joint owners of stock.....................................80
§ 218. Voting trusts and other voting agreements..80
§ 219. List of stockholders entitled to vote; penalty for refusal to produce; stock
ledger...81
§ 220. Inspection of books and records...82
§ 221. Voting, inspection and other rights of bondholders and debenture holders. 84
§ 222. Notice of meetings and adjourned meetings. 84
§ 223. Vacancies and newly created directorships..85
§ 224. Form of records..86
§ 225. Contested election of directors; proceedings to determine validity..............................86
§ 226. Appointment of custodian or receiver of corporation on deadlock or for other
cause...87
§ 227. Powers of Court in elections of directors..88
§ 228. Consent of stockholders or members in lieu of meeting. 88
§ 229. Waiver of notice. 89
§ 230. Exception to requirements of notice. 90
§ 231. Voting procedures and inspectors of elections...90
§ 232. Delivery of notice; notice by electronic transmission. 91
§ 233. Notice to stockholders sharing an address. 93

Subchapter VIII. Amendment of Certificate of Incorporation; Changes in Capital and Capital Stock..93

§ 241. Amendment of certificate of incorporation before receipt of payment for stock. 93
§ 242. Amendment of certificate of incorporation after receipt of payment for stock;
nonstock corporations. 94
§ 243. Retirement of stock..96
§ 244. Reduction of capital. 97
§ 245. Restated certificate of incorporation. 97
§ 246. [Reserved.]..98

Subchapter IX. Merger, Consolidation or Conversion..98

§ 251. Merger or consolidation of domestic corporations..98
§ 252. Merger or consolidation of domestic and foreign corporations; service of
process upon surviving or resulting corporation. 106
§ 253. Merger of parent corporation and subsidiary corporation or corporations................109
§ 254. Merger or consolidation of domestic corporations and joint-stock or other
associations. 110
§ 255. Merger or consolidation of domestic nonstock corporations. 113
§ 256. Merger or consolidation of domestic and foreign nonstock corporations;
service of process upon surviving or resulting corporation. 115
§ 257. Merger or consolidation of domestic stock and nonstock corporations. 118
§ 258. Merger or consolidation of domestic and foreign stock and nonstock
corporations..120
§ 259. Status, rights, liabilities, of constituent and surviving or resulting corporations
following merger or consolidation. 121
§ 260. Powers of corporation surviving or resulting from merger or consolidation;
issuance of stock, bonds or other indebtedness. 121
§ 261. Effect of merger upon pending actions. 122
§ 262. Appraisal rights...122
§ 263. Merger or consolidation of domestic corporations and partnerships; service of
process upon surviving or resulting corporation or partnership. 127
§ 264. Merger or consolidation of domestic corporations and limited liability
companies; service of process upon surviving or resulting corporation or
limited liability company. 130
§ 265. Conversion of other entities to a domestic corporation...134
§ 266. Conversion of a domestic corporation to other entities...135

§ 267. Merger of parent entity and subsidiary corporation or corporations. 138

Subchapter X. Sale of Assets, Dissolution and Winding Up 140

§ 271. Sale, lease or exchange of assets; consideration; procedure. 140
§ 272. Mortgage or pledge of assets. 140
§ 273. Dissolution of joint venture corporation having 2 stockholders. 140
§ 274. Dissolution before issuance of shares or beginning of business; procedure. 141
§ 275. Dissolution generally; procedure. 142
§ 276. Dissolution of nonstock corporation; procedure. 142
§ 277. Payment of franchise taxes before dissolution, merger, transfer or conversion. 143
§ 278. Continuation of corporation after dissolution for purposes of suit and winding up affairs. 143
§ 279. Trustees or receivers for dissolved corporations; appointment; powers; duties. 144
§ 280. Notice to claimants; filing of claims. 144
§ 281. Payment and distribution to claimants and stockholders. 147
§ 282. Liability of stockholders of dissolved corporations. 148
§ 283. Jurisdiction. 148
§ 284. Revocation or forfeiture of charter; proceedings. 148
§ 285. Dissolution or forfeiture of charter by decree of court; filing. 149

Subchapter XI. Insolvency; Receivers and Trustees 149

§ 291. Receivers for insolvent corporations; appointment and powers. 149
§ 292. Title to property; filing order of appointment; exception. 149
§ 293. Notices to stockholders and creditors. 150
§ 294. Receivers or trustees; inventory; list of debts and report. 150
§ 295. Creditors' proofs of claims; when barred; notice. 150
§ 296. Adjudication of claims; appeal. 150
§ 297. Sale of perishable or deteriorating property. 151
§ 298. Compensation, costs and expenses of receiver or trustee. 151
§ 299. Substitution of trustee or receiver as party; abatement of actions. 151
§ 300. Employee's lien for wages when corporation insolvent. 151
§ 301. Discontinuance of liquidation. 151
§ 302. Compromise or arrangement between corporation and creditors or stockholders. 152
§ 303. Proceeding under the Federal Bankruptcy Code of the United States; effectuation. 152

Subchapter XII. Renewal, Revival, Extension and Restoration of Certificate of Incorporation or Charter 153

§ 311. Revocation of voluntary dissolution; restoration of expired certificate of incorporation. 153
§ 312. Revival of certificate of incorporation. 155
§ 313. Revival of certificate of incorporation or charter of exempt corporations. 158
§ 314. Status of corporation. 158

Subchapter XIII. Suits Against Corporations, Directors, Officers or Stockholders 159

§ 321. Service of process on corporations. 159
§ 322. Failure of corporation to obey order of court; appointment of receiver. 160
§ 323. Failure of corporation to obey writ of mandamus; quo warranto proceedings for forfeiture of charter. 160
§ 324. Attachment of shares of stock or any option, right or interest therein; procedure; sale; title upon sale; proceeds. 160
§ 325. Actions against officers, directors or stockholders to enforce liability of corporation; unsatisfied judgment against corporation. 161

§ 326. Action by officer, director or stockholder against corporation for corporate debt paid. 162
§ 327. Stockholder's derivative action; allegation of stock ownership. 162
§ 328. Effect of liability of corporation on impairment of certain transactions. 162
§ 329. Defective organization of corporation as defense. 162
§ 330. Usury; pleading by corporation. 162

Subchapter XIV. Close Corporations; Special Provisions 163

§ 341. Law applicable to close corporation. 163
§ 342. Close corporation defined; contents of certificate of incorporation. 163
§ 343. Formation of a close corporation. 163
§ 344. Election of existing corporation to become a close corporation. 163
§ 345. Limitations on continuation of close corporation status. 164
§ 346. Voluntary termination of close corporation status by amendment of certificate of incorporation; vote required. 164
§ 347. Issuance or transfer of stock of a close corporation in breach of qualifying conditions. 164
§ 348. Involuntary termination of close corporation status; proceeding to prevent loss of status. 165
§ 349. Corporate option where a restriction on transfer of a security is held invalid. 166
§ 350. Agreements restricting discretion of directors. 166
§ 351. Management by stockholders. 166
§ 352. Appointment of custodian for close corporation. 167
§ 353. Appointment of a provisional director in certain cases. 167
§ 354. Operating corporation as partnership. 168
§ 355. Stockholders' option to dissolve corporation. 168
§ 356. Effect of this subchapter on other laws. 169

Subchapter XV. Public Benefit Corporations 169

§ 361. Law applicable to public benefit corporations; how formed. 169
§ 362. Public benefit corporation defined; contents of certificate of incorporation. 169
§ 363. Nonprofit nonstock corporations. 170
§ 364. Stock certificates; notices regarding uncertificated stock. 170
§ 365. Duties of directors. 170
§ 366. Periodic statements and third-party certification. 170
§ 367. Suits to enforce the requirements of §365(a). 171
§ 368. No effect on other corporations. 171

Subchapter XVI. Foreign Corporations 171

§ 371. Definition; qualification to do business in State; procedure. 171
§ 372. Additional requirements in case of change of name, change of business purpose or merger or consolidation. 173
§ 373. Exceptions to requirements. 173
§ 374. Annual report. 174
§ 375. Failure to file report. 175
§ 376. Service of process upon qualified foreign corporations. 175
§ 377. Change of registered agent. 176
§ 378. Penalties for noncompliance. 176
§ 379. Banking powers denied. 176
§ 380. Foreign corporation as fiduciary in this State. 177
§ 381. Withdrawal of foreign corporation from State; procedure; service of process on Secretary of State. 177
§ 382. Service of process on nonqualifying foreign corporations. 178
§ 383. Actions by and against unqualified foreign corporations. 179
§ 384. Foreign corporations doing business without having qualified; injunctions. 179
§ 385. Filing of certain instruments with recorder of deeds not required. 180

Subchapter XVII. Domestication and Transfer 180
§ 388. Domestication of non-United States entities 180
§ 389. Temporary transfer of domicile into this State. 182
§ 390. Transfer, domestication or continuance of domestic corporations 186

Subchapter XVIII. Miscellaneous Provisions 190
§ 391. Amounts payable to Secretary of State upon filing certificate or other paper 190
§ 392. [Reserved.] 195
§ 393. Rights, liabilities and duties under prior statutes. 195
§ 394. Reserved power of State to amend or repeal chapter; chapter part of corporation's charter or certificate of incorporation 195
§ 395. Corporations using "trust" in name, advertisements and otherwise; restrictions; violations and penalties; exceptions. 195
§ 396. Publication of chapter by Secretary of State; distribution 196
§ 397. Penalty for unauthorized publication of chapter. 196
§ 398. Short title. 197

Acknowledgments

Tal Greitzer's broad understanding of desk-top publishing and astonishing facility with Word made this volume possible. Deborah E. Cupples of the University of Florida Law School provided valuable comments in the editing process. Elsa Duong assisted with the editing and publishing processes. While students at the UCLA School of Law, Yvonne Stoddard, Gautam Viadyanathan, Jessop Stroman, Maxwell Michael, Jordan McClenny, Brett Drucker, and Diana Yen assisted in manuscript preparation.

Preface

Although artfully drafted, the Delaware General Corporation Law (DGCL) is unreadable. Sentences are excessively long; one rambles on for nearly two pages. The DGCL sometimes follows the standard convention that divides complex statutory sentences into multiple paragraphs. But more often the DGCL defies convention by burying several sentences on different topics in a single paragraph. Roman numerals denoting list items hide undifferentiated in the midst of long block paragraphs. Although the DGCL's section headings are informative, sections are sometimes long and subsection headings are non-existent. Add to these problems the inherent difficulty in all statutory interpretation, the complexity of corporate law, and the excruciating explicitness of the Delaware drafters, and the result is an impenetrable law. All but the most determined readers simply bounce off.

This pamphlet presents a readable version of the DGCL (the RDGCL). It does that without ambiguity as to how the readable version compares to the official version.

Readability is achieved through a combination of techniques. Some are standard typographical techniques. The RDGCL employs running heads, squares and indents entire paragraphs rather than merely the first lines of paragraphs, uses leading to visually separate paragraphs, and bolds paragraph numbers, subparagraph numbers, and those troublesome list denoters.

What most enhances the RDGCL's readability, however, is the application of a grammar-based marking system (VisiLaw) to the statutory text. The most prominent marker, a solid black box, divides sections into sentences. The second most prominent, bold text underlined or boxed, divides lengthy sentences into their constituent clauses. The ability to see at a glance—not have to figure out—where sentences and clauses begin and end facilitates statutory analysis in the most basic sense: The bold markings break the text into constituent parts that the reader can analyze one part at a time.

Within each constituent clause, the skeletal sentence—subject, verb, direct object and a few other words—are underlined. The skeletal sentence is short and can be read separately. From it, the reader can quickly get the gist, and understand the structure, of the constituent clause.

For many readers, VisiLaw markings will be intuitive. To the extent they are not, the *Key to Visilaw Markings* inside the front cover provides guidance. But VisiLaw is more than immediately meets the eye. VisiLaw markings are tools that readers can, with practice, use in non-intuitive ways to save time and improve comprehension. For suggestions in this regard, read the *Introduction to the VisiLaw Marking System* that immediately follows.

The version of the DGCL presented in this volume is current through the legislative session ending June 30, 2020. It includes House Bill 341.

Lynn M. LoPucki
Los Angeles, California

Introduction to the VisiLaw Marking System

Statutory sentence structures are often complex. Visilaw is a system for marking statutes that is designed to make them easier to read and analyze. I have applied Visilaw markings to all of the statutes in this volume.

The markings provide at least six benefits.

(1) They promote analysis by visually dividing complex sentences into clauses that can be read and analyzed one-at-a-time.

(2) The highlighting of skeletal sentence structure within each clause facilitates scanning, speeds reading, and improves comprehension.

(3) The markings improve interpretation by indicating the grammatical structure of each sentence.

(4) The markings make reading easier and reduce reader stress by identifying cohesive phrases that can be treated as single units.

(5) Highlights make it easy to find the conjunctions that indicate the relationships among listed items and subparagraphs.

(6) The markings signal the relationships among clauses and phrases.

The markings are sufficiently intuitive that most readers will benefit even without prior instruction or practice. With instruction, practice, and experimentation, the markings can provide much greater benefits. I encourage you to think of them as a set of tools, the full power and scope of which differ from person to person. The remainder of this introduction explains what each of the markings means and provides suggestions on how to use them.

1. Sentences. Sentences are the fundamental building blocks of statutory material. Each can be analyzed separately. To analyze one, it is helpful to know where it begins and ends. Knowing can be difficult. Sentences often run across the visual boundaries of subsections and the device traditionally used to mark them – the lowly period – is so small as to be nearly invisible. The solution is to add a larger, more easily visible mark if the sentence does not end at the end of a section or subsection.

> *Example: Sentence Marking*
>
> If the end of a sentence is not the end of the section or subsection in which it appears, I have marked the end of the sentence with a solid black box, like this. ■ If a sentence ends at the end of a section or subsection, no marking is necessary and none appears.

How to use sentence-end marks: Note visually where the sentence of interest begins and ends before you try to read it. Ignore surrounding text until you grasp the meaning of the sentence.

2. Primary if-then clauses. Statutes are legislative commands in sentence form. In each sentence, the legislature indicates, expressly or impliedly, that if certain conditions are met, then certain consequences follow. Although not all statutes are structured as if-then statements, if-then structure is natural and common for well-drafted statutory material.

The if-then structure of statutory sentences is often obvious. The sentence begins with the word "if" followed by a clause that specifies conditions (the "if-clause"), and finishes with the word "then" followed by a clause that specifies consequences (the "then-clause"). Typically, each of the clauses contains a subject, a verb, and perhaps a direct object. But for the dependent marker words "if" and "then," each clause could have been a sentence on its own. Together, the two clauses typically comprise the entire sentence.

I refer to such an if-then structure as a "primary" structure to distinguish it from secondary structures that appear within independent or dependent clauses. I have marked primary if-then structures by making the "if" and "then" boldface and underlining them.

> *Example: Primary If-Then Clause Marking*
>
> **<u>If</u>** this sentence were in a statute, **<u>then</u>** I would have marked it like this.

Primary ifs and thens receive the most prominent marking used within a sentence because they divide the sentence into parts that the reader can analyze separately.

The words "if" and "then" do not appear in every statute that has an if-then structure. First, statute drafters often substitute structurally equivalent words for "if." Examples include "when," "while," "until," "unless," "wherever" and "to the extent that." I have marked those equivalents in the same manner as "if." Second, drafters often leave the word "then" implied. I made each implied then express, placing it in brackets to indicate that it does not appear in the statute. An implied "then" looks like this: **[<u>then</u>]**.

How to use primary if-then marks: Primary if-then markings enable the reader to see the position of the if-then structure before starting to read. Because each clause is in essence a sentence, the reader can read one and grasp its meaning before reading the other. The reader also can read the clauses in either order, depending on the reader's interests. By scanning the if clauses in a group of statutes, a reader can determine which of those statutes will apply to his or her case. By scanning the then clauses in group of statutes, a reader can determine which statutes might yield a desired result.

3. Primary conjunctions. Two kinds of conjunctions are primary: sentence dividers and paragraph dividers. A sentence divider separates clauses. By "clause" I mean a dependent or an independent clause that contains the basic elements of a sentence – subject, verb, and perhaps direct object. The clauses separated can be multiple if-clauses (if a and if b then c), multiple then clauses (if a, then b and then c), or multiple independent clauses (a and b). Most primary conjunctions are "and" or "or."

Example: Primary Conjunction Marking

I have made primary conjunctions boldface, **and** I have boxed their texts.

In statutes, unlike in prose, a single sentence is often divided into multiple paragraphs. The motivation of the drafters is usually to group together words that should be read together because they comprise one item in a list. Thus if there is a paragraph a, there will be a paragraph b, and perhaps additional paragraphs of the series. In nearly every instance, the paragraphs are alternative requirements only one of which must be met – indicated by "or" between the last two paragraphs – or multiple requirements all of which must be met – indicated by "and" between the last two paragraphs. I refer to these conjunctions as paragraph dividers because, although they usually appear only at the end of the penultimate paragraph in the list, they implicitly appear between each pair of paragraphs in the list. Unfortunately, paragraph dividers seldom appear where statute readers need them – at the end of the first paragraph in the series. Amidst paragraphs and subparagraphs, they can be difficult to find. To make finding them easier, I have highlighted conjunctions that are primary – first level – paragraph dividers in the same manner that I highlighted conjunctions that are sentence dividers.

How to use primary conjunctions: Except when they appear at the end of a paragraph, treat primary conjunctions as sentence sub-dividers – equal to an "if" or a "then," but superior to all other dividers. For example, treat the following sentence as divided into three parts (an independent clause, an if-clause, and a then-clause:

"Sales of accounts are security interests and if security interests are in default, **then** they may be foreclosed."

4. Skeletal sentences. A "skeletal sentence" consists of the subject, verb, and direct object of an independent or dependent clause, along with the articles, adjectives, and adverbs that directly modify the subject, verb, or direct object. I have underlined the words that comprise a skeletal sentence. That marking accomplishes two things. First, it defines a short sentence or independent clause – that is, a complete thought – that, when read, conveys the gist of the entire sentence or clause. Second, it divides that sentence or independent clause into a highlighted core structure and other, un-highlighted words and phrases that modify words in the core structure.

I have highlighted at least one skeletal sentence for nearly every sentence that appears in the statutes. If a sentence is divided into primary if-then clauses, I have marked a skeletal sentence in each if-clause and in each then-clause.

> *Example: Skeletal Sentence and Primary Conjunction Markings*
>
> A security interest in property subject to a statute, regulation, or treaty described in subsection (a) may be perfected only by compliance with those requirements, and a security interest so perfected remains perfected notwithstanding a change in the use or transfer of possession of the collateral.

The primary "and" divides this sentence into two parts. The underlining indicates the gist of each part. The gist of the first is that "a security interest may be perfected." The gist of the second is that "a security interest so perfected remains perfected."

> *How to use skeletal sentences:* Begin by noting where the sentence begins and ends. Then look for primary if-then structures and primary conjunctions. If they appear, they divide the sentence into separately-analyzable parts. Each part is a clause with its own subject and verb. The smaller number of underlined words in a part constitute the skeletal sentence for that part. Focus on one such skeletal sentence. Read the skeletal sentence first to understand generally what the sentence does. Then consider how the remaining words of the sentence change its meaning. Keep in mind that the most important words in the sentence may not be in the skeletal sentence. The skeletal sentence underlining indicates *structure*, not *importance*.

5. Secondary if-then clauses. If-then structures that do not qualify as primary are secondary. An if-then structure may not qualify as primary because (1) it does not divide the sentence into sub-sentences that can be analyzed in isolation, or (2) the condition relates to only a part of the sentence. Most secondary if-clauses state conditions that, if met, result not in the primary consequence, but in some lesser consequence. I have highlighted secondary if and then clauses by double-underlining the "ifs," "thens," and equivalents.

> *Example: Secondary If-then Marking*
>
> UCC § 9-203(b)(3) provides that a security interest is enforceable only if one of the following conditions is met:
>
> **(A)** the debtor has authenticated a security agreement that provides a description of the collateral and, <u>if</u> the security interest covers timber to be cut, [<u>then</u>] a description of the land concerned;

This if-then structure is secondary because the first requirement in subsection (A) – a description of collateral – applies even if the condition is not met. The condition determines only the need for a description of the land.

Independent clauses having both a subject and a verb usually do not exist within secondary if or then clauses. Even when they do, I have not marked them as skeletal sentences to avoid confusion with primary skeletal sentences.

> *How to use secondary if-then clauses:* Locate the "if" and corresponding "then." Consider each clause separately, but keep in mind that elements of the clause may be implied from and found in, other parts of the sentence. If the condition is met, the condition becomes irrelevant. You can read the sentence as if the conditional language were not present. If the condition is not met, the entire secondary if-then clause becomes irrelevant. You can read the sentence as if the secondary if-then clause were not present.

6. Primary exceptions. A primary exception is an exception that applies to the entire sentence. That is, if the terms of the exception are met, the sentence has no application. I have used prominent parentheses that appear as half-circles to mark the beginning and end of each primary exception. They appear like ❨this❩.

> *How to use primary exceptions:* Depending on the circumstances that brought the reader to the statute, the reader can either (1) analyze the section, ignoring the exception language until the analysis is complete, or (2) analyze the exception, ignoring the remainder of the exception until the reader determines whether the exception has rendered it irrelevant.

7. Secondary exceptions. A secondary exception is an exception from part of a sentence, but not from the entire sentence. I have indicated the beginning and end of significant secondary exceptions with prominent parentheses that appear as half-diamonds. They look like ◀this▶.

> *How to use secondary exceptions:* Readers can ignore the secondary exception in analyzing the part of the sentence to which the secondary exception applies, until after the reader has analyzed that part.

8. Cohesive phrases. A cohesive phrase is a group of words that are best read as a single unit. A cohesive phrase may be a term or art, a qualification, the specification of an amount, or the specification of a hypothetical (to name just a few possibilities). Sometimes it may be helpful to think of the entire phrase as a multi-word noun. The phrase may be two or three words, or it may continue for several lines of text. I used bold parentheses to mark the beginning and end of each cohesive phrase.

Example: Cohesive Phrases

[T]he term "contractual right" includes a right set forth in a rule or bylaw of . . . **(**a securities clearing agency,**) (**a contract market designated under the Commodity Exchange Act,**) (**a derivatives transaction execution facility registered under the Commodity Exchange Act,**)** or **(**a board of trade (as defined in the Commodity Exchange Act)**)**, or in a resolution of the governing board thereof,

---

As in the above example, cohesive phrases are often items in a list. When they are, each item is likely to start with the same word and a conjunction indicating the relationship among them will appear between the last two items. When cohesive phrases are used as terms of art, they tend to repeat in the same sentence or in nearby sentences.

Cohesive phrases may be nested one within another. Each may have its own complex structure within it. To maintain simplicity in the marking system, I marked only a single level of those cohesive phrases. That is, the cohesive phrases I marked do not overlap and are not nested. Nor do they overlap with skeletal sentences. They are always in peripheral parts of the sentence.

> *How to use cohesive phrases:* Read cohesive phrases from the inside out. That is, begin by reading and understanding the phrase as a unit. Then consider that unit in the context of the sentence. If the cohesive phrase is a modifier, try to determine what it modifies. If cohesive phrases appear in a list, examine the context to determine the consequence or significance of appearing on the list. Scan surrounding sentences to see if the same cohesive phrase appears in them.

9. Secondary conjunctions. A conjunction is secondary if it indicates an important relationship, but does not qualify as a primary conjunction. (Most conjunctions qualify as neither primary nor secondary.) Secondary conjunctions appear in a smaller font and in text boxes.

I have used secondary conjunction marks in three ways. First, in skeletal sentences, they indicate the relationship between multiple subjects, verbs, or direct objects. Second, in lists composed of cohesive phrases, they indicate the relationship among the cohesive phrases. Third, where I have marked primary conjunctions to indicate the relationships among subparagraphs, I have marked secondary conjunctions to indicate the relationships among *sub*-subparagraphs.

> *Example: Secondary Conjunction*
>
> Secondary conjunctions appear in a smaller, not bolded font and in text boxes.

> *How to use secondary conjunctions:* Read secondary conjunctions that appear within the bounds of a skeletal sentence as part of the skeletal sentence (unless the context otherwise requires). Read secondary conjunctions that appear between cohesive phrases as indicating the relationship between the cohesive phrases. The "and" in the phrase "**(a)** and **(b)**" exemplifies this circumstance. When seeking to determine the relationship among items listed in sub-subparagraphs, look for the secondary conjunction at the end of the penultimate item in the list.

If the cohesive phrases are lengthy and more than two appear in the same list, in rare instances I replicated the conjunction between each pair of listed items. Of course, I put the conjunction in brackets to indicate its addition. To illustrate, if the sentence contained the structure "**(a)**, **(b)**, and **(c)**" and the second cohesive phrase was lengthy, I might render it "**(a)** [and] **(b)**, and **(c)**."

10. Custom markings. Readers may find it useful to add their own markings to this book. The most common reason for doing to is to indicate importance. Because my markings are in black, readers need only use color for their markings to be easily distinguishable.

> *Suggestions for custom markings.* Readers may wish to highlight words that are not included in the skeletal sentence, but that are crucial to the meaning of the sentence. Readers seeking to apply a statutory provision to a real or hypothetical case may wish to highlight the particular words that apply. A red or blue pen will do that nicely.

The marking system I used for this book is called "VisiLaw." I am the inventor and a patent application is pending. VisiLaw is a work-in-progress. If you have comments on the utility of VisiLaw or suggestions as to how VisiLaw can be improved, please share them with us.

NOTE ON EDITING

The official texts of the statutes seldom contain boldface, italics, underlining, or any of the other text features used in VisiLaw Markings. When Visilaw features appear, it is because I added them. In some instances, I added a single, implied word (usually "then," but on rare occasions "and" or "or") that marks an important division of a sentence. The added word appears in brackets. For example, "[then]."

TITLE 8, Corporations. Chapter 1. General Corporation Law

Subchapter I. Formation

§ 101. Incorporators; how corporation formed; purposes.

(a) <u>Any person</u>, partnership, association or corporation, singly or jointly with others, and without regard to such person's or entity's residence, domicile or state of incorporation, <u>may incorporate</u> or organize a corporation under this chapter by filing with the Division of Corporations in the Department of State a certificate of incorporation which shall be executed, acknowledged and filed in accordance with § 103 of this title.

(b) <u>A corporation may be incorporated</u> or organized under this chapter to conduct or promote any lawful business or purposes, ◄except as may otherwise be provided by the Constitution or other law of this State.►

(c) <u>Corporations</u> for constructing, maintaining and operating public utilities, whether in or outside of this State, <u>may be organized</u> under this chapter, but corporations for constructing, maintaining and operating public utilities within this State <u>shall be subject to</u>, in addition to this chapter, <u>the special provisions</u> and requirements of Title 26 applicable to such corporations.

§ 102. Contents of certificate of incorporation.

(a) <u>The certificate of incorporation shall set forth</u>:

(1) <u>The name</u> of the corporation, which (i) <u>shall contain 1</u> of the words "association," "company," "corporation," "club," "foundation," "fund," "incorporated," "institute," "society," "union," "syndicate," or "limited," (or abbreviations thereof, with or without punctuation), or <u>words</u> (or abbreviations thereof, with or without punctuation) of like import of foreign countries or jurisdictions (provided they are written in roman characters or letters); ◄provided, however, that the Division of Corporations in the Department of State may waive such requirement (unless it determines that such name is, or might otherwise appear to be, that of a natural person) if such corporation executes, acknowledges and files with the Secretary of State in accordance with § 103 of this title a certificate stating that its total assets, as defined in § 503(i) of this title, are not less than $10,000,000, or, in the sole discretion of the Division of Corporations in the Department of State, if the corporation is both a nonprofit nonstock corporation and an association of professionals,► (ii) <u>shall be such as to distinguish it</u> upon the records in the office of the Division of Corporations in the Department of State from the names that are reserved on such records and from the names on such records of each other corporation, partnership, limited partnership, limited liability company, registered series of a limited liability company, registered series of a limited partnership or statutory trust organized or registered as a domestic or foreign corporation, partnership,

limited partnership, limited liability company, registered series of a limited liability company, registered series of a limited partnership or statutory trust under the laws of this State, ◄except with the written consent of the person who has reserved such name or such other foreign corporation or domestic or foreign partnership, limited partnership, limited liability company, registered series of a limited liability company, registered series of a limited partnership or statutory trust, executed, acknowledged and filed with the Secretary of State in accordance with § 103 of this title,► or ◄except that, without prejudicing any rights of the person who has reserved such name or such other foreign corporation or domestic or foreign partnership, limited partnership, limited liability company, registered series of a limited liability company, registered series of a limited partnership or statutory trust, the Division of Corporations in the Department of State may waive such requirement if the corporation demonstrates to the satisfaction of the Secretary of State that the corporation or a predecessor entity previously has made substantial use of such name or a substantially similar name, that the corporation has made reasonable efforts to secure such written consent, and that such waiver is in the interest of the State, ► **(iii)** ◄except as permitted by § 395 of this title,► shall not contain the word "trust," and **(iv)** shall not contain the word "bank," or any variation thereof, ◄except for the name of a bank reporting to and under the supervision of the State Bank Commissioner of this State or a subsidiary of a bank or savings association (as those terms are defined in the Federal Deposit Insurance Act, as amended, at 12 U.S.C. § 1813), or a corporation regulated under the Bank Holding Company Act of 1956, as amended, 12 U.S.C. § 1841 et seq., or the Home Owners' Loan Act, as amended, 12 U.S.C. § 1461 et seq.;► ◄provided, however, that this section shall not be construed to prevent the use of the word "bank," or any variation thereof, in a context clearly not purporting to refer to a banking business or otherwise likely to mislead the public about the nature of the business of the corporation or to lead to a pattern and practice of abuse that might cause harm to the interests of the public or the State as determined by the Division of Corporations in the Department of State;►

(2) The address (which shall be stated in accordance with § 131(c) of this title) of the corporation's registered office in this State, and the name of its registered agent at such address;

(3) The nature of the business or purposes to be conducted or promoted. ■ It shall be sufficient to state, either alone or with other businesses or purposes, that **(**the purpose of the corporation is to engage in any lawful act or activity for which corporations may be organized under the General Corporation Law of Delaware,**)** and by such statement all lawful acts and activities shall be within the purposes of the corporation, ◄except for express limitations, if any;►

(4) If the corporation is to be authorized to issue only 1 class of stock, [then] the total number of shares of stock which the corporation shall have authority to issue and the par value of each of such shares, or a statement that all such shares are to be without par value. ■ If the corporation is to be authorized to issue more than 1 class of stock, [then] the certificate of incorporation shall set forth the total number of shares of all classes of stock which the corporation shall have authority to issue and the number of shares of each class and shall specify each class the shares of which are to be without par value and each class the shares of which are to have par value and the par value of the shares of each such class. ■ The certificate of incorporation shall also set forth a statement of the designations and the powers, preferences and rights, and the qualifications, limitations or restrictions thereof, which are permitted by § 151 of this title in respect of any class or classes of stock or any series of any class of stock of the corporation and the fixing of which by the certificate of incorporation is desired, and an express grant of such authority as it may then be desired to grant to the board of directors to fix by resolution or resolutions (any thereof that may be desired but which shall not be fixed by the certificate of incorporation.) ■ The foregoing provisions of this paragraph shall not apply to nonstock corporations. ■ In the case of nonstock corporations, the fact that they are not authorized to issue capital stock shall be stated in the certificate of incorporation. ■ The conditions of membership, or other criteria for identifying members, of nonstock corporations shall likewise be stated in the certificate of incorporation or the bylaws. ■ Nonstock corporations shall have members, but failure to have members shall not affect otherwise valid corporate acts or work a forfeiture or dissolution of the corporation. ■ Nonstock corporations may provide for classes or groups of members having relative rights, powers and duties, and may make provision for the future creation of additional classes or groups of members having (such relative rights, powers and duties as may from time to time be established, including rights, powers and duties senior to existing classes and groups of members.) ■ (Except as otherwise provided in this chapter,) nonstock corporations may also provide that any member or class or group of members shall have full, limited, or no voting rights or powers, including that (any member or class or group of members shall have the right to vote on a specified transaction even if that member or class or group of members does not have the right to vote for the election of the members of the governing body of the corporation.) ■ Voting by members of a nonstock corporation may be on a per capita, number, financial interest, class, group, or any other basis set forth. ■ The provisions referred to in the 3 preceding sentences may be set forth in the certificate of incorporation or the bylaws. ■ If neither the certificate of incorporation nor the bylaws of a nonstock corporation state the conditions of membership, or other criteria for identifying members, [then] the members of the corporation shall be deemed to be those entitled to vote for the election of the members of the governing body pursuant to the certificate of incorporation or bylaws of such corporation or otherwise (until thereafter otherwise provided by the certificate of incorporation or the bylaws;)

(5) The name and mailing address of the incorporator or incorporators;

(6) If the powers of the incorporator or incorporators are to terminate upon the filing of the certificate of incorporation, [then] the names and mailing addresses of the persons (who are to serve as directors until the first annual meeting of stockholders or until their successors are elected and qualify.)

(b) In addition to the matters required to be set forth in the certificate of incorporation by subsection (a) of this section, the certificate of incorporation may also contain any or all of the following matters:

(1) [Then] Any provision for the management of the business and for the conduct of the affairs of the corporation, and any provision creating, defining, limiting and regulating the powers of the corporation, the directors, and the stockholders, or any class of the stockholders, or the governing body, members, or any class or group of members

of a nonstock corporation; <u>if</u> such provisions are not contrary to the laws of this State. ■ <u>Any provision</u> which is required or permitted by any section of this chapter to be stated in the bylaws <u>may instead be stated</u> in the certificate of incorporation;

(2) The following provisions, in haec verba,

(i), for a corporation other than a nonstock corporation, viz:

"**Whenever** <u>a compromise</u> or arrangement <u>is proposed</u> between this corporation and its creditors or any class of them and/or between this corporation and its stockholders or any class of them, **[then]** <u>any court</u> of equitable jurisdiction within the State of Delaware <u>may</u>, on the application in a summary way of this corporation or of any creditor or stockholder thereof or on the application of any receiver or receivers appointed for this corporation under § 291 of Title 8 of the Delaware Code or on the application of trustees in dissolution or of any receiver or receivers appointed for this corporation under § 279 of Title 8 of the Delaware Code <u>order a meeting</u> of the creditors or class of creditors, and/or of the stockholders or class of stockholders of this corporation, as the case may be, to be summoned in such manner as the said court directs. ■ **If** <u>a majority</u> in number <u>representing three fourths</u> in value of the creditors or class of creditors, and/or of the stockholders or class of stockholders of this corporation, as the case may be, <u>agree</u> to any compromise or arrangement and to any reorganization of this corporation as consequence of such compromise or arrangement, **[then]** <u>the said compromise or arrangement</u> and <u>the said reorganization shall</u>, if sanctioned by the court to which the said application has been made, <u>be binding</u> on all the creditors or class of creditors, and/or on all the stockholders or class of stockholders, of this corporation, as the case may be, and also on this corporation"; or

(ii), for a nonstock corporation, viz:

"**Whenever** <u>a compromise or arrangement is proposed</u> between this corporation and its creditors or any class of them and/or between this corporation and its members or any class of them, **[then]** <u>any court</u> of equitable jurisdiction within the State of Delaware <u>may</u>, on the application in a summary way of this corporation or of any creditor or member thereof or on the application of any receiver or receivers appointed for this corporation under § 291 of Title 8 of the Delaware Code or on the application of trustees in dissolution or of any receiver or receivers appointed for this corporation under § 279 of Title 8 of the Delaware Code <u>order a meeting</u> of the creditors or class of creditors, and/or of the members or class of members of this corporation, as the case may be, to be summoned in such manner as the said court directs. ■ **If** <u>a majority</u> in number <u>representing three fourths</u> in value of the creditors or class of creditors, and/or of the members or class of members of this corporation, as the case may be, <u>agree</u> to any compromise or arrangement and to any reorganization of this corporation as consequence of such compromise or arrangement, **[then]** <u>the said compromise or arrangement</u> and <u>the said reorganization shall</u>, if sanctioned by the court to which the said application has been made, <u>be binding</u> on all the creditors or class of creditors, and/or on all the members or class of members, of this corporation, as the case may be, and also on this corporation";

(3) Such provisions as may be desired granting to the holders of the stock of the corporation, or the holders of any class or series of a class thereof, (the preemptive right to subscribe to any or all additional issues of stock of the corporation of any or all classes or series thereof, or to any securities of the corporation convertible into such stock.) ■ [Then] No stockholder shall have any preemptive right to subscribe to an additional issue of stock or to any security convertible into such stock **unless**, and except to the extent that, such right is expressly granted to such stockholder in the certificate of incorporation. ■ All such rights in existence on July 3, 1967, shall remain in existence unaffected by this paragraph ◄unless and until changed or terminated by appropriate action which expressly provides for the change or termination;►

(4) Provisions requiring for any corporate action, the vote of (a larger portion of the stock or of any class or series thereof, or of any other securities having voting power,) or (a larger number of the directors,) than is required by this chapter;

(5) A provision limiting the duration of the corporation's existence to a specified date; otherwise, the corporation shall have perpetual existence;

(6) A provision imposing personal liability for the debts of the corporation on its stockholders to a specified extent and upon specified conditions; otherwise, the stockholders of a corporation shall not be personally liable for the payment of the corporation's debts except as they may be liable by reason of their own conduct or acts;

(7) A provision eliminating or limiting the personal liability of a director to the corporation or its stockholders for monetary damages for breach of fiduciary duty as a director, provided that such provision shall not eliminate or limit the liability of a director:(i) For any breach of the director's duty of loyalty to the corporation or its stockholders; (ii) for acts or omissions not in good faith or which involve intentional misconduct or a knowing violation of law; (iii) under § 174 of this title; or (iv) for any transaction from which the director derived an improper personal benefit. ■ No such provision shall eliminate or limit the liability of a director for any act or omission occurring prior to the date when such provision becomes effective. ■ [Then] An amendment, repeal or elimination of such a provision shall not affect its application with respect to an act or omission by a director occurring before such amendment, repeal or elimination **unless** the provision provides otherwise at the time of such act or omission. ■ All references in this paragraph to a director shall also be deemed to refer to such other person or persons, if any, (who, pursuant to a provision of the certificate of incorporation in accordance with § 141(a) of this title, exercise or perform any of the powers or duties otherwise conferred or imposed upon the board of directors by this title.)

(c) It shall not be necessary to set forth in the certificate of incorporation any of the powers conferred on corporations by this chapter.

(d) ◄Except for provisions included pursuant to paragraphs (a)(1), (a)(2), (a)(5), (a)(6), (b)(2), (b)(5), (b)(7) of this section, and provisions included pursuant to paragraph (a)(4) of this section specifying the classes, number of shares, and par value of shares a corporation other than a nonstock corporation is authorized to issue,► any provision of the certificate of incorporation may be made dependent upon facts ascertainable outside such instrument, provided that the manner in which such facts shall operate upon the provision is clearly and explicitly set forth therein. ■ The term "facts," as used in this subsection, includes, but is not limited to, the occurrence of any event, including a determination or action by (any person or body, including the corporation).

(e) The exclusive right to the use of a name that is available for use by a domestic or foreign corporation may be reserved by or on behalf of:

(1) Any person intending to incorporate or organize a corporation with that name under this chapter or contemplating such incorporation or organization;

(2) Any domestic corporation or any foreign corporation qualified to do business in the State of Delaware, in either case, intending to change its name or contemplating such a change;

(3) Any foreign corporation intending to qualify to do business in the State of Delaware and adopt that name or contemplating such qualification and adoption; and

(4) Any person intending to organize a foreign corporation and have it qualify to do business in the State of Delaware and adopt that name or contemplating such organization, qualification and adoption.

The reservation of a specified name may be made by filing with the Secretary of State an application, executed by the applicant, (certifying that the reservation is made by or on behalf of a domestic corporation, foreign corporation or other person described in paragraphs (e)(1)-(4) of this section above,) and (specifying the name to be reserved and the name and address of the applicant.) ■ If the Secretary of State finds that the name is available for use by a domestic or foreign corporation, [then] the Secretary shall reserve the name for the use of the applicant for a period of 120 days. ■ The same applicant may renew for successive 120-day periods a reservation of a specified name by filing with the Secretary of State, prior to the expiration of such reservation (or renewal thereof), an application for renewal of such reservation, executed by the applicant, (certifying that the reservation is renewed by or on behalf of a domestic corporation, foreign corporation or other person described in paragraphs (e)(1)-(4) of this section above) and (specifying the name reservation to be renewed and the name and address of the applicant.) ■ The right to the exclusive use of a reserved name may be transferred to any other person by filing in the office of the Secretary of State a notice of the transfer, executed by the applicant for whom the name was reserved, specifying (the name reservation to be transferred) and (the name and address of the transferee.) ■ The reservation of a specified name may be cancelled by filing with the Secretary of State a notice of cancellation, executed by the applicant or transferee, specifying (the name reservation to be cancelled) and (the name and address of the applicant or transferee.) ■ Unless the Secretary of State finds that any application, application for renewal, notice of transfer, or notice of cancellation filed with the Secretary of State as required by this subsection does not conform to law, [then] upon receipt of all filing fees required by law the Secretary of State shall prepare and return to the person who filed such instrument a copy of the filed instrument with a notation thereon of the action taken by the Secretary of State. ■ A fee as set forth in § 391 of this title shall be paid (at the time of the reservation of any name,) (at the time of the renewal of any such reservation) and (at the time of the filing of a notice of the transfer or cancellation of any such reservation.)

(f) The certificate of incorporation may not contain any provision that would impose liability on a stockholder for the attorneys' fees or expenses of the corporation or any other party in connection with an internal corporate claim, as defined in § 115 of this title.

§ 103. Execution, acknowledgment, filing, recording and effective date of original certificate of incorporation and other instruments; exceptions.

(a) <u>Whenever</u> <u>any instrument is to be filed</u> with the Secretary of State or in accordance with this section or chapter, **[then]** <u>such instrument shall be executed as follows:</u>

(1) <u>The certificate of incorporation</u>, and any other instrument to be filed before the election of the initial board of directors if the initial directors were not named in the certificate of incorporation, <u>shall be signed</u> by the incorporator or incorporators (or, in the case of any such other instrument, such incorporator's or incorporators' successors and assigns). ∎ **If** <u>any incorporator is not available</u> **then** <u>any such other instrument may be signed</u>, with the same effect as if such incorporator had signed it, by any person for whom or on whose behalf such incorporator, in executing the certificate of incorporation, was acting directly or indirectly as employee or agent, `provided that` such other instrument shall state **(**that such incorporator is not available and the reason therefor**)**, **(**that such incorporator in executing the certificate of incorporation was acting directly or indirectly as employee or agent for or on behalf of such person**)**, `and` **(**that such person's signature on such instrument is otherwise authorized and not wrongful**)**.

(2) <u>All other instruments shall be signed</u>:

a. By any authorized officer of the corporation; `or`

b. <u>If</u> it shall appear from the instrument that there are no such officers, <u>then</u> by a majority of the directors or by such directors as may be designated by the board; `or`

c. <u>If</u> it shall appear from the instrument that there are no such officers or directors, <u>then</u> by the holders of record, or such of them as may be designated by the holders of record, of a majority of all outstanding shares of stock; `or`

d. By the holders of record of all outstanding shares of stock.

(b) <u>Whenever</u> <u>this chapter requires any instrument</u> to be acknowledged, **[then]** <u>such requirement is satisfied</u> by either:

(1) The formal acknowledgment by the person or 1 of the persons signing the instrument **(**that it is such person's act and deed or the act and deed of the corporation**)**, `and` **(**that the facts stated therein are true**)**. ∎ <u>Such acknowledgment shall be made</u> before a person who is authorized by the law of the place of execution to take acknowledgments of deeds. ∎ **If** <u>such person has a seal</u> of office **[then]** <u>such person shall affix it</u> to the instrument.

(2) The signature, without more, of the person or persons signing the instrument, in which case such signature or signatures shall constitute the affirmation or acknowledgment of the signatory, under penalties of perjury, **(**that the instrument is such person's act and deed or the act and deed of the corporation**)**, `and` **(**that the facts stated therein are true**)**.

(c) Whenever any instrument is to be filed with the Secretary of State or in accordance with this section or chapter, [then] such requirement means that:

(1) The signed instrument shall be delivered to the office of the Secretary of State;

(2) All taxes and fees authorized by law to be collected by the Secretary of State in connection with the filing of the instrument shall be tendered to the Secretary of State; and

(3) Upon delivery of the instrument, the Secretary of State shall record the date and time of its delivery. ■ Upon such delivery and tender of the required taxes and fees, the Secretary of State shall certify that the instrument has been filed in the Secretary of State's office by endorsing upon the signed instrument the word "Filed", and the date and time of its filing. ■ This endorsement is the "filing date" of the instrument, and is conclusive of the date and time of its filing in the absence of actual fraud. ■ The Secretary of State shall file and index the endorsed instrument. ■ (Except as provided in paragraph (c)(4) of this section and in subsection (i) of this section), such filing date of an instrument shall be the date and time of delivery of the instrument.

(4) Upon request made upon or prior to delivery, the Secretary of State may, to the extent deemed practicable, establish as the filing date of an instrument a date and time after its delivery. ■ If the Secretary of State refuses to file any instrument due to an error, omission or other imperfection, [then] the Secretary of State may hold such instrument in suspension, and in such event, upon (delivery of a replacement instrument in proper form for filing) and (tender of the required taxes and fees) within 5 business days after notice of such suspension is given to the filer, the Secretary of State shall establish as the filing date of such instrument the date and time that would have been the filing date of the rejected instrument had it been accepted for filing. ■ The Secretary of State shall not issue a certificate of good standing with respect to any corporation with an instrument held in suspension pursuant to this subsection. ■ [Then] The Secretary of State may establish as the filing date of an instrument the date and time at which information from such instrument is entered pursuant to paragraph (c)(8) of this section if such instrument is delivered on the same date and within 4 hours after such information is entered.

(5) The Secretary of State, acting as agent for the recorders of each of the counties, shall collect and deposit in a separate account established exclusively for that purpose a county assessment fee with respect to each filed instrument and shall thereafter weekly remit from such account to the recorder of each of the said counties the amount or amounts of such fees as provided for in paragraph (c)(6) of this section or as elsewhere provided by law. ■ Said fees shall be for the purposes of defraying certain costs incurred by the counties (in merging the information and images of such filed documents with the document information systems of each of the recorder's offices in the counties) and (in retrieving, maintaining and displaying such information and images in the offices of the recorders and at remote locations in each of such counties). ■ In consideration for its acting as the agent for the recorders with respect to the collection and payment of the county assessment fees, the Secretary of State shall retain and pay over to the General Fund of the State an administrative charge of 1 percent of the total fees collected.

(6) The assessment fee to the counties shall be $24 for each 1-page instrument filed with the Secretary of State in accordance with this section and $9.00 for each additional page for instruments with more than 1 page. ■ The recorder's office to receive the assessment fee shall be the recorder's office in the county in which the corporation's registered office in this State is, or is to be, located, ◄except that an assessment fee shall not be charged for either a certificate of dissolution qualifying for treatment under § 391(a)(5)b. of this title or a document filed in accordance with subchapter XVI of this chapter.►

(7) The Secretary of State, acting as agent, shall collect and deposit in a separate account established exclusively for that purpose a courthouse municipality fee with respect to each filed instrument and shall thereafter monthly remit funds from such account to the treasuries of the municipalities designated in § 301 of Title 10. ■ Said fees shall be for the purposes of defraying certain costs incurred by such municipalities in hosting the primary locations for the Delaware courts. ■ The fee to such municipalities shall be $20 for each instrument filed with the Secretary of State in accordance with this section. ■ The municipality to receive the fee shall be the municipality designated in § 301 of Title 10 in the county in which the corporation's registered office in this State is, or is to be, located, ◄except that a fee shall not be charged for a certificate of dissolution qualifying for treatment under § 391(a)(5)b. of this title, a resignation of agent without appointment of a successor under § 136 of this title, or a document filed in accordance with subchapter XVI of this chapter.►

(8) The Secretary of State shall cause to be entered such information from each instrument as the Secretary of State deems appropriate into the Delaware Corporation Information System or any system which is a successor thereto in the office of the Secretary of State, and such information and a copy of each such instrument shall be permanently maintained as a public record on a suitable medium. ■ The Secretary of State is authorized to grant direct access to such system to registered agents (subject to the execution of an operating agreement between the Secretary of State and such registered agent). ■ Any registered agent granted such access shall demonstrate the existence of policies to ensure that information entered into the system accurately reflects the content of instruments in the possession of the registered agent at the time of entry.

(d) Any instrument filed in accordance with subsection (c) of this section shall be effective upon its filing date. ■ Any instrument may provide that it is not to become effective until a specified time subsequent to the time it is filed, but such time shall not be later than a time on the ninetieth day after the date of its filing. ■ If any instrument filed in accordance with subsection (c) of this section provides for a future effective date or time and if the transaction is terminated or its terms are amended to change the future effective date or time prior to the future effective date or time, [then] the instrument shall be terminated or amended by the filing, prior to the future effective date or time set forth in such instrument, of a certificate of termination or amendment of the original instrument, executed in accordance with subsection (a) of this section, which (shall identify the instrument which has been terminated or amended) and (shall state that the instrument has been terminated or the manner in which it has been amended).

(e) If another section of this chapter specifically prescribes a manner of executing, acknowledging or filing a specified instrument [or] a time when such instrument shall become effective which differs from the corresponding provisions of this section, **then** such other section shall govern.

(f) Whenever any instrument authorized to be filed with the Secretary of State under any provision of this title, has been so filed and is an inaccurate record of the corporate action therein referred to, [or] was defectively or erroneously executed, sealed or acknowledged, [then] the instrument may be corrected by filing with the Secretary of State a certificate of correction of the instrument which shall be executed, acknowledged and filed in accordance with this section. ■ The certificate of correction shall specify the inaccuracy or defect to be corrected [and] shall set forth the portion of the instrument in corrected form. ■ In lieu of filing a certificate of correction the instrument may be corrected by filing with the Secretary of State a corrected instrument which shall be executed, acknowledged and filed in accordance with this section. ■ The corrected instrument shall be specifically designated as such in its heading, shall specify the inaccuracy or defect to be corrected, [and] shall set forth the entire instrument in corrected form. ■ An instrument corrected in accordance with this section shall be effective as of the date the original instrument was filed, ◄except as to those persons who are substantially and adversely affected by the correction and as to those persons the instrument as corrected shall be effective from the filing date►.

(g) Notwithstanding that any instrument authorized to be filed with the Secretary of State under this title is when filed inaccurately, defectively or erroneously executed, sealed or acknowledged, or otherwise defective in any respect, the Secretary of State shall have no liability to any person for **(**the preclearance for filing**)**, **(**the acceptance for filing**)** [or] **(**the filing and indexing of such instrument**)** by the Secretary of State.

(h) Any signature on any instrument authorized to be filed with the Secretary of State under this title may be a facsimile, a conformed signature [or] an electronically transmitted signature.

(i) (1) If:

    a. Together with the actual delivery of an instrument and tender of the required taxes and fees, there is delivered to the Secretary of State a separate affidavit (which in its heading shall be designated as an "affidavit of extraordinary condition") attesting, on the basis of personal knowledge of the affiant or a reliable source of knowledge identified in the affidavit, that an earlier effort to deliver such instrument and tender such taxes and fees was made in good faith, specifying the nature, date and time of such good faith effort [and] requesting that the Secretary of State establish such date and time as the filing date of such instrument; [or]

    b. Upon the actual delivery of an instrument and tender of the required taxes and fees, the Secretary of State in the Secretary's discretion provides a written waiver of the requirement for such an affidavit **(**stating that it appears to the Secretary of State that an earlier effort to deliver such instrument and tender such taxes and fees was made in good faith**)** and **(**specifying the date and time of such effort**)**; [and]

    c. The Secretary of State determines **(**that an extraordinary condition existed at such date and time**)**, **(**that such earlier effort was unsuccessful as a result of the existence of such extraordinary condition), and (that such actual delivery and tender were made within a reasonable period (not to exceed 2 business days) after the cessation of such extraordinary condition),

then the Secretary of State may establish such date and time as the filing date of such instrument. ■ No fee shall be paid to the Secretary of State for receiving an affidavit of extraordinary condition.

(2) For purposes of this subsection, an "extraordinary condition" means: any emergency resulting from an attack on, invasion or occupation by foreign military forces of, or disaster, catastrophe, war or other armed conflict, revolution or insurrection, or rioting or civil commotion in, the United States or a locality (in which the Secretary of State conducts its business) or (in which the good faith effort to deliver the instrument and tender the required taxes and fees is made), or the immediate threat of any of the foregoing; or any malfunction or outage of the electrical or telephone service to the Secretary of State's office, or weather or other condition in or about a locality in which the Secretary of State conducts its business, as a result of which the Secretary of State's office is not open for the purpose of the filing of instruments under this chapter or such filing cannot be effected without extraordinary effort. ■ The Secretary of State may require such proof as it deems necessary to make the determination required under paragraph (i)(1)c. of this section, and any such determination shall be conclusive in the absence of actual fraud.

(3) If the Secretary of State establishes the filing date of an instrument pursuant to this subsection, **[then]** the date and time of delivery of the affidavit of extraordinary condition or the date and time of the Secretary of State's written waiver of such affidavit shall be endorsed on such affidavit or waiver and such affidavit or waiver, so endorsed, shall be attached to the filed instrument to which it relates. ■ Such filed instrument shall be effective as of the date and time established as the filing date by the Secretary of State pursuant to this subsection, (except as to those persons who are substantially and adversely affected by such establishment and, as to those persons, the instrument shall be effective from the date and time endorsed on the affidavit of extraordinary condition or written waiver attached thereto).

(j) Notwithstanding any other provision of this chapter, it shall not be necessary for any corporation to amend its certificate of incorporation, or any other document, that has been filed prior to August 1, 2011, to comply with § 131(c) of this title, provided that any certificate or other document filed under this chapter on or after August 1, 2011, and changing the address of a registered office shall comply with § 131(c) of this title.

§ 104. Certificate of incorporation; definition.

The term "certificate of incorporation," as used in this chapter, unless the context requires otherwise, includes not only the original certificate of incorporation filed to create a corporation but also all other certificates, agreements of merger or consolidation, plans of reorganization, or other instruments, howsoever designated, (which are filed pursuant to § 102, §§ 133-136, § 151, §§ 241-243, § 245, §§ 251-258, §§ 263-264, § 267, § 303, §§ 311-313, or any other section of this title), and (which have the effect of amending or supplementing in some respect a corporation's certificate of incorporation).

§ 105. Certificate of incorporation and other certificates; evidence.

A copy of a certificate of incorporation, or a restated certificate of incorporation, or of any other certificate which has been filed in the office of the Secretary of State as required by any provision of this title shall, when duly certified by the Secretary of State, be received in all courts, public offices and official bodies as prima facie evidence of:

(1) Due execution, acknowledgment and filing of the instrument;

(2) Observance and performance of all acts and conditions necessary to have been observed and performed precedent to the instrument becoming effective; and

(3) Any other facts required or permitted by law to be stated in the instrument.

§ 106. Commencement of corporate existence.

Upon the filing with the Secretary of State of the certificate of incorporation, executed and acknowledged in accordance with § 103 of this title, the incorporator or incorporators who signed the certificate, and such incorporator's or incorporators' successors and assigns, shall, from the date of such filing, be and constitute a body corporate, by the name set forth in the certificate, (subject to § 103(d) of this title) and (subject to dissolution or other termination of its existence as provided in this chapter).

§ 107. Powers of incorporators.

If the persons who are to serve as directors until the first annual meeting of stockholders have not been named in the certificate of incorporation, [then] the incorporator or incorporators, until the directors are elected, shall manage the affairs of the corporation and may do whatever is necessary and proper to perfect the organization of the corporation, including (the adoption of the original bylaws of the corporation) and (the election of directors).

§ 108. Organization meeting of incorporators or directors named in certificate of incorporation.

(a) After the filing of the certificate of incorporation an organization meeting of the incorporator or incorporators, or of the board of directors if the initial directors were named in the certificate of incorporation, shall be held, either within or without this State, at the call of a majority of the incorporators or directors, as the case may be, for the purposes of (adopting bylaws), (electing directors (if the meeting is of the incorporators) to serve or hold office until the first annual meeting of stockholders or until their successors are elected and qualify), (electing officers if the meeting is of the directors), (doing any other or further acts to perfect the organization of the corporation), and (transacting such other business as may come before the meeting).

(b) The persons calling the meeting shall give to each other incorporator or director, as the case may be, at least 2 days' notice thereof in writing or by electronic transmission by any usual means of communication, which notice shall state the time, place and purposes of the meeting as fixed by the persons calling it. ■ Notice of the meeting need not be given to anyone (who attends the meeting) or (who waives notice either before or after the meeting).

(c) **[Then]** Unless otherwise restricted by the certificate of incorporation, **(1)** any action permitted to be taken at the organization meeting of the incorporators or directors, as the case may be, may be taken without a meeting **if** each incorporator or director, where there is more than 1, or the sole incorporator or director where there is only 1, consents thereto in writing or by electronic transmission and **(2)** a consent may be documented, signed and delivered in any manner permitted by § 116 of this title. ■ Any person (whether or not then an incorporator or director) may provide, whether through instruction to an agent or otherwise, that a consent to action will be effective at a future time (including a time determined upon the happening of an event), no later than 60 days after such instruction is given or such provision is made and such consent shall be deemed to have been given for purposes of this subsection at such effective time (so long as such person is then an incorporator or director, as the case may be, and did not revoke the consent prior to such time). ■ Any such consent shall be revocable prior to its becoming effective..

(d) **If** any incorporator is not available to act, **then** any person for whom or on whose behalf the incorporator was acting directly or indirectly as employee or agent, may take any action that such incorporator would have been authorized to take under this section or § 107 of this title; **provided that** any instrument signed by such other person, or any record of the proceedings of a meeting in which such person participated, shall state (that such incorporator is not available and the reason therefor), (that such incorporator was acting directly or indirectly as employee or agent for or on behalf of such person), and (that such person's signature on such instrument or participation in such meeting is otherwise authorized and not wrongful).

§ 109. Bylaws.

(a) The original or other bylaws of a corporation may be adopted, amended or repealed by the incorporators, [then] by the initial directors of a corporation other than a nonstock corporation or initial members of the governing body of a nonstock corporation if they were named in the certificate of incorporation, or, (before a corporation other than a nonstock corporation has received any payment for any of its stock, by its board of directors). ■ **After** a corporation other than a nonstock corporation has received any payment for any of its stock, **[then]** the power to adopt, amend or repeal bylaws shall be in the stockholders entitled to vote. ■ In the case of a nonstock corporation, the power to adopt, amend or repeal bylaws shall be in its members entitled to vote. ■ Notwithstanding the foregoing, any corporation may, in its certificate of incorporation, confer the power to adopt, amend or repeal bylaws upon the directors or, in the case of a nonstock corporation, upon its governing body. ■ The fact that such power has been so conferred upon the directors or governing body, as the case may be, shall not divest the stockholders or members of the power, nor limit their power to adopt, amend or repeal bylaws.

(b) The bylaws may contain any provision, not inconsistent with law or with the certificate of incorporation, relating to (the business of the corporation,) (the conduct of its affairs), and (its rights or powers or the rights or powers of its stockholders, directors, officers or employees). The bylaws may not contain any provision that would impose liability on a stockholder for the attorneys' fees or expenses of the corporation or any other party in connection with an internal corporate claim, as defined in § 115 of this title.

§ 110. Emergency bylaws and other powers in emergency.

(a) The board of directors of any corporation may adopt emergency bylaws, subject to repeal or change by action of the stockholders, which notwithstanding any different provision elsewhere in this chapter or in Chapters 3 [repealed] and 5 [repealed] of Title 26, or in Chapter 7 of Title 5, or in the certificate of incorporation or bylaws, shall be operative (during any emergency resulting from an attack on the United States or on a locality in which the corporation conducts its business or customarily holds meetings of its board of directors or its stockholders), or (during any nuclear or atomic disaster), or (during the existence of any catastrophe, including, but not limited to, an epidemic or pandemic, and a declaration of a national emergency by the United States government, or other similar emergency condition), irrespective of whether a quorum of the board of directors or a standing committee thereof can readily be convened for action. ∎ The emergency bylaws contemplated by this section may be adopted by the board of directors or, if a quorum cannot be readily convened for a meeting, by a majority of the directors present. ∎ The emergency bylaws may make any provision that may be practical and necessary for the circumstances of the emergency, including provisions that:

(1) A meeting of the board of directors or a committee thereof may be called by any officer or director in such manner and under such conditions as shall be prescribed in the emergency bylaws;

(2) The director or directors in attendance at the meeting, or any greater number fixed by the emergency bylaws, shall constitute a quorum; and

(3) The officers or other persons designated on a list approved by the board of directors before the emergency, all in such order of priority and subject to such conditions and for such period of time (not longer than reasonably necessary after the termination of the emergency) as may be provided in the emergency bylaws or in the resolution approving the list, shall, to the extent required to provide a quorum at any meeting of the board of directors, be deemed directors for such meeting.

(b) The board of directors, either before or during any such emergency, may provide, and from time to time modify, lines of succession in the event that during such emergency any or all officers or agents of the corporation shall for any reason be rendered incapable of discharging their duties.

(c) The board of directors, either before or during any such emergency, may, effective in the emergency, change the head office or designate several alternative head offices or regional offices, or authorize the officers so to do.

(d) No officer, director or employee acting in accordance with any emergency bylaws shall be liable ◄except for wilful misconduct►.

(e) To the extent not inconsistent with any emergency bylaws so adopted, the bylaws of the corporation shall remain in effect during any emergency and upon its termination the emergency bylaws shall cease to be operative.

(f) **Unless** otherwise provided in emergency bylaws, **[then]** notice of any meeting of the board of directors during such an emergency may be given only to such of the directors as it may be feasible to reach at the time and by such means as may be feasible at the time, including publication or radio.

(g) To the extent required to constitute a quorum at any meeting of the board of directors during such an emergency, the officers of the corporation who are present shall, unless otherwise provided in emergency bylaws, be deemed, in order of rank and within the same rank in order of seniority, directors for such meeting.

(h) Nothing contained in this section shall be deemed exclusive of any other provisions for emergency powers consistent with other sections of this title which have been or may be adopted by corporations created under this chapter.

(i) During any emergency condition of a type described in paragraph (a) of this section, the board of directors (or, if a quorum cannot be readily convened for a meeting, a majority of the directors present) may **(i)** take any action that it determines to be practical and necessary to address the circumstances of such emergency condition with respect to a meeting of stockholders of the corporation notwithstanding anything to the contrary in this chapter or in Chapter 7 of Title 5 or in the certificate of incorporation or bylaws, including, but not limited to, **(1)** to postpone any such meeting to a later time or date (with the record date for determining the stockholders entitled to notice of, and to vote at, such meeting applying to the postponed meeting irrespective of § 213 of this title), and **(2) (**with respect to a corporation subject to the reporting requirements of § 13(a) or § 15(d) of the Securities Exchange Act of 1934, as amended, and the rules and regulations promulgated thereunder,**)** to notify stockholders of any postponement or a change of the place of the meeting (or a change to hold the meeting solely by means of remote communication) solely by a document publicly filed by the corporation with the Securities and Exchange Commission pursuant to § 13, § 14 or § 15(d) of such Act and such rules and regulations; and **(ii)** with respect to any dividend that has been declared as to which the record date has not occurred, change each of the record date and payment date to a later date or dates (provided the payment date as so changed is not more than 60 days after the record date as so changed); provided that, in either case, the corporation gives notice of such change to stockholders as promptly as practicable thereafter (and in any event before the record date theretofore in effect), which notice, in the case of a corporation subject to the reporting requirements of § 13(a) or § 15(d) of the Securities Exchange Act of 1934, as amended, and the rules and regulations promulgated thereunder, may be given solely by a document publicly filed with the Securities and Exchange Commission pursuant to § 13, § 14 or § 15(d) of such Act and such rules and regulations. ■ No person shall be liable, and no meeting of stockholders shall be postponed or voided, for the failure to make a stocklist available pursuant to § 219 of this title if it was not practicable to allow inspection during any such emergency condition.

§ 111. Jurisdiction to interpret, apply, enforce or determine the validity of corporate instruments and provisions of this title.

(a) Any civil action to interpret, apply, enforce or determine the validity of the provisions of:

(1) The certificate of incorporation or the bylaws of a corporation;

(2) Any instrument, document or agreement **(i)** by which a corporation creates or sells, or offers to create or sell, any of its stock, or any rights or options respecting its stock , or **(ii)** to which a corporation and 1 or more holders of its stock are parties, and pursuant to which any such holder or holders sell or offer to sell any of such stock, or **(iii)** by which a corporation agrees to sell, lease or exchange any of its property or assets, and which by its terms provides that 1 or more holders of its stock approve of or consent to such sale, lease or exchange;

(3) Any written restrictions on the transfer, registration of transfer or ownership of securities under § 202 of this title;

(4) Any proxy under § 212 or § 215 of this title;

(5) Any voting trust or other voting agreement under § 218 of this title;

(6) Any agreement, certificate of merger or consolidation, or certificate of ownership and merger governed by §§ 251-253, §§ 255-258, §§ 263-264, or § 267 of this title;

(7) Any certificate of conversion under § 265 or § 266 of this title;

(8) Any certificate of domestication, transfer or continuance under § 388, § 389 or § 390 of this title; or

(9) Any other instrument, document, agreement, or certificate required by any provision of this title;

may be brought in the Court of Chancery, ◄except to the extent that a statute confers exclusive jurisdiction on a court, agency or tribunal other than the Court of Chancery►.

(b) Any civil action to interpret, apply or enforce any provision of this title may be brought in the Court of Chancery.

§ 112. Access to proxy solicitation materials.

The bylaws may provide that if the corporation solicits proxies with respect to an election of directors, [then] it may be required, to the extent and subject to such procedures or conditions as may be provided in the bylaws, to include in its proxy solicitation materials (including any form of proxy it distributes), in addition to (individuals nominated by the board of directors), (1 or more individuals nominated by a stockholder). ■ Such procedures or conditions may include any of the following:

(1) A provision requiring a minimum record or beneficial ownership, or duration of ownership, of shares of the corporation's capital stock, by the nominating stockholder, and defining beneficial ownership to take into account options or other rights in respect of or related to such stock;

(2) A provision requiring the nominating stockholder to submit specified information concerning the stockholder and the stockholder's nominees, including information concerning ownership by such persons of shares of the corporation's capital stock, or options or other rights in respect of or related to such stock;

(3) A provision conditioning eligibility to require inclusion in the corporation's proxy solicitation materials upon (the number or proportion of directors nominated by stockholders) or (whether the stockholder previously sought to require such inclusion);

(4) [Then] A provision precluding nominations by any person if such person, any nominee of such person, or any affiliate or associate of such person or nominee, has acquired or publicly proposed to acquire (shares constituting a specified percentage of the voting power of the corporation's outstanding voting stock) (within a specified period before the election of directors);

(5) A provision requiring that the nominating stockholder undertake to indemnify the corporation in respect of (any loss arising as a result of any false or misleading information or statement submitted by the nominating stockholder in connection with a nomination); and

(6) Any other lawful condition.

§ 113. Proxy expense reimbursement.

(a) The bylaws may provide for the reimbursement by the corporation of (expenses incurred by a stockholder in soliciting proxies in connection with an election of directors), subject to such procedures or conditions as the bylaws may prescribe, including:

(1) Conditioning eligibility for reimbursement upon (the number or proportion of persons nominated by the stockholder seeking reimbursement) or (whether such stockholder previously sought reimbursement for similar expenses);

(2) Limitations on the amount of reimbursement based (upon the proportion of votes cast in favor of 1 or more of the persons nominated by the stockholder seeking reimbursement), or (upon the amount spent by the corporation in soliciting proxies in connection with the election);

(3) Limitations concerning elections of directors by cumulative voting pursuant to § 214 of this title; or

(4) Any other lawful condition.

(b) No bylaw so adopted shall apply to elections for which any record date precedes its adoption.

§ 114. Application of chapter to nonstock corporations.

(a) ❰Except as otherwise provided in subsections (b) and (c) of this section,❱ the provisions of this chapter and of chapter 5 of this title shall apply to nonstock corporations in the manner specified in the following paragraphs (a)(1)-(4) of this section:

(1) All references to stockholders of the corporation shall be deemed to refer to members of the corporation;

(2) All references to the board of directors of the corporation shall be deemed to refer to the governing body of the corporation;

(3) All references to directors or to members of the board of directors of the corporation shall be deemed to refer to members of the governing body of the corporation; and

(4) All references to stock, capital stock, or shares thereof of a corporation authorized to issue capital stock shall be deemed to refer (to memberships of a nonprofit nonstock corporation) and (to membership interests of any other nonstock corporation).

(b) Subsection (a) of this section shall not apply to:

(1) Sections 102(a)(4), (b)(1) and (2), 109(a), 114, 141, 154, 215, 228, 230(b), 241, 242, 253, 254, 255, 256, 257, 258, 271, 276, 311, 312, 313, 390 and 503 of this title, which apply to nonstock corporations by their terms;

(2) Sections 102(f), 109(b) (last sentence), 151, 152, 153, 155, 156, 157(d), 158, 161, 162, 163, 164, 165, 166, 167, 168, 203, 211, 212, 213, 214, 216, 219, 222, 231, 243, 244, 251, 252, 267, 274, 275, 324, 364, 366(a), 391, and 502(a)(5) of this title; and

(3) Subchapter XIV and subchapter XVI of this chapter.

(c) In the case of a nonprofit nonstock corporation, subsection (a) of this section shall not apply to:

(1) The sections and subchapters listed in subsection (b) of this section;

(2) Sections 102(b)(3), 111(a)(2) and (3), 144(a)(2), 217, 218(a) and (b), and 262 of this title; and

(3) Subchapter V, subchapter VI (other than Sections 204 and 205) and subchapter XV of this chapter.

(d) For purposes of this chapter:

(1) A "charitable nonstock corporation" is any nonprofit nonstock corporation that is exempt from taxation under § 501(c)(3) of the United States Internal Revenue Code [26 U.S.C. § 501(c)(3)], or any successor provisions.

(2) A "membership interest" is, unless otherwise provided in a nonstock corporation's certificate of incorporation, a member's share of the profits and losses of a nonstock corporation, or a member's right to receive distributions of the nonstock corporation's assets, or both;

(3) A "nonprofit nonstock corporation" is a nonstock corporation that does not have membership interests; and

(4) A "nonstock corporation" is any corporation organized under this chapter that is not authorized to issue capital stock.

§ 115 Forum selection provisions.

The certificate of incorporation or the bylaws may require, consistent with applicable jurisdictional requirements, that any or all internal corporate claims shall be brought solely and exclusively in any or all of the courts in this State, and no provision of the certificate of incorporation or the bylaws may prohibit bringing such claims in the courts of this State.
■ "Internal corporate claims" means claims, including claims in the right of the corporation, **(i)** that are based upon a violation of a duty by a current or former director or officer or stockholder in such capacity, or **(ii)** as to which this title confers jurisdiction upon the Court of Chancery.

§ 116. Document Form, Signature and Delivery.

(a) ❮Except as provided in subsection (b) of this section,❯ without limiting the manner in which any act or transaction may be documented, or the manner in which a document may signed or delivered:

(1) Any act or transaction contemplated or governed by this chapter or the certificate of incorporation or bylaws may be provided for in a document, and an electronic transmission shall be deemed the equivalent of a written document. ■ "Document" means:

(i) Any tangible medium on which information is inscribed, and includes handwritten, typed, printed or similar instruments, and copies of such instruments and

(ii) An electronic transmission.

(2) Whenever this chapter or the certificate of incorporation or bylaws requires or permits a signature, the signature may be a manual, facsimile, conformed or electronic signature. ■ "Electronic signature" means an electronic symbol or process that is attached to, or logically associated with, a document and executed or adopted by a person with an intent to execute authenticate or adopt the document. ■ A person may execute a document with such person's signature.

(3) ❨Unless otherwise agreed between the sender and recipient (and in the case of proxies or consents given by or on behalf of a stockholder, subject to the additional requirements set forth in § 212(c)(2) & (3) and § 228(d)(1), respectively, of this title),❩ an electronic transmission shall be deemed delivered to a person for purposes of this chapter and the certificate of incorporation and bylaws when it enters an information processing system that the person has designated for the purpose of receiving electronic transmissions of the type delivered, ❨so long as the electronic transmission is in a form capable of being processed by that system and such person is able to retrieve the electronic transmission.❩ ■ Whether a person has so designated an information processing system is determined by the certificate of incorporation, the bylaws or from the context and surrounding circumstances, including the parties' conduct. ■ An electronic transmission is delivered under this section even if no person is aware of its receipt. ■ Receipt of an electronic acknowledgment from an information processing system establishes that an electronic transmission was received but, by itself, does not establish that the content sent corresponds to the content received.

This chapter shall not prohibit one or more persons from conducting a transaction in accordance with Chapter 12A of Title 6 ❨so long as the part or parts of the transaction that are governed by this chapter are documented, signed and delivered in accordance with this subsection (a) or otherwise in accordance with this chapter❩. ■ This subsection (a) shall apply solely for purposes of determining whether an act or transaction has been documented, and the document has been signed and delivered, in accordance with this chapter, the certificate of incorporation and the bylaws.

(b) Subsection (a) of this section shall not apply to:

(1) a document filed with or submitted to the Secretary of State, the Register in Chancery, or a court or other judicial or governmental body of this State;

(2) a document comprising part of the stock ledger;

(3) a certificate representing a security;

(4) any document expressly referenced as a notice (or waiver of notice) by this chapter, the certificate of incorporation or bylaws;

(5) a ballot to vote on actions at a meeting of stockholders; and

(6) an act or transaction effected pursuant to Section 280 or subchapters III, XIII or XVI of this chapter. ■

The foregoing shall not create any presumption about the lawful means to document a matter addressed by this subsection (b), or the lawful means to sign or deliver a document addressed by this subsection (b). ■ No provision of the certificate of incorporation or bylaws shall limit the application of subsection (a) of this section ◄except for a provision that expressly restricts or prohibits the use of an electronic transmission or electronic signature (or any form thereof) or expressly restricts or prohibits the delivery of an electronic transmission to an information processing system.▶

(c) **In the event** that any provision of this chapter is deemed to modify, limit or supersede the Electronic Signatures in Global and National Commerce Act, [15 U.S.C. [§§] 7001 et. Seq.], **[then]** the provisions of this chapter shall control to the fullest extent permitted by section 7002(a)(2) of such act.

Subchapter II. Powers

§ 121. General powers.

(a) In addition to the powers enumerated in § 122 of this title, every corporation, its officers, directors and stockholders shall possess and may exercise all the powers and privileges granted by this chapter or by any other law or by its certificate of incorporation, together with any powers incidental thereto, ❨so far as such powers and privileges are necessary or convenient to the conduct, promotion or attainment of the business or purposes set forth in its certificate of incorporation❩.

(b) Every corporation shall be governed by the provisions and be subject to the restrictions and liabilities contained in this chapter.

§ 122. Specific powers.

Every corporation created under this chapter shall have power to:

    (1) [Then] Have perpetual succession by its corporate name, unless a limited period of duration is stated in its certificate of incorporation;

    (2) Sue and be sued in all courts and participate, as a party or otherwise, in any judicial, administrative, arbitrative or other proceeding, in its corporate name;

    (3) Have a corporate seal, which may be altered at pleasure, and use the same by causing it or a facsimile thereof, to be impressed or affixed or in any other manner reproduced;

    (4) Purchase, receive, take by grant, gift, devise, bequest or otherwise, lease, or otherwise acquire, own, hold, improve, employ, use and otherwise deal in and with real or personal property, or any interest therein, wherever situated, and to sell, convey, lease, exchange, transfer or otherwise dispose of, or mortgage or pledge, all or any of its property and assets, or any interest therein, wherever situated;

    (5) Appoint such officers and agents as the business of the corporation requires and to pay or otherwise provide for them suitable compensation;

    (6) Adopt, amend and repeal bylaws;

    (7) Wind up and dissolve itself in the manner provided in this chapter;

(8) Conduct its business, carry on its operations and have offices and exercise its powers within or without this State;

(9) Make donations for the public welfare or for charitable, scientific or educational purposes, and in time of war or other national emergency in aid thereof;

(10) Be an incorporator, promoter or manager of other corporations of any type or kind;

(11) Participate with others **(**in any corporation, partnership, limited partnership, joint venture or other association of any kind**)**, or **(**in any transaction, undertaking or arrangement which the participating corporation would have power to conduct by itself**)**, whether or not such participation involves sharing or delegation of control with or to others;

(12) Transact any lawful business which the corporation's board of directors shall find to be in aid of governmental authority;

(13) Make contracts, including contracts of guaranty and suretyship, incur liabilities, borrow money at such rates of interest as the corporation may determine, issue its notes, bonds and other obligations, and secure any of its obligations by mortgage, pledge or other encumbrance of all or any of its property, franchises and income, and make contracts of guaranty and suretyship which are necessary or convenient to the conduct, promotion or attainment of the business of

    (a) a corporation all of the outstanding stock of which is owned, directly or indirectly, by the contracting corporation, or

    (b) a corporation which owns, directly or indirectly, all of the outstanding stock of the contracting corporation, or

    (c) a corporation all of the outstanding stock of which is owned, directly or indirectly, by a corporation which owns, directly or indirectly, all of the outstanding stock of the contracting corporation,

which contracts of guaranty and suretyship shall be deemed to be necessary or convenient to the conduct, promotion or attainment of the business of the contracting corporation, and make other contracts of guaranty and suretyship which are necessary or convenient to the conduct, promotion or attainment of the business of the contracting corporation;

(14) Lend money for its corporate purposes, invest and reinvest its funds, and take, hold and deal with real and personal property as security for the payment of funds so loaned or invested;

(15) Pay pensions and establish and carry out pension, profit sharing, stock option, stock purchase, stock bonus, retirement, benefit, incentive and compensation plans, trusts and provisions for any or all of its directors, officers and employees, and for any or all of the directors, officers and employees of its subsidiaries;

(16) Provide insurance for its benefit on the life of any of its directors, officers or employees, or on the life of any stockholder for the purpose of acquiring at such stockholder's death shares of its stock owned by such stockholder.

(17) Renounce, **(**in its certificate of incorporation**)** or **(**by action of its board of directors**)**, any interest or expectancy of the corporation in, or in being offered an opportunity to participate in, specified business opportunities or specified classes or categories of business opportunities that are presented to the corporation or 1 or more of its officers, directors or stockholders.

§ 123. Powers respecting securities of other corporations or entities.

Any corporation organized under the laws of this State may guarantee, purchase, take, receive, subscribe for or otherwise acquire; own, hold, use or otherwise employ; sell, lease, exchange, transfer or otherwise dispose of; mortgage, lend, pledge or otherwise deal in and with, bonds and other obligations of, or shares or other securities or interests in, or issued (by, any other domestic or foreign corporation, partnership, association or individual), or (by any government or agency or instrumentality thereof). ■ A corporation while owner of any such securities may exercise all the rights, powers and privileges of ownership, including the right to vote.

§ 124. Effect of lack of corporate capacity or power; ultra vires.

No act of a corporation and no conveyance or transfer of real or personal property to or by a corporation shall be invalid by reason of the fact that the corporation was without capacity or power to do such act or to make or receive such conveyance or transfer, but such lack of capacity or power may be asserted:

(1) In a proceeding by a stockholder against the corporation to enjoin the doing of any act or acts or the transfer of real or personal property by or to the corporation. ■ **If** the unauthorized acts or transfer sought to be enjoined are being, or are to be, performed or made pursuant to any contract to which the corporation is a party, **[then]** the court may, if all of the parties to the contract are parties to the proceeding and if it deems the same to be equitable, set aside and enjoin the performance of such contract, and in so doing may allow to the corporation or to the other parties to the contract, as the case may be, such compensation as may be equitable for the loss or damage sustained by any of them which may result from the action of the court in setting aside and enjoining the performance of such contract, but anticipated profits to be derived from the performance of the contract shall not be awarded by the court as a loss or damage sustained;

(2) In a proceeding by the corporation, whether acting directly or through a receiver, trustee or other legal representative, or through stockholders in a representative suit, (against an incumbent or former officer or director of the corporation), for loss or damage due to such incumbent or former officer's or director's unauthorized act;

(3) In a proceeding by the Attorney General (to dissolve the corporation), or (to enjoin the corporation from the transaction of unauthorized business).

§ 125. Conferring academic or honorary degrees.

No corporation organized after April 18, 1945, shall have power to confer academic or honorary degrees **unless** the certificate of incorporation or an amendment thereof shall so provide and **unless** the certificate of incorporation or an amendment thereof prior to its being filed in the office of the Secretary of State shall have endorsed thereon the approval of the Department of Education of this State. ■ No corporation organized before April 18, 1945, any provision in its certificate of incorporation to the contrary notwithstanding, shall possess the power aforesaid without first filing in the office of the Secretary of State a certificate of amendment so providing, the filing of which certificate of amendment in the office of the Secretary of State shall be subject to prior approval of the Department of Education, evidenced as hereinabove provided. ■ **[Then]** Approval shall be granted **only when** it appears to the reasonable satisfaction of the Department of Education (that the corporation is engaged in conducting a bona fide institution of higher learning, giving instructions in arts and letters, science or the professions), or (that the corporation proposes, in good faith, to engage in that field and has or will have the resources, including personnel, requisite for the conduct of an institution of higher learning). ■ Upon dissolution, all such corporations shall comply with § 8530 of Title 14. ■ **[Then]** Notwithstanding any provision herein to the contrary, no corporation shall have the power to conduct a private business or trade school **unless** the certificate of incorporation or an amendment thereof, prior to its being filed in the office of the Secretary of State, shall have endorsed thereon the approval of the Department of Education pursuant to Chapter 85 of Title 14.

Notwithstanding the foregoing provisions, any corporation conducting a law school, (which has its principal place of operation in Delaware), and (which intends to meet the standards of approval of the American Bar Association), may, after it has been in actual operation for not less than 1 year, retain at its own expense a dean or dean emeritus of a law school fully approved by the American Bar Association to make an on-site inspection and report concerning the progress of the corporation toward meeting the standards for approval by the American Bar Association. ■ Such dean or dean emeritus shall be chosen by the Attorney General from a panel of 3 deans whose names are presented to the Attorney General as being willing to serve. ■ One such dean on this panel shall be nominated by the trustees of said law school corporation; [and] another dean shall be nominated by a committee of the Student Bar Association of said law school; and the other dean shall be nominated by a committee of lawyers who are parents of students attending such law school. ■ **If** any of the above-named groups cannot find a dean, **[then]** it may substitute 2 full professors of accredited law schools for the dean it is entitled to nominate, and in such a case if the Attorney General chooses 1 of such professors, such professor shall serve the function of a dean as herein prescribed. ■ **If** the dean so retained shall report in writing that, (in such dean's professional judgment, the corporation is attempting, in good faith, to comply with the standards for approval of the American Bar Association and is making reasonable progress toward meeting such standards), **[then]** the corporation may file a copy of the report with the Secretary of Education and with the Attorney General. ■ Any corporation which complies with these provisions by filing such report shall be deemed to have temporary approval from the State and shall be entitled to amend its certificate of incorporation to authorize the granting of standard academic law degrees. ■ Thereafter, **until** the law school operated by the corporation is approved by the American Bar Association, **[then]** the corporation shall file once during each academic year a new report, in the same manner as the first report. ■ **If**, at any time, the corporation fails to file such a report, or **if** the dean retained to render such report states that, (in such dean's opinion, the corporation is not continuing to make reasonable progress toward accreditation), **[then]** the Attorney General, at the request of the Secretary of Education, may file a complaint in the Court of Chancery to suspend said temporary approval and degree-granting power until a further report is filed by a dean or dean emeritus of an accredited law school that (the school has resumed its progress towards meeting the standards for approval**)**. ■ Upon approval of the law school by the American Bar Association, temporary approval shall become final, and shall no longer be subject to suspension or vacation under this section.

§ 126. Banking power denied.

(a) No corporation organized under this chapter shall possess the power of issuing bills, notes, or other evidences of debt for circulation as money, or the power of carrying on the business of receiving deposits of money.

(b) Corporations organized under this chapter to buy, sell and otherwise deal in notes, open accounts and other similar evidences of debt, or to loan money and to take notes, open accounts and other similar evidences of debt as collateral security therefor, shall not be deemed to be engaging in the business of banking.

§ 127. Private foundation; powers and duties.

A corporation of this State which is a private foundation under the United States internal revenue laws and whose certificate of incorporation does not expressly provide that this section shall not apply to it is required to act or to refrain from acting so as not to subject itself to the taxes imposed by **(**26 U.S.C. § 4941 (relating to taxes on self-dealing)**)**, **(**§ 4942 (relating to taxes on failure to distribute income)**)**, **(**§ 4943 (relating to taxes on excess business holdings)**)**, **(**§ 4944 (relating to taxes on investments which jeopardize charitable purpose)**)**, or **(**§ 4945 (relating to taxable expenditures)**)**, or **(**corresponding provisions of any subsequent United States internal revenue law**)**.

Subchapter III. Registered Office and Registered Agent

§ 131. Registered office in State; principal office or place of business in State.

(a) Every corporation shall have and maintain in this State a registered office which may, but need not be, the same as its place of business.

(b) Whenever the term "corporation's principal office or place of business in this State" or "principal office or place of business of the corporation in this State," or other term of like import, is or has been used in a corporation's certificate of incorporation, or in any other document, or in any statute, **[then]** it shall be deemed to mean and refer to, unless the context indicates otherwise, the corporation's registered office required by this section; and it shall not be necessary for any corporation to amend its certificate of incorporation or any other document to comply with this section.

(c) As contained in any certificate of incorporation or other document filed with the Secretary of State under this chapter, the address of a registered office shall include the street, number, city, county and postal code.

§ 132. Registered agent in State; resident agent.

(a) Every corporation shall have and maintain in this State a registered agent, which agent may be any of:

(1) The corporation itself;

(2) An individual resident in this State;

(3) A domestic corporation (other than the corporation itself), a domestic partnership (whether general (including a limited liability partnership) or limited (including a limited liability limited partnership)), a domestic limited liability company or a domestic statutory trust; or

(4) A foreign corporation, a foreign limited liability partnership, a foreign limited partnership, a foreign limited liability limited partnership, a foreign limited liability company or a foreign statutory trust.

(b) Every registered agent for a domestic corporation or a foreign corporation shall:

(1) If an entity, [then] maintain a business office in this State which is generally open, or if an individual, [then] be generally present at a designated location in this State, at sufficiently frequent times to accept service of process and otherwise perform the functions of a registered agent;

(2) If a foreign entity, [then] be authorized to transact business in this State;

(3) Accept service of process and other communications directed to the corporations for which it serves as registered agent [and] forward same to the corporation to which the service or communication is directed;

(4) Forward to the corporations for which it serves as registered agent the annual report required by § 502 of this title [or] an electronic notification of same in a form satisfactory to the Secretary of State ("Secretary") [and]

(5) Satisfy and adhere to regulations established by the Secretary regarding the verification of both the identity of the entity's contacts and individuals for which the registered agent maintains a record for the reduction of risk of unlawful business purposes.

(c) Any registered agent who at any time serves as registered agent for more than 50 entities (a "commercial registered agent"), whether domestic or foreign, shall satisfy [and] comply with the following qualifications.

(1) A natural person serving as a commercial registered agent shall:

a. Maintain a principal residence [or] a principal place of business in this State;

b. Maintain a Delaware business license;

c. Be generally present at a designated location within this State during normal business hours to accept service of process and otherwise perform the functions of a registered agent as specified in subsection (b) of this section;

d. Provide the Secretary upon request with such information identifying and enabling communication with such commercial registered agent as the Secretary shall require; [and]

e. Satisfy and adhere to regulations established by the Secretary regarding the verification of both the identity of the entity's contacts and individuals for which the natural person maintains a record for the reduction of risk of unlawful business purposes.

(2) A domestic or foreign corporation, a domestic or foreign partnership ((whether general (including a limited liability partnership) or limited (including a limited liability limited partnership))), a domestic or foreign limited liability company, or a domestic or foreign statutory trust serving as a commercial registered agent shall:

a. Have a business office within this State which is generally open during normal business hours to (accept service of process) and (otherwise perform the functions of a registered agent as specified in subsection (b) of this section);

b. Maintain a Delaware business license;

c. Have generally present at such office during normal business hours an officer, director or managing agent who is a natural person;

d. Provide the Secretary upon request with such information identifying and enabling communication with such commercial registered agent as the Secretary shall require and

e. Satisfy and adhere to regulations established by the Secretary regarding the verification of both the identity of the entity's contacts and individuals for which it maintains a record for the reduction of risk of unlawful business purposes.

(3) [Then] For purposes of this subsection and paragraph (f)(2)a. of this section, a commercial registered agent shall also include any registered agent which has an officer, director or managing agent in common with any other registered agent or agents **if** such registered agents at any time during such common service as officer, director or managing agent collectively served as registered agents for more than 50 entities, whether domestic or foreign.

(d) Every corporation formed under the laws of this State or qualified to do business in this State shall provide to its registered agent and update from time to time as necessary the name, business address and business telephone number of a natural person (who is an officer, director, employee, or designated agent of the corporation), (who is then authorized to receive communications from the registered agent). ■ Such person shall be deemed the communications contact for the corporation. ■ Every registered agent shall retain (in paper or electronic form) the above information concerning the current communications contact for each corporation for which he, she or it serves as a registered agent. ■ **If** the corporation fails to provide the registered agent with a current communications contact, **[then]** the registered agent may resign as the registered agent for such corporation pursuant to § 136 of this title.

(e) The Secretary is fully authorized to issue such regulations as may be necessary or appropriate to carry out the enforcement of subsections (b), (c) and (d) of this section, and to take actions reasonable and necessary to assure registered agents' compliance with subsections (b), (c) and (d) of this section. ■ Such actions may include refusal to file documents submitted by a registered agent, including the refusal to file any documents regarding an entity's formation.

(f) Upon application of the Secretary, the Court of Chancery may enjoin any person or entity from serving as a registered agent or as an officer, director or managing agent of a registered agent.

(1) Upon the filing of a complaint by the Secretary pursuant to this section, the Court may make such orders respecting such proceeding as it deems appropriate, and may enter such orders granting interim or final relief as it deems proper under the circumstances.

(2) Any one or more of the following grounds shall be a sufficient basis to grant an injunction pursuant to this section:

    a. With respect to any registered agent who at any time within 1 year immediately prior to the filing of the Secretary's complaint is a commercial registered agent, failure after notice and warning to comply with (the qualifications set forth in subsection (b) of this section) and/or (the requirements of subsection (c) or (d) of this section above);

    b. The person serving as a registered agent, or any person who is an officer, director or managing agent of an entity registered agent, has been convicted of a felony [or] any crime which includes an element of dishonesty or fraud or involves moral turpitude;

    c. The registered agent has engaged in conduct in connection with acting as a registered agent that is intended to or likely to deceive or defraud the public.

(3) With respect to any order the court enters pursuant to this section with respect to an entity that has acted as a registered agent, the court may also direct such order to any person who has served as an officer, director, or managing agent of such registered agent. ■ Any person who, on or after January 1, 2007, serves as an officer, director, or managing agent of an entity acting as a registered agent in this State shall be deemed thereby to have consented to the appointment of such registered agent as agent upon whom service of process may be made in any action brought pursuant to this section, [and] service as an officer, director, or managing agent of an entity acting as a registered agent in this State shall be a signification of the consent of such person that (any process when so served shall be of the same legal force and validity as if served upon such person within this State), [and] such appointment of the registered agent shall be irrevocable.

(4) Upon the entry of an order by the Court enjoining any person or entity from acting as a registered agent, the Secretary shall mail or deliver notice of such order to each affected corporation at the address of its principal place of business as specified in its most recent franchise tax report or other record of the Secretary. ■ If such corporation is a domestic corporation [and] fails to obtain and designate a new registered agent within 30 days after such notice is given, [then] the Secretary shall declare the charter of such corporation forfeited. ■ If such corporation is a foreign corporation, [and] fails to obtain and designate a new registered agent within 30 days after such notice is given, [then] the Secretary shall forfeit its qualification to do business in this State. ■ If the court enjoins a person or entity from acting as a registered agent as provided in this section [and] no new registered agent shall have been obtained and designated in the time and manner aforesaid, [then] service of legal process against the corporation for which the registered agent had been acting shall thereafter be upon the Secretary in accordance with § 321 of this title. ■ The Court of Chancery may, upon application of the Secretary on notice to the former registered agent, enter such orders as it deems appropriate to give the Secretary access to information in the former registered agent's possession in order to facilitate communication with the corporations the former registered agent served.

(g) The Secretary is authorized to make a list of registered agents available to the public, and to establish such qualifications and issue such rules and regulations with respect to such listing as the Secretary deems necessary or appropriate.

(h) Whenever the term "resident agent" or "resident agent in charge of a corporation's principal office or place of business in this State," or other term of like import which refers to a corporation's agent required by statute to be located in this State, is or has been used in a corporation's certificate of incorporation, or in any other document, or in any statute, [then] it shall be deemed to mean and refer to, unless the context indicates otherwise, the corporation's registered agent required by this section; and it shall not be necessary for any corporation to amend its certificate of incorporation or any other document to comply with this section.

§ 133. Change of location of registered office; change of registered agent.

Any corporation may, by resolution of its board of directors, change the location of its registered office in this State to any other place in this State. ■ By like resolution, the registered agent of a corporation may be changed to any other person or corporation including itself. ■ In either such case, the resolution shall be as detailed in its statement as is required by § 102(a)(2) of this title. ■ Upon the adoption of such a resolution, a certificate certifying the change shall be executed, acknowledged, and filed in accordance with § 103 of this title.

§ 134. Change of address or name of registered agent.

(a) A registered agent may change the address of the registered office of the corporation or corporations for which the agent is a registered agent to another address in this State by filing with the Secretary of State a certificate, executed and acknowledged by such registered agent, (setting forth the address at which such registered agent has maintained the registered office for each of the corporations for which it is a registered agent), and further (certifying to the new address to which each such registered office will be changed on a given day, and at which new address such registered agent will thereafter maintain the registered office for each of the corporations for which it is a registered agent). ■ Thereafter, or until further change of address, as authorized by law, the registered office in this State of each of the corporations for which the agent is a registered agent shall be located at the new address of the registered agent thereof as given in the certificate.

(b) In the event of a change of name of any person or corporation acting as registered agent in this State, such registered agent shall file with the Secretary of State a certificate, executed and acknowledged by such registered agent, setting forth (the new name of such registered agent), (the name of such registered agent before it was changed), and (the address at which such registered agent has maintained the registered office for each of the corporations for which it acts as a registered agent). ■ A change of name of any person or corporation acting as a registered agent as a result of a merger or consolidation of the registered agent, with or into another person or corporation which succeeds to its assets by operation of law, shall be deemed a change of name for purposes of this section.

§ 135. Resignation of registered agent coupled with appointment of successor.

The registered agent of 1 or more corporations may resign and appoint a successor registered agent by filing a certificate with the Secretary of State, stating the name and address of the successor agent, in accordance with § 102(a)(2) of this title. ■ There shall be attached to such certificate a statement of each affected corporation ratifying and approving such change of registered agent. ■ Each such statement shall be executed and acknowledged in accordance with § 103 of this title. ■ Upon such filing, the successor registered agent shall become the registered agent of such corporations as have ratified and approved such substitution and the successor registered agent's address, as stated in such certificate, shall become the address of each such corporation's registered office in this State.

§ 136. Resignation of registered agent not coupled with appointment of successor.

(a) The registered agent of a corporation, including a corporation which has become void pursuant to Section 510 of this title, may resign without appointing a successor by filing a certificate of resignation with the Secretary of State, but such resignation shall not become effective until 30 days after the certificate is filed. ■ The certificate shall be executed and acknowledged by the registered agent, shall contain a statement that written notice of resignation was given to the corporation at least 30 days prior to the filing of the certificate by mailing or delivering such notice to the corporation at its address last known to the registered agent and shall set forth the date of such notice. ■ The certificate shall include such information last provided to the registered agent pursuant to Section 132(d) of this title for a communications contact for the affected corporation. ■ Such information regarding the communications contact shall not be deemed public. ■ A certificate filed pursuant to this section must be on the form prescribed by the Secretary of State.

(b) After receipt of the notice of the resignation of its registered agent, provided for in subsection (a) of this section, the corporation for which such registered agent was acting shall obtain and designate a new registered agent to take the place of the registered agent so resigning in the same manner as provided in § 133 of this title for change of registered agent. ■ If such corporation, being a corporation of this State, fails to obtain and designate a new registered agent as aforesaid prior to the expiration of the period of 30 days after the filing by the registered agent of the certificate of resignation, [then] the Secretary of State shall declare the charter of such corporation forfeited. ■ If such corporation, being a foreign corporation, fails to obtain and designate a new registered agent as aforesaid prior to the expiration of the period of 30 days after the filing by the registered agent of the certificate of resignation, [then] the Secretary of State shall forfeit its authority to do business in this State.

(c) After the resignation of the registered agent shall have become effective as provided in this section and if no new registered agent shall have been obtained and designated in the time and manner aforesaid, [then] service of legal process against the corporation for which the resigned registered agent had been acting shall thereafter be upon the Secretary of State in accordance with § 321 of this title.

Subchapter IV. Directors and Officers

§ 141. Board of directors; powers; number, qualifications, terms and quorum; committees; classes of directors; nonstock corporations; reliance upon books; action without meeting; removal.

(a) <u>The business and affairs</u> of every corporation organized under this chapter <u>shall be managed</u> by or under the direction of a board of directors, ❪except as may be otherwise provided in this chapter or in its certificate of incorporation❫. ■ **If** <u>any such provision is made</u> in the certificate of incorporation, **[then]** <u>the powers</u> and <u>duties</u> conferred or imposed upon the board of directors by this chapter <u>shall be exercised</u> or <u>performed</u> to such extent and by such person or persons as shall be provided in the certificate of incorporation.

(b) <u>The board of directors</u> of a corporation <u>shall consist of 1 or more members</u>, each of whom shall be a natural person. ■ <u>The number</u> of directors <u>shall be fixed</u> by, or in the manner provided in, the bylaws, ❪unless the certificate of incorporation fixes the number of directors, in which case a change in the number of directors shall be made only by amendment of the certificate❫. ■ <u>Directors need not be stockholders</u> unless so required by the certificate of incorporation or the bylaws. ■ <u>The certificate of incorporation</u> or <u>bylaws may prescribe other qualifications</u> for directors. ■ <u>Each director shall hold office</u> **until** <u>such director's successor is elected</u> and <u>qualified</u> or **until** <u>such director's earlier resignation</u> or <u>removal</u>. ■ <u>Any director may resign</u> at any time ❪upon notice given in writing❫ or ❪by electronic transmission❫ to the corporation. ■ **[Then]** <u>A resignation is effective</u> **when** <u>the resignation is delivered</u> **unless** <u>the resignation specifies a later effective date</u> or <u>an effective date determined</u> upon the happening of an event or events. ■ <u>A resignation</u> which is conditioned upon the director failing to receive a specified vote for reelection as a director <u>may provide</u> that it is irrevocable. ■ **[Then]** <u>A majority</u> of the total number of directors <u>shall constitute a quorum</u> for the transaction of business **unless** <u>the certificate of incorporation</u> or <u>the bylaws require a greater number</u>. ■ **Unless** <u>the certificate of incorporation provides otherwise,</u> **[then]** <u>the bylaws may provide</u> that a number less than a majority shall constitute a quorum which in no case shall be less than 1/3 of the total number of directors. ■ <u>The vote</u> of the majority of the directors present at a meeting at which a quorum is present <u>shall be the act of the board of directors</u> **unless** <u>the certificate of incorporation</u> or <u>the bylaws shall require a vote</u> of a greater number.

(c)(1) <u>All corporations</u> incorporated prior to July 1, 1996, <u>shall be governed by this paragraph (c)(1)</u> of this section, **provided that** <u>any such corporation may</u> by a resolution adopted by a majority of the whole board <u>elect to be governed by paragraph (c)(2)</u> of this section, in which case this paragraph (c)(1) of this section shall not apply to such corporation. ■ <u>All corporations</u> incorporated on or after July 1, 1996, <u>shall be governed by paragraph (c)(2)</u> of this section. ■ <u>The board of directors may</u>, by resolution passed by a majority of the whole board, <u>designate 1 or more committees</u>, each committee to consist of 1 or more of the directors of the corporation. ■ <u>The board may designate 1 or more directors</u> as alternate members of any committee, who may replace any absent or disqualified member at any meeting of the committee. ■ <u>The bylaws may provide</u> that in the absence or disqualification of a member of a committee, the member or members present at any meeting and not disqualified from voting, whether or not the member or members present constitute a quorum, may unanimously appoint another member of the board of directors to act at the meeting in the place of any such absent or disqualified member. ■ Any such committee, to the extent provided in the resolution of the board of directors, or in the bylaws of the corporation, shall have and may exercise all the powers and authority of the board of directors in the management of the business and affairs of the corporation, and may authorize the seal of the corporation to be affixed to all papers which may require it; but no such committee shall have the power or authority in reference to (amending the certificate of incorporation) ◀(except that a committee may, to the extent authorized in the resolution or resolutions providing for the issuance of shares of stock adopted by the board of directors as provided in § 151(a) of this title, fix the designations and any of the preferences or rights of such shares relating to dividends, redemption, dissolution, any distribution of assets of the corporation or the conversion into, or the exchange of such shares for, shares of any other class or classes or any other series of the same or any other class or classes of stock of the corporation or fix the number of shares of any series of stock or authorize the increase or decrease of the shares of any series)▶, (adopting an agreement of merger or consolidation under § 251, § 252, § 254, § 255, § 256, § 257, § 258, § 263 or § 264 of this title), (recommending to the stockholders the sale, lease or exchange of all or substantially all of the corporation's property and assets), (recommending to the stockholders a dissolution of the corporation or a revocation of a dissolution), or (amending the bylaws of the corporation); and, **unless** the resolution, bylaws or certificate of incorporation expressly so provides, **[then]** no such committee shall have the power or authority (to declare a dividend), (to authorize the issuance of stock) or (to adopt a certificate of ownership and merger pursuant to § 253 of this title).

(2) The board of directors may designate 1 or more committees, each committee to consist of 1 or more of the directors of the corporation. ■ The board may designate 1 or more directors as alternate members of any committee, who may replace any absent or disqualified member at any meeting of the committee. ■ The bylaws may provide that in the absence or disqualification of a member of a committee, the member or members present at any meeting and not disqualified from voting, whether or not such member or members constitute a quorum, may unanimously appoint another member of the board of directors to act at the meeting in the place of any such absent or disqualified member. ■ Any such committee, to the extent provided in the resolution of the board of directors, or in the bylaws of the corporation, shall have and may exercise all the powers and authority of the board of directors in the management of the business and affairs of the corporation, and may authorize the seal of the corporation to be affixed to all papers which may require it; but no such committee shall have the power or authority in reference to the following matter: **(i)** approving or adopting, or recommending to the stockholders, any action or matter (other than the election or removal of directors) expressly required by this chapter to be submitted to stockholders for approval or **(ii)** adopting, amending or repealing any bylaw of the corporation.

(3) ◀Unless otherwise provided in the certificate of incorporation, the bylaws or the resolution of the board of directors designating the committee,▶ a committee may create 1 or more subcommittees, each subcommittee to consist of 1 or more members of the committee, and delegate to a subcommittee any or all of the powers and authority of the committee. ■ ◀Except for references to committees and members of committees in

subsection (c) of this section,▸ every reference in this chapter to a committee of the board of directors or a member of a committee shall be deemed to include a reference to a subcommittee or member of a subcommittee.

(4) **[Then]** A majority of the directors then serving on a committee of the board of directors or on a subcommittee of a committee shall constitute a quorum for the transaction of business by the committee or subcommittee, **unless** the certificate of incorporation, the bylaws, a resolution of the board of directors or a resolution of a committee that created the subcommittee requires a greater or lesser number, provided that in no case shall a quorum be less than 1/3 of the directors then serving on the committee or subcommittee. ■ **[Then]** The vote of the majority of the members of a committee or subcommittee present at a meeting at which a quorum is present shall be the act of the committee or subcommittee, **unless** the certificate of incorporation, the bylaws, a resolution of the board of directors or a resolution of a committee that created the subcommittee requires a greater number.

(d) The directors of any corporation organized under this chapter may, by the certificate of incorporation or by an initial bylaw, or by a bylaw adopted by a vote of the stockholders, be divided into 1, 2 or 3 classes; the term of office of those of the first class to expire at the first annual meeting held after such classification becomes effective; of the second class 1 year thereafter; of the third class 2 years thereafter; and at each annual election held after such classification becomes effective, directors shall be chosen for a full term, as the case may be, to succeed those whose terms expire. ■ The certificate of incorporation or bylaw provision dividing the directors into classes may authorize the board of directors to assign members of the board already in office to such classes at the time such classification becomes effective. ■ The certificate of incorporation may confer upon holders of any class or series of stock the right to elect 1 or more directors who (shall serve for such term), and (have such voting powers as shall be stated in the certificate of incorporation). ■ The terms of office and voting powers of the directors elected separately by the holders of any class or series of stock may be greater than or less than those of any other director or class of directors. ■ In addition, the certificate of incorporation may confer upon 1 or more directors, whether or not elected separately by the holders of any class or series of stock, voting powers greater than or less than those of other directors. ■ Any such provision conferring greater or lesser voting power shall apply to voting in any committee, (unless otherwise provided in the certificate of incorporation or bylaws). ■ **If** the certificate of incorporation provides that 1 or more directors shall have more or less than 1 vote per director on any matter, **[then]** every reference in this chapter to a majority or other proportion of the directors shall refer to a majority or other proportion of the votes of the directors.

(e) A member of the board of directors, or a member of any committee designated by the board of directors, shall, in the performance of such member's duties, be fully protected in relying in good faith upon the records of the corporation and upon such information, opinions, reports or statements presented to the corporation (by any of the corporation's officers or employees, or committees of the board of directors), or (by any other person as to matters the member reasonably believes are within such other person's professional or expert competence) and who has been selected with reasonable care by or on behalf of the corporation.

Subchapter IV. Directors and Officers § 141

(f) [Then] Unless otherwise restricted by the certificate of incorporation or bylaws, **(1)** any action required or permitted to be taken at any meeting of the board of directors or of any committee thereof may be taken without a meeting if all members of the board or committee, as the case may be, consent thereto in writing, or by electronic transmission, and **(2)** a consent may be documented, signed and delivered in any manner permitted by § 116 of this title. ■ Any person (whether or not then a director) may provide, whether through instruction to an agent or otherwise, that (a consent to action will be effective at a future time (including a time determined upon the happening of an event), no later than 60 days after such instruction is given or such provision is made) and such consent shall be deemed to have been given for purposes of this subsection at such effective time (so long as such person is then a director and did not revoke the consent prior to such time). ■ Any such consent shall be revocable prior to its becoming effective. ■ After an action is taken, the consent or consents relating thereto shall be filed with the minutes of the proceedings of the board of directors, or the committee thereof, in the same paper or electronic form as the minutes are maintained.

(g) ◄Unless otherwise restricted by the certificate of incorporation or bylaws►, the board of directors of any corporation organized under this chapter may hold its meetings, and have an office or offices, outside of this State.

(h) ◄Unless otherwise restricted by the certificate of incorporation or bylaws►, the board of directors shall have the authority to fix the compensation of directors.

(i) ◄Unless otherwise restricted by the certificate of incorporation or bylaws►, members of the board of directors of any corporation, or any committee designated by the board, may participate in a meeting of such board, or committee by means of (conference telephone or other communications equipment by means of which all persons participating in the meeting can hear each other), and participation in a meeting pursuant to this subsection shall constitute presence in person at the meeting.

(j) The certificate of incorporation of any nonstock corporation may provide that less than 1/3 of the members of the governing body may constitute a quorum thereof and may otherwise provide that the business and affairs of the corporation shall be managed in a manner different from that provided in this section. ■ ◄Except as may be otherwise provided by the certificate of incorporation,► this section shall apply to such a corporation, and when so applied, all references (to the board of directors,) (to members thereof,) and (to stockholders) shall be deemed to refer (to the governing body of the corporation,) (the members thereof) and (the members of the corporation,) respectively; and all references to stock, capital stock, or shares thereof shall be deemed to refer (to memberships of a nonprofit nonstock corporation) and (to membership interests of any other nonstock corporation).

(k) Any director or the entire board of directors may be removed, with or without cause, by the holders of a majority of the shares then entitled to vote at an election of directors, except as follows:

> **(1)** Unless the certificate of incorporation otherwise provides, (in the case of a corporation whose board is classified as provided in subsection (d) of this section), stockholders may effect such removal only for cause; or

(2) (In the case of a corporation having cumulative voting,**)** if less than the entire board is to be removed, no director may be removed without cause if the votes cast against such director's removal would be sufficient to elect such director if then cumulatively voted at an election of the entire board of directors, or, if there be classes of directors, at an election of the class of directors of which such director is a part.

Whenever the holders of any class or series are entitled to elect 1 or more directors by the certificate of incorporation, **[then]** this subsection shall apply, in respect to the removal without cause of a director or directors so elected, to the vote of the holders of the outstanding shares of that class or series and not to the vote of the outstanding shares as a whole.

§ 142. Officers; titles, duties, selection, term; failure to elect; vacancies.

(a) Every corporation organized under this chapter shall have such officers with such titles and duties **(**as shall be stated in the bylaws or in a resolution of the board of directors which is not inconsistent with the bylaws**)** and **(**as may be necessary to enable it to sign instruments and stock certificates which comply with §§ 103(a)(2) and 158 of this title**)**. ■ One of the officers shall have the duty to record the proceedings of the meetings of the stockholders and directors in a book to be kept for that purpose. ■ **[Then]** Any number of offices may be held by the same person **unless** the certificate of incorporation or bylaws otherwise provide.

(b) Officers shall be chosen in such manner and shall hold their offices for such terms as are prescribed by the bylaws or determined by the board of directors or other governing body. ■ Each officer shall hold office **(**until such officer's successor is elected and qualified**)** or **(**until such officer's earlier resignation or removal**)**. ■ Any officer may resign at any time upon written notice to the corporation.

(c) The corporation may secure the fidelity of any or all of its officers or agents by bond or otherwise.

(d) A failure to elect officers shall not dissolve or otherwise affect the corporation.

(e) Any vacancy occurring in any office of the corporation by death, resignation, removal or otherwise, shall be filled as the bylaws provide. ■ In the absence of such provision, the vacancy shall be filled by the board of directors or other governing body.

§ 143. Loans to employees and officers; guaranty of obligations of employees and officers.

Any corporation may lend money to, or guarantee any obligation of, or otherwise assist any officer or other employee of the corporation or of its subsidiary, including any officer or employee who is a director of the corporation or its subsidiary, **whenever**, in the judgment of the directors, such loan, guaranty or assistance may reasonably be expected to benefit the corporation. ■ The loan, guaranty or other assistance may be with or without interest, and may be unsecured, or secured in such manner as the board of directors shall approve, including, without limitation, a pledge of shares of stock of the corporation. ■ Nothing in this section contained shall be deemed to deny, limit or restrict the powers of guaranty or warranty of any corporation at common law or under any statute.

§ 144. Interested directors; quorum.

(a) [Then] No contract or transaction between (a corporation) and (1 or more of its directors or officers), or between (a corporation) and (any other corporation, partnership, association, or other organization in which 1 or more of its directors or officers, are directors or officers, or have a financial interest), shall be void or voidable solely for this reason, or solely because the director or officer is present at or participates in the meeting of the board or committee which authorizes the contract or transaction, or solely because any such director's or officer's votes are counted for such purpose, if:

(1) The material facts as to the director's or officer's relationship or interest and as to the contract or transaction are disclosed or are known to the board of directors or the committee, and the board or committee in good faith authorizes the contract or transaction (by the affirmative votes of a majority of the disinterested directors, even though the disinterested directors be less than a quorum); or

(2) The material facts as to the director's or officer's relationship or interest and as to the contract or transaction are disclosed or are known to the stockholders entitled to vote thereon, and the contract or transaction is specifically approved in good faith (by vote of the stockholders); or

(3) The contract or transaction is fair as to the corporation as of the time it is authorized, approved or ratified, by the board of directors, a committee or the stockholders.

(b) Common or interested directors may be counted in determining the presence of a quorum at a meeting of the board of directors or of a committee which authorizes the contract or transaction.

§ 145. Indemnification of officers, directors, employees and agents; insurance.

(a) [Then] A corporation shall have power to indemnify (any person who was or is a party or is threatened to be made a party to any threatened, pending or completed action, suit or proceeding, whether civil, criminal, administrative or investigative (other than an action by or in the right of the corporation)) by reason of the fact that the person (is or was a director, officer, employee or agent of the corporation), or (is or was serving at the request of the corporation as a director, officer, employee or agent of another corporation, partnership, joint venture, trust or other enterprise), (against expenses (including attorneys' fees), judgments, fines and amounts paid in settlement actually and reasonably incurred by the person in connection with such action, suit or proceeding) if the person acted in good faith and in a manner the person reasonably believed to be in or not opposed to the best interests of the corporation, and, with respect to any criminal action or proceeding, had no reasonable cause to believe the person's conduct was unlawful. ■ The termination of any action, suit or proceeding by judgment, order, settlement, conviction, or upon a plea of nolo contendere or its equivalent, shall not, of itself, create a presumption that the person (did not act in good faith and in a manner which the person reasonably believed to be in or not opposed to the best interests of the corporation), and, with respect to any criminal action or proceeding, (had reasonable cause to believe that the person's conduct was unlawful).

(b) [Then] A corporation shall have power to indemnify (any person who was or is a party or is threatened to be made a party to any threatened, pending or completed action or suit by or in the right of the corporation to procure a judgment in its favor) by reason of the fact that the person (is or was a director, officer, employee or agent of the corporation), or (is or was serving at the request of the corporation as a director, officer, employee or agent of another corporation, partnership, joint venture, trust or other enterprise) (against expenses (including attorneys' fees) actually and reasonably incurred by the person in connection with the defense or settlement of such action or suit) **if** the person acted in good faith and in a manner the person reasonably believed to be in or not opposed to the best interests of the corporation and ◀except that no indemnification shall be made in respect of any claim, issue or matter as to which such person shall have been adjudged to be liable to the corporation unless and only to the extent that the Court of Chancery or the court in which such action or suit was brought shall determine upon application that, despite the adjudication of liability but in view of all the circumstances of the case, such person is fairly and reasonably entitled to indemnity for such expenses which the Court of Chancery or such other court shall deem proper▶.

(c)(1) To the extent that a present or former director or officer of a corporation has been successful on the merits or otherwise (in defense of any action, suit or proceeding referred to in subsections (a) and (b) of this section), or (in defense of any claim, issue or matter therein), **[then]** such person shall be indemnified (against expenses (including attorneys' fees) actually and reasonably incurred by such person in connection therewith). ■ For indemnification with respect to any act or omission occurring after December 31, 2020, references to "officer" for purposes of this subsection (c)(1) and (2) shall mean only a person who at the time of such act or omission is deemed to have consented to service by the delivery of process to the registered agent of the corporation pursuant to section 3114(b) of title 10 (for purposes of this sentence only, treating residents of this State as if they were nonresidents to apply section 3114(b) of title 10 to this sentence).

(2) [Then] The corporation may indemnify any other person who is not a present or former director or officer of the corporation against expenses (including attorneys' fees) actually and reasonably incurred by such person **to the extent** he or she has been successful on the merits or otherwise in defense of any action, suit or proceeding referred to in subsections (a) and (b) of this section, or in defense of any claim, issue or matter therein.

(d) Any indemnification under subsections (a) and (b) of this section (unless ordered by a court) shall be made by the corporation only as authorized in the specific case upon a determination that (indemnification of the present or former director, officer, employee or agent is proper in the circumstances because the person has met the applicable standard of conduct set forth in subsections (a) and (b) of this section). ■ Such determination shall be made, with respect to a person who is a director or officer of the corporation at the time of such determination:

(1) By a majority vote of the directors who are not parties to such action, suit or proceeding, even though less than a quorum; or

(2) By a committee of such directors designated by majority vote of such directors, even though less than a quorum; or

(3) If there are no such directors, or if such directors so direct, [then] by independent legal counsel in a written opinion; or

(4) By the stockholders.

(e) Expenses (including attorneys' fees) incurred by an officer or director of the corporation in defending any civil, criminal, administrative or investigative action, suit or proceeding may be paid by the corporation in advance of the final disposition of such action, suit or proceeding (upon receipt of an undertaking by or on behalf of such director or officer to repay such amount if it shall ultimately be determined that such person is not entitled to be indemnified by the corporation as authorized in this section). ■ Such expenses (including attorneys' fees) incurred (by former directors and officers or other employees and agents of the corporation) or (by persons serving at the request of the corporation as directors, officers, employees or agents of another corporation, partnership, joint venture, trust or other enterprise) may be so paid upon such terms and conditions, if any, as the corporation deems appropriate.

(f) The indemnification [and] advancement of expenses provided by, or granted pursuant to, the other subsections of this section shall not be deemed exclusive of any other rights to which those seeking indemnification or advancement of expenses may be entitled under any bylaw, agreement, vote of stockholders or disinterested directors or otherwise, both (as to action in such person's official capacity) and (as to action in another capacity while holding such office). ■ [Then] A right to indemnification or to advancement of expenses arising under a provision of the certificate of incorporation or a bylaw shall not be eliminated or impaired by an amendment to or repeal or elimination of the certificate of incorporation or the bylaws after the occurrence of the act or omission that is the subject of the civil, criminal, administrative or investigative action, suit or proceeding for which indemnification or advancement of expenses is sought, **unless** the provision in effect at the time of such act or omission explicitly authorizes such elimination or impairment after such action or omission has occurred.

(g) A corporation shall have power to purchase and maintain insurance on behalf of any person who (is or was a director, officer, employee or agent of the corporation), [or] (is or was serving at the request of the corporation as a director, officer, employee or agent of another corporation, partnership, joint venture, trust or other enterprise) against any liability (asserted against such person and incurred by such person in any such capacity), [or] (arising out of such person's status as such), whether or not the corporation would have the power to indemnify such person against such liability under this section.

(h) For purposes of this section, references to "the corporation" shall include, in addition to the resulting corporation, any constituent corporation (including any constituent of a constituent) absorbed in a consolidation or merger which, if its separate existence had continued, would have had power and authority to indemnify its directors, officers, and employees or agents, [so that] any person who (is or was a director, officer, employee or agent of such constituent corporation), or (is or was serving at the request of such constituent corporation as a director, officer, employee or agent of another corporation, partnership, joint venture, trust or other enterprise), shall stand in the same position under this section with respect to the resulting or surviving corporation as such person would have with respect to such constituent corporation if its separate existence had continued.

(i) For purposes of this section, references to "other enterprises" shall include employee benefit plans; references to "fines" shall include any excise taxes assessed on a person with respect to any employee benefit plan; and references to "serving at the request of the corporation" shall include any service as a director, officer, employee or agent of the corporation which imposes duties on, or involves services by, such director, officer, employee or agent with respect to an employee benefit plan, its participants or beneficiaries; and a person who acted (in good faith) and (in a manner such person reasonably believed to be in the interest of the participants and beneficiaries of an employee benefit plan) shall be deemed to have acted in a manner "not opposed to the best interests of the corporation" as referred to in this section.

(j) The indemnification and advancement of expenses provided by, or granted pursuant to, this section shall, unless otherwise provided when authorized or ratified, continue as to a person who has ceased to be a director, officer, employee or agent and shall inure to the benefit of the heirs, executors and administrators of such a person.

(k) The Court of Chancery is hereby vested with exclusive jurisdiction to hear and determine all actions for advancement of expenses or indemnification brought (under this section) or (under any bylaw, agreement, vote of stockholders or disinterested directors), or (otherwise). ■ The Court of Chancery may summarily determine a corporation's obligation to advance expenses (including attorneys' fees).

§ 146. Submission of matters for stockholder vote.

A corporation may agree to submit a matter to a vote of its stockholders whether or not the board of directors (determines at any time subsequent to approving such matter that such matter is no longer advisable) and (recommends that the stockholders reject or vote against the matter).

Subchapter V. Stock and Dividends

§ 151. Classes and series of stock; redemption; rights.

(a) Every corporation may issue 1 or more classes of stock or 1 or more series of stock within any class thereof, any or all of which classes may be of stock with par value or stock without par value and which classes or series may have (such voting powers, full or limited, or no voting powers,) and (such designations, preferences and relative, participating, optional or other special rights, and qualifications, limitations or restrictions thereof), as shall be stated and expressed in the (certificate of incorporation) or of (any amendment thereto), or (in the resolution or resolutions providing for the issue of such stock adopted by the board of directors pursuant to authority expressly vested in it by the provisions of its certificate of incorporation). ■ Any of the voting powers, designations, preferences, rights and qualifications, limitations or restrictions of any such class or series of stock may be made dependent upon facts ascertainable outside the certificate of incorporation or of any amendment thereto, or outside the resolution or resolutions providing for the issue of such stock adopted by the board of directors pursuant to authority expressly vested in it by its certificate of incorporation, provided that the manner in which such facts shall operate upon the voting powers, designations, preferences, rights and qualifications, limitations or restrictions of such class or series of stock <u>is clearly and expressly set forth</u> (in the certificate of incorporation) or (in the resolution or resolutions providing for the issue of such stock adopted by the board of directors). ■ <u>The term "facts,"</u> as used in this subsection, <u>includes</u>, but is not limited to, <u>the occurrence</u> of any event, including a determination or action by (any person or body, including the corporation). ■ <u>The power</u> to increase or decrease or otherwise adjust the capital stock as provided in this chapter <u>shall apply to all or any</u> such classes of stock.

(b) <u>Any stock</u> of any class or series <u>may be made subject to redemption</u> (by the corporation at its option) or (at the option of the holders of such stock) or (upon the happening of a specified event); ⌈provided however, that⌉ immediately following any such redemption <u>the corporation shall have outstanding 1 or more shares</u> of 1 or more classes or series of stock, which share, or shares together, shall have full voting powers. ■ Notwithstanding the limitation stated in the foregoing proviso:

> (1) <u>Any stock</u> of a regulated investment company registered under the Investment Company Act of 1940 [15 U.S.C. § 80 a-1 et seq.], as heretofore or hereafter amended, <u>may be made subject to redemption</u> by the corporation at its option or at the option of the holders of such stock.

> (2) <u>Any stock</u> of a corporation which (holds (directly or indirectly) a license or franchise from a governmental agency to conduct its business) or (is a member of a national securities exchange), which license, franchise or membership is conditioned upon some or all of the holders of its stock possessing prescribed qualifications, <u>may be made subject to redemption</u> by the corporation to the extent necessary to prevent the loss of such license, franchise or membership or to reinstate it.

<u>Any stock</u> which may be made redeemable under this section <u>may be redeemed</u> for cash, property or rights, including securities of the same or another corporation, at such time or times, price or prices, or rate or rates, and with such adjustments, as shall be stated in (the certificate of incorporation) or (in the resolution or resolutions providing for the issue of such stock adopted by the board of directors pursuant to subsection (a) of this section).

(c) <u>The holders</u> of preferred or special stock of any class or of any series thereof <u>shall be entitled to receive dividends</u> (at such rates, on such conditions and at such times as shall be stated in the certificate of incorporation or in the resolution or resolutions providing for the issue of such stock adopted by the board of directors as hereinabove provided), (payable in preference to, or in such relation to, the dividends payable on any other class or classes or of any other series of stock), ⌈and⌉ (cumulative or noncumulative as shall be so stated and expressed). ■ <u>When</u> <u>dividends</u> upon the preferred and special stocks, if any, to the extent of the preference to which such stocks are entitled, <u>shall have been paid</u> ⌈or⌉ <u>declared and set apart for payment,</u> <u>[then]</u> <u>a dividend</u> on the remaining class or classes or series of stock <u>may then be paid</u> out of the remaining assets of the corporation available for dividends as elsewhere in this chapter provided.

(d) <u>The holders</u> of the preferred or special stock of any class or of any series thereof <u>shall be entitled to such rights</u> upon the dissolution of, or upon any distribution of the assets of, the corporation as shall be stated (in the certificate of incorporation) or (in the resolution or resolutions providing for the issue of such stock adopted by the board of directors as hereinabove provided).

§ 151   Subchapter V. Stock and Dividends

(e) <u>Any stock</u> of any class or of any series thereof <u>may be made convertible</u> into, [or] <u>exchangeable</u> for, (at the option of either the holder or the corporation) or (upon the happening of a specified event), shares of any other class or classes or any other series of the same or any other class or classes of stock of the corporation, at such price or prices or at such rate or rates of exchange and with such adjustments as shall be stated (in the certificate of incorporation) or (in the resolution or resolutions providing for the issue of such stock adopted by the board of directors as hereinabove provided).

(f) <u>If</u> any corporation shall be authorized to issue more than 1 class of stock [or] more than 1 series of any class, **[then]** the powers, designations, preferences and relative, participating, optional, or other special rights of each class of stock or series thereof and the qualifications, limitations or restrictions of such preferences and/or rights <u>shall be set forth</u> in full or summarized on the face or back of the certificate which the corporation shall issue to represent such class or series of stock, [provided that], ◀except as otherwise provided in § 202 of this title▶, in lieu of the foregoing requirements, <u>there may be set forth</u> on the face or back of the certificate which the corporation shall issue to represent such class or series of stock, <u>a statement</u> (that the corporation will furnish without charge to each stockholder who so requests the powers, designations, preferences and relative, participating, optional, or other special rights of each class of stock or series thereof and the qualifications, limitations or restrictions of such preferences and/or rights). ■ Within a reasonable time after the issuance or transfer of uncertificated stock, <u>the registered owner</u> thereof <u>shall be given a notice</u>, in writing or by electronic transmission, <u>containing</u> (the information required to be set forth or stated on certificates pursuant to this section or § 156, § 202(a), § 218(a) or § 364 of this title) or (with respect to this section a statement that the corporation will furnish without charge to each stockholder who so requests the powers, designations, preferences and relative participating, optional or other special rights of each class of stock or series thereof and the qualifications, limitations or restrictions of such preferences and/or rights). ■ ◀Except as otherwise expressly provided by law▶, <u>the rights and obligations</u> of the holders of uncertificated stock [and] <u>the rights and obligations</u> of the holders of certificates representing stock of the same class and series <u>shall be identical</u>.

(g) <u>When</u> <u>any corporation desires to issue any shares</u> of stock of any class or of any series of any class of which the powers, designations, preferences and relative, participating, optional or other rights, if any, or the qualifications, limitations or restrictions thereof, if any, (shall not have been set forth in the certificate of incorporation or in any amendment thereto) but (shall be provided for in a resolution or resolutions adopted by the board of directors pursuant to authority expressly vested in it by the certificate of incorporation or any amendment thereto), **[then]** <u>a certificate</u> of designations setting forth a copy of such resolution or resolutions and the number of shares of stock of such class or series as to which the resolution or resolutions apply <u>shall be executed, acknowledged, filed and shall become effective</u>, in accordance with § 103 of this title. ■ Unless otherwise provided in any such resolution or resolutions, <u>the number</u> of shares of stock of any such series to which such resolution or resolutions apply <u>may be increased</u> (but not above the total number of authorized shares of the class) [or] <u>decreased</u> (but not below the number of shares thereof then outstanding) by a certificate likewise executed, acknowledged and filed setting forth a statement (that a specified increase or decrease therein had been authorized and directed by a resolution or resolutions likewise adopted by the board of directors). ■ In case the number of such shares shall be decreased <u>the number</u> of shares so specified in the certificate <u>shall resume the status</u> which they had prior to the adoption of the first resolution or resolutions. ■ <u>**When**</u> <u>no shares</u> of any such class or series <u>are outstanding</u>, either because none were issued or because no issued shares of any such class or series remain outstanding, <u>[then]</u> <u>a certificate</u> setting forth a resolution or resolutions adopted by the board of directors that none of the authorized shares of such class or series are outstanding, and that none will be issued subject to the certificate of designations previously filed with respect to such class or series, <u>may be executed, acknowledged and filed</u> in accordance with § 103 of this title and, <u>**when**</u> such certificate becomes effective, <u>[then]</u> <u>it shall have the effect</u> of eliminating from the certificate of incorporation all matters set forth in the certificate of designations with respect to such class or series of stock. ■ Unless otherwise provided in the certificate of incorporation, <u>**if**</u> <u>no shares</u> of stock <u>have been issued</u> of a class or series of stock established by a resolution of the board of directors, <u>[then]</u> <u>the voting powers</u>, designations, preferences and relative, participating, optional or other rights, if any, or the qualifications, limitations or restrictions thereof, <u>may be amended</u> by a resolution or resolutions adopted by the board of directors. ■ A certificate which:

(1) States that no shares of the class or series have been issued;

(2) Sets forth a copy of the resolution or resolutions; and

(3) If the designation of the class or series is being changed, indicates the original designation and the new designation,

<u>shall be executed, acknowledged and filed</u> and <u>shall become effective</u>, in accordance with § 103 of this title. ■ <u>**When**</u> <u>any certificate filed</u> under this subsection <u>becomes effective</u>, <u>[then]</u> <u>it shall have the effect</u> of amending the certificate of incorporation; ◄except that neither the filing of such certificate nor the filing of a restated certificate of incorporation pursuant to § 245 of this title shall prohibit the board of directors from subsequently adopting such resolutions as authorized by this subsection.►

§ 152. Issuance of stock; lawful consideration; fully paid stock.

<u>The consideration</u>, as determined pursuant to § 153(a) and (b) of this title, for subscriptions to, or the purchase of, the capital stock to be issued by a corporation <u>shall be paid</u> in such form and in such manner as the board of directors shall determine. ■ <u>The board of directors may authorize capital stock to be issued</u> for consideration consisting of cash, any tangible or intangible property or any benefit to the corporation, or any combination thereof. ■ <u>The resolution</u> authorizing the issuance of capital stock <u>may provide</u> that any stock to be issued pursuant to such resolution may be issued in 1 or more transactions in such numbers and at such times as are set forth in or determined by or in the manner set forth in the resolution, (which may include a determination or action by any person or body, including the corporation), provided <u>the resolution fixes a maximum number</u> of shares that may be issued pursuant to such resolution, <u>a time period</u> during which such shares may be issued and <u>a minimum amount</u> of consideration for which such shares may be issued. ■ <u>The board of directors may determine the amount</u> of consideration for which shares may be issued by (setting a minimum amount of consideration) or (approving a formula by which the amount or minimum amount of consideration is determined). ■ <u>The formula may include</u> or <u>be made dependent upon</u> facts ascertainable outside the formula, provided <u>the manner</u> in

which such facts shall operate upon the formula is clearly and expressly set forth in the formula or in the resolution approving the formula. ∎ In the absence of actual fraud in the transaction, the judgment of the directors as to the value of such consideration shall be conclusive. ∎ The capital stock so issued shall be deemed to be fully paid and nonassessable stock upon receipt by the corporation of such consideration; provided, however, nothing contained herein shall prevent the board of directors from issuing partly paid shares under § 156 of this title.

§ 153. Consideration for stock.

(a) Shares of stock with par value may be issued for such consideration, having a value not less than the par value thereof, as determined from time to time by the board of directors, or [then] by the stockholders if the certificate of incorporation so provides.

(b) Shares of stock without par value may be issued for such consideration as is determined from time to time by the board of directors, or [then] by the stockholders if the certificate of incorporation so provides.

(c) Treasury shares may be disposed of by the corporation for such consideration as may be determined from time to time by the board of directors, or [then] by the stockholders if the certificate of incorporation so provides.

(d) If the certificate of incorporation reserves to the stockholders the right to determine the consideration for the issue of any shares, **[then]** the stockholders shall, unless the certificate requires a greater vote, do so by a vote of a majority of the outstanding stock entitled to vote thereon.

§ 154. Determination of amount of capital; capital, surplus and net assets defined.

Any corporation may, by resolution of its board of directors, determine that only a part of the consideration which shall be received by the corporation for any of the shares of its capital stock which it shall issue from time to time shall be capital; but, **in case** any of the shares issued shall be shares having a par value, **[then]** the amount of the part of such consideration so determined to be capital shall be in excess of the aggregate par value of the shares issued for such consideration having a par value, **unless** all the shares issued shall be shares having a par value, **in which case** the amount of the part of such consideration so determined to be capital need be only equal to the aggregate par value of such shares. ∎ In each such case the board of directors shall specify in dollars the part of such consideration which shall be capital. ∎ **If** the board of directors shall not have determined **(1)** at the time of issue of any shares of the capital stock of the corporation issued for cash or **(2)** within 60 days after the issue of any shares of the capital stock of the corporation issued for consideration other than cash what part of the consideration for such shares shall be capital, **[then]** the capital of the corporation in respect of such shares shall be an amount equal to the aggregate par value of such shares having a par value, plus the amount of the consideration for such shares without par value. ∎ The amount of the consideration so determined to be capital in respect of any shares without par value shall be the stated capital of such shares. ∎ The capital of the corporation may be increased from time to time by resolution of the board of directors directing that (a portion of the net assets of the corporation in excess of the amount so determined to be capital be transferred to the capital account). ■ The board of directors may direct that the portion of such net assets so transferred shall be treated as capital in respect of any shares of the corporation of any designated class or classes. ■ The excess, if any, at any given time, of (the net assets of the corporation) over (the amount so determined to be capital) shall be surplus. ■ Net assets means the amount by which total assets exceed total liabilities. ■ Capital and surplus are not liabilities for this purpose. ■ Notwithstanding anything in this section to the contrary, for purposes of this section and §§ 160 and 170 of this title, the capital of any nonstock corporation shall be deemed to be zero.

§ 155. Fractions of shares.

A corporation may, but shall not be required to, issue fractions of a share. ■ If it does not issue fractions of a share, [then] it shall (1) arrange for the disposition of fractional interests by those entitled thereto, (2) pay in cash the fair value of fractions of a share as of the time when those entitled to receive such fractions are determined or (3) issue scrip or warrants in registered form (either represented by a certificate or uncertificated) or in bearer form (represented by a certificate) which shall entitle the holder to receive a full share upon the surrender of such scrip or warrants aggregating a full share. ■ A certificate for a fractional share or an uncertificated fractional share shall, but scrip or warrants shall not unless otherwise provided therein, entitle the holder (to exercise voting rights), (to receive dividends thereon) and (to participate in any of the assets of the corporation in the event of liquidation). ■ The board of directors may cause scrip or warrants to be issued (subject to the conditions that they shall become void if not exchanged for certificates representing the full shares or uncertificated full shares before a specified date), or (subject to the conditions that the shares for which scrip or warrants are exchangeable may be sold by the corporation and the proceeds thereof distributed to the holders of scrip or warrants), or (subject to any other conditions which the board of directors may impose).

§ 156. Partly paid shares.

Any corporation may issue the whole or any part of its shares as (partly paid) and (subject to call for the remainder of the consideration to be paid therefor). ■ (Upon the face or back of each stock certificate issued to represent any such partly paid shares), or (upon the books and records of the corporation in the case of uncertificated partly paid shares), the total amount of the consideration to be paid therefor and the amount paid thereon shall be stated. ■ Upon the declaration of any dividend on fully paid shares, the corporation shall declare a dividend upon partly paid shares of the same class, but only upon the basis of the percentage of the consideration actually paid thereon.

§ 157. Rights and options respecting stock.

(a) Subject to any provisions in the certificate of incorporation, every corporation may create and issue, whether or not in connection with the issue and sale of any shares of stock or other securities of the corporation, rights or options entitling the holders thereof to acquire from the corporation any shares of its capital stock of any class or classes, (such rights or options to be evidenced by or in such instrument or instruments as shall be approved by the board of directors).

(b) The terms upon which, including the time or times which may be limited or unlimited in duration, at or within which, and the consideration (including a formula by which such consideration may be determined) for which any such shares may be acquired from the corporation upon the exercise of any such right or option, shall be such as shall be stated in the certificate of incorporation, or in a resolution adopted by the board of directors providing for the creation and issue of such rights or options, and, in every case, shall be set forth or incorporated by reference in the instrument or instruments evidencing such rights or options. ■ A formula by which such consideration may be determined may include or be made dependent upon facts ascertainable outside the formula, provided the manner in which such facts shall operate upon the formula is clearly and expressly set forth in the formula or in the resolution approving the formula. ■ In the absence of actual fraud in the transaction, the judgment of the directors as to the consideration for the issuance of such rights or options and the sufficiency thereof shall be conclusive.

(c) The board of directors may, by a resolution adopted by the board, authorize 1 or more officers of the corporation to do 1 or both of the following: **(i)** designate officers and employees of the corporation or of any of its subsidiaries to be recipients of such rights or options created by the corporation, and **(ii)** determine the number of such rights or options to be received by such officers and employees; provided, however, that the resolution so authorizing such officer or officers shall specify the total number of rights or options such officer or officers may so award. ■ The board of directors may not authorize an officer to designate himself or herself as a recipient of any such rights or options.

(d) In case the shares of stock of the corporation to be issued upon the exercise of such rights or options shall be shares having a par value, **[then]** the consideration so to be received therefor shall have a value not less than the par value thereof. ■ **In case** the shares of stock so to be issued shall be shares of stock without par value, **[then]** the consideration therefor shall be determined in the manner provided in § 153 of this title.

§ 158. Stock certificates; uncertificated shares.

The shares of a corporation shall be represented by certificates, provided that the board of directors of the corporation may provide by resolution or resolutions that **(**some or all of any or all classes or series of its stock shall be uncertificated shares**)**. ■ **[Then]** Any such resolution shall not apply to shares represented by a certificate **until** such certificate is surrendered to the corporation. ■ Every holder of stock represented by certificates shall be entitled to have a certificate **(**signed by, or in the name of, the corporation by any 2 authorized officers of the corporation**)** **(**representing the number of shares registered in certificate form**)**. ■ Any or all the signatures on the certificate may be a facsimile. ■ **In case** any officer, transfer agent or registrar who has signed or whose facsimile signature has been placed upon a certificate shall have ceased to be such officer, transfer agent or registrar before such certificate is issued, **[then]** it may be issued by the corporation with the same effect as if such person were such officer, transfer agent or registrar at the date of issue. ■ A corporation shall not have power to issue a certificate in bearer form.

§ 159. Shares of stock; personal property, transfer and taxation.

The shares of stock in every corporation shall be deemed personal property and transferable as provided in Article 8 of subtitle I of Title 6. ■ **[Then]** No stock or bonds issued by any corporation organized under this chapter shall be taxed by this State when the same shall be owned by nonresidents of this State, or by foreign corporations. ■ Whenever any transfer of shares shall be made for collateral security, and not absolutely, [then] it shall be so expressed in the entry of transfer if, when the certificates are presented to the corporation for transfer or uncertificated shares are requested to be transferred, both the transferor and transferee request the corporation to do so.

§ 160. Corporation's powers respecting ownership, voting, etc., of its own stock; rights of stock called for redemption.

(a) Every corporation may purchase, redeem, receive, take or otherwise acquire, own and hold, sell, lend, exchange, transfer or otherwise dispose of, pledge, use and otherwise deal in and with its own shares; provided, however, that no corporation shall:

> (1) [Then] Purchase or redeem its own shares of capital stock for cash or other property (when the capital of the corporation is impaired) or (when such purchase or redemption would cause any impairment of the capital of the corporation), ◄except that a corporation other than a nonstock corporation may purchase or redeem out of capital any of its own shares which are entitled upon any distribution of its assets, whether by dividend or in liquidation, to a preference over another class or series of its stock, or, if no shares entitled to such a preference are outstanding, any of its own shares, if such shares will be retired upon their acquisition and the capital of the corporation reduced in accordance with §§ 243 and 244 of this title.► ■ [Then] Nothing in this subsection shall invalidate or otherwise affect a note, debenture or other obligation of a corporation given by it as consideration for its acquisition by purchase, redemption or exchange of its shares of stock if at the time such note, debenture or obligation was delivered by the corporation its capital was not then impaired or did not thereby become impaired;
>
> (2) Purchase, for more than the price at which they may then be redeemed, any of its shares which are redeemable at the option of the corporation; or
>
> (3) a. [Then] In the case of a corporation other than a nonstock corporation, redeem any of its shares, unless their redemption is authorized by § 151(b) of this title and then only in accordance with such section and the certificate of incorporation, or
>
> b. [Then] In the case of a nonstock corporation, redeem any of its membership interests, unless their redemption is authorized by the certificate of incorporation and then only in accordance with the certificate of incorporation.

(b) Nothing in this section limits or affects a corporation's right to resell any of its shares theretofore purchased or redeemed out of surplus and which have not been retired, for such consideration as shall be fixed by the board of directors.

(c) Shares of its own capital stock belonging (to the corporation) or (to another corporation, if a majority of the shares entitled to vote in the election of directors of such other corporation is held, directly or indirectly, by the corporation,) shall neither be entitled to vote nor be counted for quorum purposes. ■ Nothing in this section shall be construed as limiting the right of any corporation to vote stock, including but not limited to its own stock, held by it in a fiduciary capacity.

(d) Shares which have been called for redemption shall not be deemed to be outstanding shares for the purpose of voting or determining the total number of shares entitled to vote on any matter on and after the date on which (notice of redemption has been sent to holders thereof) and (a sum sufficient to redeem such shares has been irrevocably deposited or set aside to pay the redemption price to the holders of the shares upon surrender of certificates therefor.)

§ 161. Issuance of additional stock; when and by whom.

The directors may, at any time and from time to time, (if all of the shares of capital stock which the corporation is authorized by its certificate of incorporation to issue have not been issued, subscribed for, or otherwise committed to be issued,) issue or take subscriptions for additional shares of its capital stock up to the amount authorized in its certificate of incorporation.

§ 162. Liability of stockholder or subscriber for stock not paid in full.

(a) When the whole of the consideration payable for shares of a corporation has not been paid in, and the assets shall be insufficient to satisfy the claims of its creditors, **[then]** each holder of or subscriber for such shares shall be bound to pay on each share held or subscribed for by such holder or subscriber (the sum necessary to complete the amount of the unpaid balance of the consideration for which such shares were issued or are to be issued by the corporation).

(b) The amounts which shall be payable as provided in subsection (a) of this section may be recovered as provided in § 325 of this title, after a writ of execution against the corporation has been returned unsatisfied as provided in said § 325.

(c) Any person becoming an assignee or transferee of shares or of a subscription for shares in good faith and (without knowledge or notice that the full consideration therefor has not been paid) shall not be personally liable for any unpaid portion of such consideration, but the transferor shall remain liable therefor.

(d) No person holding shares in any corporation as collateral security shall be personally liable as a stockholder but the person pledging such shares shall be considered the holder thereof and shall be so liable. ■ No executor, administrator, guardian, trustee or other fiduciary shall be personally liable as a stockholder, but the estate or funds held by such executor, administrator, guardian, trustee or other fiduciary in such fiduciary capacity shall be liable.

(e) No liability under this section or under § 325 of this title shall be asserted more than 6 years after (the issuance of the stock) or (the date of the subscription upon which the assessment is sought).

(f) In any action (by a receiver or trustee of an insolvent corporation) or (by a judgment creditor) to obtain an assessment under this section, any stockholder or subscriber for stock of the insolvent corporation may appear and contest the claim or claims of such receiver or trustee.

§ 163. Payment for stock not paid in full.

The capital stock of a corporation shall be paid for in such amounts and at such times as the directors may require. ■ The directors may, from time to time, demand payment, in respect of each share of stock not fully paid, of such sum of money as the necessities of the business may, in the judgment of the board of directors, require, not exceeding in the whole the balance remaining unpaid on said stock, and such sum so demanded shall be paid to the corporation at such times and by such installments as the directors shall direct. ■ The directors shall give notice of the time and place of such payments, which notice shall be given at least 30 days before the time for such payment, to each holder of or subscriber for stock which is not fully paid at such holder's or subscriber's last known address.

§ 164. Failure to pay for stock; remedies.

When any stockholder fails to pay any installment or call upon such stockholder's stock which may have been properly demanded by the directors, [then] at the time when such payment is due, the directors may collect the amount of any such installment or call or any balance thereof remaining unpaid, from the said stockholder by an action at law, or they shall sell at public sale such part of the shares of such delinquent stockholder as will pay all demands then due from such stockholder with interest and all incidental expenses, and shall transfer the shares so sold to the purchaser, who shall be entitled to a certificate therefor.

Notice of the time and place of such sale and of the sum due on each share shall be given by advertisement at least 1 week before the sale, in a newspaper of the county in this State where such corporation's registered office is located, and such notice shall be mailed by the corporation to such delinquent stockholder at such stockholder's last known post-office address, at least 20 days before such sale.

If no bidder can be had to pay the amount due on the stock, and if the amount is not collected by an action at law, which may be brought within the county where the corporation has its registered office, within 1 year from the date of the bringing of such action at law, [then] the said stock and the amount previously paid in by the delinquent stockholder on the stock shall be forfeited to the corporation.

§ 165. Revocability of preincorporation subscriptions.

◀Unless otherwise provided by the terms of the subscription,▶ a subscription for stock of a corporation to be formed shall be irrevocable, ◀except with the consent of all other subscribers or the corporation,▶ for a period of 6 months from its date.

§ 166. Formalities required of stock subscriptions.

A subscription for stock of a corporation, whether made before or after the formation of a corporation, shall not be enforceable against a subscriber, ◀unless in writing and signed by the subscriber or by such subscriber's agent.▶

§ 167. Lost, stolen or destroyed stock certificates; issuance of new certificate or uncertificated shares.

A corporation may issue a new certificate of stock or uncertificated shares in place of any certificate theretofore issued by it, alleged to have been lost, stolen or destroyed, and the corporation may require the owner of the lost, stolen or destroyed certificate, or such owner's legal representative to give the corporation a bond sufficient to indemnify it against any claim that may be made against it on account of ◀the alleged loss, theft or destruction of any such certificate) or (the issuance of such new certificate or uncertificated shares).

§ 168. Judicial proceedings to compel issuance of new certificate or uncertificated shares.

(a) If a corporation refuses to issue new uncertificated shares [or] a new certificate of stock in place of a certificate theretofore issued by it, or by any corporation of which it is the lawful successor, alleged to have been lost, stolen or destroyed, [then] the owner of the lost, stolen or destroyed certificate or such owner's legal representatives may apply to the Court of Chancery for an order requiring the corporation to show cause why it should not issue new uncertificated shares or a new certificate of stock in place of the certificate so lost, stolen or destroyed. ■ Such application shall be by a complaint which shall state (the name of the corporation), (the number and date of the certificate, if known or ascertainable by the plaintiff), (the number of shares of stock represented thereby and to whom issued), and (a statement of the circumstances attending such loss, theft or destruction). ■ Thereupon the court shall make an order requiring the corporation to show cause at a time and place therein designated, why it should not issue new uncertificated shares or a new certificate of stock in place of the one described in the complaint. ■ A copy of the complaint and order shall be served upon the corporation at least 5 days before the time designated in the order.

(b) If, upon hearing, the court is satisfied (that the plaintiff is the lawful owner of the number of shares of capital stock, or any part thereof, described in the complaint), and (that the certificate therefor has been lost, stolen or destroyed, and no sufficient cause has been shown why new uncertificated shares or a new certificate should not be issued in place thereof), [then] it shall make an order requiring the corporation to issue and deliver to the plaintiff new uncertificated shares or a new certificate for such shares. ■ In its order the court shall direct that, prior to the issuance and delivery to the plaintiff of such new uncertificated shares or a new certificate, the plaintiff give the corporation (a bond in such form and with such security as to the court appears sufficient to indemnify the corporation against any claim that may be made against it on account of the alleged loss, theft or destruction of any such certificate or the issuance of such new uncertificated shares or new certificate). ■ No corporation which has issued uncertificated shares or a certificate pursuant to an order of the court entered hereunder shall be liable in an amount in excess of the amount specified in such bond.

§ 169. Situs of ownership of stock.

(For all purposes of title, action, attachment, garnishment and jurisdiction of all courts held in this State), but not (for the purpose of taxation), the situs of the ownership of the capital stock of all corporations existing under the laws of this State, whether organized under this chapter or otherwise, shall be regarded as in this State.

§ 170. Dividends; payment; wasting asset corporations.

(a) The directors of every corporation, subject to any restrictions contained in its certificate of incorporation, may declare and pay dividends upon the shares of its capital stock either:

(1) Out of its surplus, as defined in and computed in accordance with §§ 154 and 244 of this title; or

(2) In case there shall be no such surplus, out of its net profits for the fiscal year in which the dividend is declared and/or the preceding fiscal year. ■

If the capital of the corporation, computed in accordance with §§ 154 and 244 of this title, shall have been diminished by depreciation in the value of its property, or by losses, or otherwise, to (an amount less than the aggregate amount of the capital represented by the issued and outstanding stock of all classes having a preference upon the distribution of assets), [then] the directors of such corporation shall not declare and pay out of such net profits any dividends upon any shares of any classes of its capital stock until the deficiency in the amount of capital represented by the issued and outstanding stock of all classes having a preference upon the distribution of assets shall have been repaired. ■ [Then] Nothing in this subsection shall invalidate or otherwise affect a note, debenture or other obligation of the corporation paid by it as a dividend on shares of its stock, or any payment made thereon, if at the time such note, debenture or obligation was delivered by the corporation, the corporation had either surplus or net profits as provided in (a)(1) or (2) of this section from which the dividend could lawfully have been paid.

(b) Subject to any restrictions contained in its certificate of incorporation, the directors of any corporation engaged in the exploitation of wasting assets (including but not limited to a corporation engaged in the exploitation of natural resources or other wasting assets, including patents, or engaged primarily in the liquidation of specific assets) may determine the net profits derived from the exploitation of such wasting assets or the net proceeds derived from such liquidation without taking into consideration the depletion of such assets resulting from lapse of time, consumption, liquidation or exploitation of such assets.

§ 171. Special purpose reserves.

The directors of a corporation may set apart out of any of the funds of the corporation available for dividends a reserve or reserves for any proper purpose and may abolish any such reserve.

§ 172. Liability of directors and committee members as to dividends or stock redemption.

A member of the board of directors, or a member of any committee designated by the board of directors, shall be fully protected in relying in good faith (upon the records of the corporation) and (upon such information, opinions, reports or statements presented to the corporation by any of its officers or employees, or committees of the board of directors, or by any other person as to matters the director reasonably believes are within such other person's professional or expert competence and who has been selected with reasonable care by or on behalf of the corporation), as to (the value and amount of the assets, liabilities and/or net profits of the corporation) or (any other facts pertinent to the existence and amount of surplus or other funds from which dividends might properly be declared and paid, or with which the corporation's stock might properly be purchased or redeemed).

§ 173. Declaration and payment of dividends.

No corporation shall pay dividends ❨except in accordance with this chapter❩. ■ Dividends may be paid in cash, in property, or in shares of the corporation's capital stock. ■ If the dividend is to be paid in shares of the corporation's theretofore unissued capital stock [then] the board of directors shall, by resolution, direct that there be designated as capital in respect of such shares ❨an amount which is not less than the aggregate par value of par value shares being declared as a dividend❩ and, in the case of shares without par value being declared as a dividend, ❨such amount as shall be determined by the board of directors❩. ■ [Then] No such designation as capital shall be necessary if shares are being distributed by a corporation pursuant to a split-up or division of its stock rather than as payment of a dividend declared payable in stock of the corporation.

§ 174. Liability of directors for unlawful payment of dividend or unlawful stock purchase or redemption; exoneration from liability; contribution among directors; subrogation.

(a) In case of any wilful or negligent violation of § 160 or § 173 of this title, the directors under whose administration the same may happen shall be jointly and severally liable, at any time within 6 years ❨after paying such unlawful dividend❩ or ❨after such unlawful stock purchase or redemption❩, to the corporation, and to its creditors in the event of its dissolution or insolvency, ❨to the full amount of the dividend unlawfully paid❩, or ❨to the full amount unlawfully paid for the purchase or redemption of the corporation's stock❩, with interest from the time such liability accrued. ■ Any director who may have been absent when the same was done, or who may have dissented from the act or resolution by which the same was done, may be exonerated from such liability ❨by causing his or her dissent to be entered on the books containing the minutes of the proceedings of the directors❩ at the time the same was done, or immediately after such director has notice of the same.

(b) Any director against whom a claim is successfully asserted under this section shall be entitled to contribution from the other directors who voted for or concurred in the unlawful dividend, stock purchase or stock redemption.

(c) Any director against whom a claim is successfully asserted under this section shall be entitled, to the extent of the amount paid by such director as a result of such claim, to be subrogated to the rights of the corporation against stockholders who received ❨the dividend on❩, or ❨assets for the sale or redemption of❩, their stock ❨with knowledge of facts indicating that such dividend, stock purchase or redemption was unlawful under this chapter❩, in proportion to the amounts received by such stockholders respectively.

Subchapter VI. Stock Transfers

§ 201. Transfer of stock, stock certificates and uncertificated stock.

❨Except as otherwise provided in this chapter,❩ the transfer of stock and the certificates of stock which represent the stock or uncertificated stock shall be governed by Article 8 of subtitle I of Title 6. ■ **To the extent that** any provision of this chapter is inconsistent with any provision of subtitle I of Title 6, [then] this chapter shall be controlling.

§ 202. Restrictions on transfer and ownership of securities.

(a) A written restriction or restrictions (on the transfer or registration of transfer of a security of a corporation), or (on the amount of the corporation's securities that may be owned by any person or group of persons), if permitted by this section and (noted conspicuously on the certificate or certificates representing the security or securities so restricted) or, in the case of uncertificated shares, (contained in the notice or notices given pursuant to § 151(f) of this title), may be enforced against the holder of the restricted security or securities or any successor or transferee of the holder including an executor, administrator, trustee, guardian or other fiduciary entrusted with like responsibility for the person or estate of the holder. ■ Unless (noted conspicuously on the certificate or certificates representing the security or securities so restricted) or, in the case of uncertificated shares, (contained in the notice or notices given pursuant to § 151(f) of this title), a restriction, even though permitted by this section, is ineffective ◄except against a person with actual knowledge of the restriction.▶

(b) A restriction (on the transfer or registration of transfer of securities of a corporation), or (on the amount of a corporation's securities that may be owned by any person or group of persons), may be imposed by the certificate of incorporation or by the bylaws or by an agreement (among any number of security holders) or (among such holders and the corporation). ■ **[Then]** No restrictions so imposed shall be binding with respect to securities issued prior to the adoption of the restriction **unless** the holders of the securities are parties to an agreement [or] voted in favor of the restriction.

(c) [Then] A restriction (on the transfer or registration of transfer of securities of a corporation) or (on the amount of such securities that may be owned by any person or group of persons) is permitted by this section **if** it:

> **(1)** Obligates the holder of the restricted securities to offer to the corporation or to any other holders of securities of the corporation or to any other person or to any combination of the foregoing, a prior opportunity, to be exercised within a reasonable time, to acquire the restricted securities; [or]
>
> **(2)** Obligates the corporation [or] any holder of securities of the corporation [or] any other person [or] any combination of the foregoing, to purchase the securities which are the subject of an agreement respecting the purchase and sale of the restricted securities; [or]
>
> **(3)** Requires the corporation [or] the holders of any class or series of securities of the corporation to consent to any proposed transfer of the restricted securities [or] to approve the proposed transferee of the restricted securities, [or] to approve the amount of securities of the corporation that may be owned by any person or group of persons; [or]
>
> **(4)** Obligates the holder of the restricted securities to sell or transfer an amount of restricted securities (to the corporation) or (to any other holders of securities of the corporation) or (to any other person) or (to any combination of the foregoing), [or] causes or results in the automatic sale or transfer of an amount of restricted securities (to the corporation) or (to any other holders of securities of the corporation) or (to any other person) or (to any combination of the foregoing); [or]

(5) Prohibits or restricts the transfer of the restricted securities to, [or] the ownership of restricted securities by, designated persons or classes of persons or groups of persons, [and] such designation is not manifestly unreasonable.

(d) Any restriction on the transfer or the registration of transfer of the securities of a corporation, or on the amount of securities of a corporation that may be owned by a person or group of persons, for any of the following purposes shall be conclusively presumed to be for a reasonable purpose:

(1) Maintaining any local, state, federal or foreign tax advantage to the corporation or its stockholders, including without limitation:

a. Maintaining the corporation's status as an electing small business corporation under subchapter S of the United States Internal Revenue Code [26 U.S.C. § 1371 et seq.], [or]

b. Maintaining or preserving any tax attribute (including without limitation net operating losses), [or]

c. Qualifying or maintaining the qualification of the corporation as a real estate investment trust pursuant to the United States Internal Revenue Code or regulations adopted pursuant to the United States Internal Revenue Code, [or]

(2) Maintaining any statutory or regulatory advantage or complying with any statutory or regulatory requirements under applicable local, state, federal or foreign law.

(e) Any other lawful restriction **(**on transfer or registration of transfer of securities**)**, or **(**on the amount of securities that may be owned by any person or group of persons**)**, is permitted by this section.

§ 203. Business combinations with interested stockholders.

(a) **[Then]** Notwithstanding any other provisions of this chapter, a corporation shall not engage in any business combination with any interested stockholder for a period of 3 years following the time that such stockholder became an interested stockholder, **unless**:

(1) Prior to such time the board of directors of the corporation approved either the business combination or the transaction which resulted in the stockholder becoming an interested stockholder;

(2) Upon consummation of the transaction which resulted in the stockholder becoming an interested stockholder, the interested stockholder owned at least 85% of the voting stock of the corporation outstanding at the time the transaction commenced, excluding for purposes of determining the voting stock outstanding (but not the outstanding voting stock owned by the interested stockholder) those shares owned **(i)** by persons who are directors and also officers [and] **(ii)** employee stock plans in which employee participants do not have the right to determine confidentially whether shares held subject to the plan will be tendered in a tender or exchange offer; [or]

(3) At or subsequent to such time the business combination is approved by the board of directors and authorized at an annual or special meeting of stockholders, and not by written consent, **(**by the affirmative vote of at least 66 2/3% of the outstanding voting stock which is not owned by the interested stockholder**)**.

(b) **[Then]** The restrictions contained in this section shall not apply **if**:

(1) <u>The corporation's original certificate of incorporation contains a provision</u> expressly electing not to be governed by this section;

(2) <u>The corporation</u>, by action of its board of directors, <u>adopts an amendment</u> to its bylaws within 90 days of February 2, 1988, expressly electing not to be governed by this section, which amendment shall not be further amended by the board of directors;

(3) <u>The corporation</u>, by action of its stockholders, <u>adopts an amendment</u> to its certificate of incorporation or bylaws expressly electing not to be governed by this section; `provided that`, in addition to any other vote required by law, <u>such amendment</u> to the certificate of incorporation or bylaws <u>must be adopted</u> by the affirmative vote of a majority of the outstanding stock entitled to vote thereon. ■ In the case of a corporation that both **(i)** has never had a class of voting stock that falls within any of the 2 categories set out in paragraph (b)(4) of this section, and **(ii)** has not elected by a provision in its original certificate of incorporation or any amendment thereto to be governed by this section, <u>such amendment shall become effective</u> upon **(i)** in the case of an amendment to the certificate of incorporation, the date and time at which the certificate filed in accordance with § 103 of this title becomes effective thereunder or **(ii)** in the case of an amendment to the bylaws, the date of the adoption of such amendment. ■ In all other cases, <u>an amendment adopted</u> pursuant to this paragraph <u>shall</u> become effective **(i)** in the case of an amendment to the certificate of incorporation, 12 months after the date and time at which the certificate filed in accordance with § 103 of this title becomes effective thereunder or **(ii)** in the case of an amendment to the bylaws, 12 months after the date of the adoption of such amendment, `and` , in either case, <u>the election not to be governed</u> by this section <u>shall not apply to any business combination</u> between such corporation and any person who became an interested stockholder of such corporation on or before **(A)** in the case of an amendment to the certificate of incorporation, the date and time at which the certificate filed in accordance with § 103 of this title becomes effective thereunder; or **(B)** in the case of an amendment to the bylaws, the date of the adoption of such amendment. ■ <u>A bylaw amendment adopted</u> pursuant to this paragraph <u>shall not be further amended</u> by the board of directors;

(4) <u>[Then]</u> <u>The corporation does not have a class</u> of voting stock that is: **(i)** Listed on a national securities exchange; or **(ii)** held of record by more than 2,000 stockholders, <u>unless</u> any of the foregoing results from action taken, directly or indirectly, by an interested stockholder or from a transaction in which a person becomes an interested stockholder;

(5) <u>A stockholder becomes an interested stockholder inadvertently</u> `and` **(i)** as soon as practicable <u>divests itself</u> of ownership of sufficient shares so that the stockholder ceases to be an interested stockholder; `and` **(ii)** <u>would not</u>, at any time within the 3-year period immediately prior to a business combination between the corporation and such stockholder, <u>have been an interested stockholder</u> but for the inadvertent acquisition of ownership;

(6) <u>The business combination is proposed</u> **(**prior to the consummation or abandonment of**)** `and` **(**subsequent to the earlier of the public announcement or the notice required hereunder of**)** a proposed transaction which **(i)** constitutes 1 of the transactions described in the second sentence of this paragraph; **(ii)** is with or by a person who either **(**was not an interested stockholder during the previous 3 years**)** `or` **(**who became an interested stockholder with the approval of the corporation's board of directors or during the period described in paragraph (b)(7) of this section); `and` **(iii)** is approved or not opposed by a majority of the members of the board of directors then in office (but not less than 1) who (were directors prior to any person becoming an interested stockholder during the previous 3 years) `or` (were recommended for election or elected to succeed such directors by a majority of such directors). The proposed transactions referred to in the preceding sentence are limited to **(x)** a merger or consolidation of the corporation (except for a merger in respect of which, pursuant to § 251(f) of this title, no vote of the stockholders of the corporation is required); **(y)** a sale, lease, exchange, mortgage, pledge, transfer `or` other disposition (in 1 transaction or a series of transactions), whether as part of a dissolution or otherwise, of assets of the corporation or of any direct or indirect majority-owned subsidiary of the corporation (other than to any direct or indirect wholly-owned subsidiary or to the corporation) having an aggregate market value equal to 50% or more of either (that aggregate market value of all of the assets of the corporation determined on a consolidated basis) or (the aggregate market value of all the outstanding stock of the corporation); `or` **(z)** a proposed tender or exchange offer for 50% or more of the outstanding voting stock of the corporation. ■ The corporation shall give not less than 20 days' notice to all interested stockholders prior to the consummation of any of the transactions described in clause (x) or (y) of the second sentence of this paragraph; `or`

(7) The business combination is with an interested stockholder who became an interested stockholder at a time when the restrictions contained in this section did not apply by reason of any of paragraphs (b)(1) through (4) of this section, `provided, however, that` [then] this paragraph (b)(7) shall not apply **if**, at the time such interested stockholder became an interested stockholder, the corporation's certificate of incorporation contained a provision authorized by the last sentence of this subsection (b).

Notwithstanding paragraphs (b)(1), (2), (3) and (4) of this section, a corporation may elect by a provision of its original certificate of incorporation or any amendment thereto to be governed by this section; `provided that` [then] any such amendment to the certificate of incorporation shall not apply to restrict a business combination between the corporation and an interested stockholder of the corporation **if** the interested stockholder became such before the date and time at which the certificate filed in accordance with § 103 of this title becomes effective thereunder.

(c) As used in this section only, the term:

(1) "Affiliate" means a person that directly, or indirectly through 1 or more intermediaries, controls, or is controlled by, or is under common control with, another person.

(2) "Associate," when used to indicate a relationship with any person, means: **(i)** Any corporation, partnership, unincorporated association `or` other entity of which such person is a director, officer or partner or is, directly or indirectly, the owner of 20% or more of any class of voting stock; **(ii)** any trust `or` other estate in which such person has at least a 20% beneficial interest or as to which such person serves as trustee or in a similar fiduciary capacity; and (iii) any relative or spouse of such person, or any relative of such spouse, who has the same residence as such person.

(3) "Business combination," when used in reference to any corporation and any interested stockholder of such corporation, means:

(i) Any merger or consolidation of the corporation or any direct or indirect majority-owned subsidiary of the corporation with **(A)** the interested stockholder, or **(B)** [then] with any other corporation, partnership, unincorporated association or other entity if the merger or consolidation is caused by the interested stockholder and as a result of such merger or consolidation subsection (a) of this section is not applicable to the surviving entity;

(ii) Any sale, lease, exchange, mortgage, pledge, transfer or other disposition (in 1 transaction or a series of transactions), ◄except proportionately as a stockholder of such corporation►, to or with the interested stockholder, whether as part of a dissolution or otherwise, of assets of the corporation or of any direct or indirect majority-owned subsidiary of the corporation which assets have an aggregate market value equal to 10% or more of either **(**the aggregate market value of all the assets of the corporation determined on a consolidated basis**)** or **(**the aggregate market value of all the outstanding stock of the corporation**)**;

(iii) Any transaction which results in the issuance or transfer by the corporation or by any direct or indirect majority-owned subsidiary of the corporation of any stock of the corporation or of such subsidiary to the interested stockholder, ◄except: **(A)** Pursuant to the exercise, exchange or conversion of securities exercisable for, exchangeable for or convertible into stock of such corporation or any such subsidiary which securities were outstanding prior to the time that the interested stockholder became such; **(B)** pursuant to a merger under § 251(g) of this title; **(C)** pursuant to a dividend or distribution paid or made, or the exercise, exchange or conversion of securities exercisable for, exchangeable for or convertible into stock of such corporation or any such subsidiary which security is distributed, pro rata to all holders of a class or series of stock of such corporation subsequent to the time the interested stockholder became such; **(D)** pursuant to an exchange offer by the corporation to purchase stock made on the same terms to all holders of said stock; or **(E)** any issuance or transfer of stock by the corporation►; provided however, that in no case under items (C)-(E) of this subparagraph shall there be an increase in the interested stockholder's proportionate share **(**of the stock of any class or series of the corporation**)** or **(**of the voting stock of the corporation**)**;

(iv) Any transaction involving the corporation or any direct or indirect majority-owned subsidiary of the corporation which has the effect, directly or indirectly, of increasing the proportionate share of the stock of any class or series, or securities convertible into the stock of any class or series, of the corporation or of any such subsidiary which is owned by the interested stockholder, ◄except as a result of immaterial changes due to fractional share adjustments or as a result of any purchase or redemption of any shares of stock not caused, directly or indirectly, by the interested stockholder►; or

(v) Any receipt by the interested stockholder of the benefit, directly or indirectly (except proportionately as a stockholder of such corporation), of any loans, advances, guarantees, pledges or other financial benefits (other than those expressly permitted in paragraphs (c)(3)(i)-(iv) of this section) provided by or through the corporation or any direct or indirect majority-owned subsidiary.

(4) "Control," including the terms "controlling," "controlled by" and "under common control with," means the possession, directly or indirectly, of the power to direct or cause the direction of the management and policies of a person, whether through the ownership of voting stock, by contract or otherwise. ■ A person who is the owner of 20% or more of the outstanding voting stock of any corporation, partnership, unincorporated association or other entity shall be presumed to have control of such entity, in the absence of proof by a preponderance of the evidence to the contrary; Notwithstanding the foregoing, a presumption of control shall not apply where such person holds voting stock, in good faith and not for the purpose of circumventing this section, as an agent, bank, broker, nominee, custodian or trustee for 1 or more owners who do not individually or as a group have control of such entity.

(5) "Interested stockholder" means any person (other than the corporation and any direct or indirect majority-owned subsidiary of the corporation) that (i) is the owner of 15% or more of the outstanding voting stock of the corporation, or (ii) is an affiliate or associate of the corporation and was the owner of 15% or more of the outstanding voting stock of the corporation at any time within the 3-year period immediately prior to (the date on which it is sought to be determined whether such person is an interested stockholder), and the affiliates and associates of such person; provided, however, that the term "interested stockholder" shall not include (x) any person who (A) owned shares in excess of the 15% limitation set forth herein as of, or acquired such shares (pursuant to a tender offer commenced prior to, December 23, 1987), or (pursuant to an exchange offer announced prior to the aforesaid date and commenced within 90 days thereafter) and either (I) continued to own shares in excess of such 15% limitation or would have but for action by the corporation or (II) is an affiliate or associate of the corporation and so continued (or so would have continued but for action by the corporation) to be the owner of 15% or more of the outstanding voting stock of the corporation at any time within the 3-year period immediately prior to (the date on which it is sought to be determined whether such a person is an interested stockholder) or (B) acquired said shares from a person described in item (A) of this paragraph by gift, inheritance or in a transaction in which no consideration was exchanged; or (y) any person whose ownership of shares in excess of the 15% limitation set forth herein is the result of action taken solely by the corporation; provided that [then] such person shall be an interested stockholder if thereafter such person acquires additional shares of voting stock of the corporation, ◀except as a result of further corporate action not caused, directly or indirectly, by such person▶. For the purpose of determining whether a person is an interested stockholder, the voting stock of the corporation deemed to be outstanding shall include stock deemed to be owned by the person through application of paragraph (9) of this subsection but shall not include any other unissued stock of such corporation which may be issuable pursuant to any agreement, arrangement or understanding, or upon exercise of conversion rights, warrants or options, or otherwise.

(6) "Person" means any individual, corporation, partnership, unincorporated association or other entity.

(7) "Stock" means, with respect to any corporation, capital stock and, with respect to any other entity, any equity interest.

(8) "Voting stock" means, with respect to any corporation, stock of any class or series entitled to vote generally in the election of directors and, with respect to any entity that is not a corporation, any equity interest entitled to vote generally in the election of the governing body of such entity. ■ Every reference to a percentage of voting stock shall refer to such percentage of the votes of such voting stock.

(9) "Owner," including the terms "own" and "owned," when used with respect to any stock, means a person that individually or with or through any of its affiliates or associates:

(i) Beneficially owns such stock, directly or indirectly; or

(ii) Has (A) the right to acquire such stock (whether such right is exercisable immediately or only after the passage of time) pursuant to any agreement, arrangement or understanding, or upon the exercise of conversion rights, exchange rights, warrants or options, or otherwise; provided, however, that [then] a person shall not be deemed the owner of stock tendered pursuant to a tender or exchange offer made by such person or any of such person's affiliates or associates until such tendered stock is accepted for purchase or exchange; or (B) the right to vote such stock pursuant to any agreement, arrangement or understanding; provided, however, that [then] a person shall not be deemed the owner of any stock because of such person's right to vote such stock if the agreement, arrangement or understanding to vote such stock arises solely from a revocable proxy or consent given in response to a proxy or consent solicitation made to 10 or more persons; or

(iii) Has any agreement, arrangement or understanding (for the purpose of acquiring, holding, voting (except voting pursuant to a revocable proxy or consent as described in item (B) of subparagraph (ii) of this paragraph), or disposing of such stock) with any other person that beneficially owns, or whose affiliates or associates beneficially own, directly or indirectly, such stock.

(d) No provision of a certificate of incorporation or bylaw shall require, for any vote of stockholders required by this section, a greater vote of stockholders than that specified in this section.

(e) The Court of Chancery is hereby vested with exclusive jurisdiction to hear and determine all matters with respect to this section.

§ 204. Ratification of defective corporate acts and stock.

(a) Subject to subsection (f) of this section, no defective corporate act or putative stock shall be void or voidable solely as a result of a failure of authorization if (ratified as provided in this section) or (validated by the Court of Chancery in a proceeding brought under § 205 of this title).

(b)(1) In order to ratify 1 or more defective corporate acts pursuant to this section (other than the ratification of an election of the initial board of directors pursuant to paragraph (b)(2) of this section), the board of directors of the corporation shall adopt resolutions stating:

 (A) The defective corporate act or acts to be ratified;

 (B) The date of each defective corporate act or acts;

 (C) If such defective corporate act or acts involved the issuance of shares of putative stock, [then] the number and type of shares of putative stock issued and the date or dates upon which such putative shares were purported to have been issued;

 (D) The nature of the failure of authorization in respect of each defective corporate act to be ratified; and

 (E) That the board of directors approves the ratification of the defective corporate act or acts. ■

Such resolutions may also provide that, at any time before the validation effective time in respect of any defective corporate act set forth therein, notwithstanding the approval of the ratification of such defective corporate act by stockholders, the board of directors may abandon the ratification of such defective corporate act without further action of the stockholders. ■ The quorum and voting requirements applicable to the ratification by the board of directors of any defective corporate act shall be the quorum and voting requirements applicable to the type of defective corporate act proposed to be ratified at the time the board adopts the resolutions ratifying the defective corporate act; provided that if the certificate of incorporation or bylaws of the corporation, any plan or agreement to which the corporation was a party or any provision of this title, in each case as in effect as of the time of the defective corporate act, would have required a larger number or portion of directors or of specified directors for a quorum to be present or to approve the defective corporate act, [then] such larger number or portion of such directors or such specified directors shall be required for a quorum to be present or to adopt the resolutions to ratify the defective corporate act, as applicable, except that the presence or approval of any director elected, appointed or nominated by holders of any class or series of which no shares are then outstanding, or by any person that is no longer a stockholder, shall not be required.

(2) In order to ratify a defective corporate act in respect of the election of the initial board of directors of the corporation pursuant to § 108 of this title, a majority of the persons who, at the time the resolutions required by this paragraph (b)(2) of this section are adopted, are exercising the powers of directors under claim and color of an election or appointment as such may adopt resolutions stating:

 (A) The name of the person or persons who first took action in the name of the corporation as the initial board of directors of the corporation;

 (B) The earlier of the date on which such persons first took such action or were purported to have been elected as the initial board of directors; and

 (C) That the ratification of the election of such person or persons as the initial board of directors is approved.

(c) [Then] Each defective corporate act ratified pursuant to paragraph (b)(1) of this section shall be submitted to stockholders for approval as provided in subsection (d) of this section, **unless**:

(1) (A) No other provision of this title, and no provision of the certificate of incorporation or bylaws of the corporation, or of any plan or agreement to which the corporation is a party, would have required stockholder approval of such defective corporate act to be ratified, either (at the time of such defective corporate act) or (at the time the board of directors adopts the resolutions ratifying such defective corporate act pursuant to paragraph (b)(1) of this section); and (B) such defective corporate act did not result from a failure to comply with § 203 of this title; or

(2) As of the record date for determining the stockholders entitled to vote on the ratification of such defective corporate act, there are no shares of valid stock outstanding and entitled to vote thereon, regardless of whether there then exist any shares of putative stock.

(d) If the ratification of a defective corporate act is required to be submitted to stockholders for approval pursuant to subsection (c) of this section, [then] due notice of the time, place, if any, and purpose of the meeting shall be given at least 20 days before the date of the meeting to each holder of valid stock and putative stock, whether voting or nonvoting, at the address of such holder as it appears or most recently appeared, as appropriate, on the records of the corporation. ■ The notice shall also be given to the holders of record of valid stock and putative stock, whether voting or nonvoting, as of the time of the defective corporate act (or, in the case of any defective corporate act that involved the establishment of a record date for notice of or voting at any meeting of stockholders, for action by written consent of stockholders in lieu of a meeting, or for any other purpose, the record date for notice of or voting at such meeting, the record date for action by written consent, or the record date for such other action, as the case may be), other than holders whose identities or addresses cannot be determined from the records of the corporation. ■ The notice shall contain a copy of (the resolutions adopted by the board of directors pursuant to paragraph (b)(1) of this section) or (the information required by paragraph (b)(1)(A) through (E) of this section) and a statement that any claim (that the defective corporate act or putative stock ratified hereunder is void or voidable due to the failure of authorization), or (that the Court of Chancery should declare in its discretion that a ratification in accordance with this section not be effective or be effective only on certain conditions) must be brought within 120 days from the applicable validation effective time. ■ At such meeting, the quorum and voting requirements applicable to ratification of such defective corporate act shall be the quorum and voting requirements applicable to the type of defective corporate act proposed to be ratified at the time of the approval of the ratification, except that:

(1) If the certificate of incorporation or bylaws of the corporation, any plan or agreement to which the corporation was a party or any provision of this title in effect as of the time of the defective corporate act would have required a larger number or portion of stock or of any class or series thereof or of specified stockholders for a quorum to be present or to approve the defective corporate act, [then] the presence or approval of such larger number or portion of stock or of such class or series thereof or of such specified stockholders shall be required for a quorum to be present or to approve the ratification of the defective corporate act, as applicable, ◄except that the presence or approval of shares of any class or series of which no shares are then outstanding, or of any person that is no longer a stockholder, shall not be required;▶

(2) The approval by stockholders of the ratification of the election of a director shall require the affirmative vote of the majority of shares present at the meeting and entitled to vote on the election of such director, ◄except that if the certificate of incorporation or bylaws of the corporation then in effect or in effect at the time of the defective election require or required a larger number or portion of stock or of any class or series thereof or of specified stockholders to elect such director, the affirmative vote of such larger number or portion of stock or of any class or series thereof or of such specified stockholders shall be required to ratify the election of such director, except that the presence or approval of shares of any class or series of which no shares are then outstanding, or of any person that is no longer a stockholder, shall not be required;► and

(3) In the event of a failure of authorization resulting from failure to comply with the provisions of § 203 of this title, [then] the ratification of the defective corporate act shall require the vote set forth in § 203(a)(3) of this title, regardless of whether such vote would have otherwise been required.

Shares of putative stock on the record date for determining stockholders entitled to vote on any matter submitted to stockholders pursuant to subsection (c) of this section (and without giving effect to any ratification that becomes effective after such record date) shall neither be entitled to vote nor counted for quorum purposes in any vote to ratify any defective corporate act.

(e) If a defective corporate act ratified pursuant to this section would have required under any other section of this title the filing of a certificate in accordance with § 103 of this title, **then**, whether or not a certificate was previously filed in respect of such defective corporate act and in lieu of filing the certificate otherwise required by this title, the corporation shall file a certificate of validation with respect to such defective corporate act in accordance with § 103 of this title. ■ A separate certificate of validation shall be required for each defective corporate act requiring the filing of a certificate of validation under this section, ◄except that **(i)** 2 or more defective corporate acts may be included in a single certificate of validation if the corporation filed, or to comply with this title would have filed, a single certificate under another provision of this title to effect such acts, and **(ii)** 2 or more overissues of shares of any class, classes or series of stock may be included in a single certificate of validation►, provided that the increase in the number of authorized shares of each such class or series set forth in the certificate of validation shall be effective as of the date of the first such overissue. ■ The certificate of validation shall set forth:

(1) Each defective corporate act that is the subject of the certificate of validation (including, in the case of any defective corporate act involving the issuance of shares of putative stock, the number and type of shares of putative stock issued and the date or dates upon which such putative shares were purported to have been issued), the date of such defective corporate act, and the nature of the failure of authorization in respect of such defective corporate act;

(2) A statement that such defective corporate act was ratified in accordance with this section, including the date on which the board of directors ratified such defective corporate act and the date, if any, on which the stockholders approved the ratification of such defective corporate act; and

(3) Information required by 1 of the following paragraphs:

a. If a certificate was previously filed under § 103 of this title in respect of such defective corporate act and no changes to such certificate are required to give effect to such defective corporate act in accordance with this section, [then] the certificate of validation shall set forth **(x)** the name, title and filing date of the certificate previously filed and of any certificate of correction thereto and **(y)** a statement that a copy of the certificate previously filed, together with any certificate of correction thereto, is attached as an exhibit to the certificate of validation;

b. If a certificate was previously filed under § 103 of this title in respect of the defective corporate act and such certificate requires any change to give effect to the defective corporate act in accordance with this section (including a change to the date and time of the effectiveness of such certificate), [then] the certificate of validation shall set forth **(x)** the name, title and filing date of the certificate so previously filed and of any certificate of correction thereto, **(y)** a statement that a certificate containing all of the information required to be included under the applicable section or sections of this title to give effect to the defective corporate act is attached as an exhibit to the certificate of validation, and **(z)** the date and time that such certificate shall be deemed to have become effective pursuant to this section; or

c. If a certificate was not previously filed under § 103 of this title in respect of the defective corporate act and the defective corporate act ratified pursuant to this section would have required under any other section of this title the filing of a certificate in accordance with § 103 of this title, [then] the certificate of validation shall set forth **(x)** a statement that a certificate containing all of the information required to be included under the applicable section or sections of this title to give effect to the defective corporate act is attached as an exhibit to the certificate of validation, and **(y)** the date and time that such certificate shall be deemed to have become effective pursuant to this section.

A certificate attached to a certificate of validation pursuant to paragraph (e)(3)b. or c. of this section need not be separately executed and acknowledged and need not include any statement required by any other section of this title that such instrument has been approved and adopted in accordance with the provisions of such other section.

(f) From and after the validation effective time, unless otherwise determined in an action brought pursuant to § 205 of this title:

(1) Subject to the last sentence of subsection (d) of this section, each defective corporate act ratified in accordance with this section shall no longer be deemed void or voidable as a result of the failure of authorization described in the resolutions adopted pursuant to subsection (b) of this section and such effect shall be retroactive to the time of the defective corporate act; and

(2) Subject to the last sentence of subsection (d) of this section, each share or fraction of a share of putative stock issued or purportedly issued pursuant to any such defective corporate act shall no longer be deemed void or voidable and shall be deemed to be an identical share or fraction of a share of outstanding stock as of the time it was purportedly issued.

(g) In respect of each defective corporate act ratified by the board of directors pursuant to subsection (b) of this section, prompt notice of the ratification shall be given to all holders of valid stock and putative stock, whether voting or nonvoting, (as of the date the board of directors adopts the resolutions approving such defective corporate act), or (as of a date within 60 days after such date of adoption), as established by the board of directors, at the address of such holder as it appears or most recently appeared, as appropriate, on the records of the corporation. ■ The notice shall also be given to the holders of record of valid stock and putative stock, whether voting or nonvoting, as of the time of the defective corporate act, other than holders whose identities or addresses cannot be determined from the records of the corporation. ■ The notice shall contain a copy of the resolutions adopted pursuant to subsection (b) of this section or the information specified in paragraphs (b)(1)(A) through (E) or paragraphs (b)(2)(A) through (C) of this section, as applicable, and a statement that any claim (that the defective corporate act or putative stock ratified hereunder is void or voidable due to the failure of authorization), or (that the Court of Chancery should declare in its discretion that a ratification in accordance with this section not be effective or be effective only on certain conditions) must be brought within 120 days from the later of the validation effective time or the time at which the notice required by this subsection is given. ■ **[Then]** Notwithstanding the foregoing, **(i)** no such notice shall be required **if** notice of the ratification of the defective corporate act is to be given in accordance with subsection (d) of this section, and **(ii)** in the case of a corporation that has a class of stock listed on a national securities exchange, the notice required by this subsection and the second sentence of subsection (d) of this section may be deemed given if disclosed in a document publicly filed by the corporation with the Securities and Exchange Commission pursuant to (§§ 13, 14 or 15(d) [15 U.S.C. §§ 78m, 77n or 78o(d)] of the Securities Exchange Act of 1934, as amended, and the rules and regulations promulgated thereunder, or the corresponding provisions of any subsequent United States federal securities laws, rules or regulations). ■ **If** any defective corporate act has been approved by stockholders acting pursuant to § 228 of this title, **[then]** the notice required by this subsection may be included in any notice required to be given pursuant to § 228(e) of this title and, if so given, shall be sent (to the stockholders entitled thereto under § 228(e)) and (to all holders of valid and putative stock to whom notice would be required under this subsection if the defective corporate act had been approved at a meeting) other than any stockholder who approved the action by consent in lieu of a meeting pursuant to § 228 of this title or any holder of putative stock who otherwise consented thereto in writing. ■ Solely for purposes of subsection (d) of this section and this subsection, notice to holders of putative stock, and notice to holders of valid stock and putative stock as of the time of the defective corporate act, shall be treated as notice to holders of valid stock for purposes of §§ 222 and 228, 229, 230, 232 and 233 of this title.

(h) As used in this section and in § 205 of this title only, the term:

    (1) "Defective corporate act" means an overissue, an election or appointment of directors that is void or voidable due to a failure of authorization, or any act or transaction purportedly taken by or on behalf of the corporation that (is, and at the time such act or transaction was purportedly taken would have been, within the power of a corporation under subchapter II of this chapter (without regard to the failure of authorization identified in § 204(b)(1)(D) of this title)), but (is void or voidable due to a failure of authorization);

(2) "Failure of authorization" means: **(i)** the failure to authorize or effect an act or transaction in compliance with **(A)** the provisions of this title, **(B)** the certificate of incorporation or bylaws of the corporation, or **(C)** any plan or agreement to which the corporation is a party or the disclosure set forth in any proxy or consent solicitation statement, if and to the extent such failure would render such act or transaction void or voidable; or **(ii)** the failure of the board of directors or any officer of the corporation to authorize or approve any act or transaction taken by or on behalf of the corporation that would have required for its due authorization the approval of the board of directors or such officer;

(3) "Overissue" means the purported issuance of:

    a. Shares of capital stock of a class or series in excess of the number of shares of such class or series the corporation has the power to issue under § 161 of this title at the time of such issuance; or

    b. Shares of any class or series of capital stock that is not then authorized for issuance by the certificate of incorporation of the corporation;

(4) "Putative stock" means the shares of any class or series of capital stock of the corporation (including shares issued upon exercise of options, rights, warrants or other securities convertible into shares of capital stock of the corporation, or interests with respect thereto that were created or issued pursuant to a defective corporate act) that:

    a. But for any failure of authorization, would constitute valid stock; or

    b. Cannot be determined by the board of directors to be valid stock;

(5) "Time of the defective corporate act" means the date and time the defective corporate act was purported to have been taken;

(6) "Validation effective time" with respect to any defective corporate act ratified pursuant to this section means the latest of:

    a. (The time at which the defective corporate act submitted to the stockholders for approval pursuant to subsection (c) of this section is approved by such stockholders) or (if no such vote of stockholders is required to approve the ratification of the defective corporate act, the time at which the board of directors adopts the resolutions required by paragraph (b)(1) or (b)(2) of this section);

    b. Where no certificate of validation is required to be filed pursuant to subsection (e) of this section, [then] the time, if any, specified by the board of directors in the resolutions adopted pursuant to paragraph (b)(1) or (b)(2) of this section, which time shall not precede the time at which such resolutions are adopted; and

    c. The time at which any certificate of validation filed pursuant to subsection (e) of this section shall become effective in accordance with § 103 of this title.

(7) "Valid stock" means the shares of any class or series of capital stock of the corporation that have been duly authorized and validly issued in accordance with this title.

In the absence of actual fraud in the transaction, the judgment of the board of directors that shares of stock are valid stock or putative stock shall be conclusive, unless otherwise determined by the Court of Chancery in a proceeding brought pursuant to § 205 of this title.

(i) Ratification under this section or validation under § 205 of this title shall not be deemed to be the exclusive means (of ratifying or validating any act or transaction taken by or on behalf of the corporation, including any defective corporate act, or any issuance of stock, including any putative stock), or (of adopting or endorsing any act or transaction taken by or in the name of the corporation prior to the commencement of its existence), and the absence or failure of ratification in accordance with either this section or validation under § 205 of this title shall not, of itself, affect the validity or effectiveness of any act or transaction or the issuance of any stock properly ratified under common law or otherwise, nor shall it create a presumption that any such act or transaction is or was a defective corporate act or that such stock is void or voidable.

§ 205. Proceedings regarding validity of defective corporate acts and stock.

(a) Subject to subsection (f) of this section, upon application by (the corporation), (any successor entity to the corporation), (any member of the board of directors), (any record or beneficial holder of valid stock or putative stock), (any record or beneficial holder of valid or putative stock as of the time of a defective corporate act ratified pursuant to § 204 of this title), (or any other person claiming to be substantially and adversely affected by a ratification pursuant to § 204 of this title), the Court of Chancery may:

(1) Determine the validity and effectiveness of any defective corporate act ratified pursuant to § 204 of this title;

(2) Determine the validity and effectiveness of the ratification of any defective corporate act pursuant to § 204 of this title;

(3) Determine the validity and effectiveness of any defective corporate act not ratified or not ratified effectively pursuant to § 204 of this title;

(4) Determine the validity of any corporate act or transaction and any stock, rights or options to acquire stock; and

(5) Modify or waive any of the procedures set forth in § 204 of this title to ratify a defective corporate act.

(b) In connection with an action under this section, the Court of Chancery may:

(1) Declare that a ratification in accordance with and pursuant to § 204 of this title (is not effective) or (shall only be effective at a time or upon conditions established by the Court);

(2) Validate and declare effective any defective corporate act or putative stock and impose conditions upon such validation by the Court;

(3) Require measures to remedy or avoid harm (to any person substantially and adversely affected by a ratification pursuant to § 204 of this title) or (from any order of the Court pursuant to this section), excluding any harm that would have resulted if the defective corporate act had been valid when approved or effectuated;

(4) Order the Secretary of State to accept an instrument for filing with an effective time specified by the Court, which effective time may be prior or subsequent to the time of

such order, **provided that** the filing date of such instrument shall be determined in accordance with § 103(c)(3) of this title;

(5) Approve a stock ledger for the corporation that includes any stock ratified or validated in accordance with this section or with § 204 of this title;

(6) Declare that shares of putative stock are shares of valid stock or require a corporation to issue and deliver shares of valid stock in place of any shares of putative stock;

(7) Order that a meeting of holders of valid stock or putative stock be held and exercise the powers provided to the Court under § 227 of this title with respect to such a meeting;

(8) Declare that a defective corporate act validated by the Court shall be effective as of the time of the defective corporate act or at such other time as the Court shall determine;

(9) Declare that putative stock validated by the Court shall be deemed to be an identical share or fraction of a share of valid stock as of the time originally issued or purportedly issued or at such other time as the Court shall determine; and

(10) Make such other orders regarding such matters as it deems proper under the circumstances.

(c) Service of the application under subsection (a) of this section upon the registered agent of the corporation shall be deemed to be service upon the corporation, and no other party need be joined in order for the Court of Chancery to adjudicate the matter. ■ In an action filed by the corporation, the Court may require notice of the action be provided to other persons specified by the Court and permit such other persons to intervene in the action.

(d) In connection with the resolution of matters pursuant to subsections (a) and (b) of this section, the Court of Chancery may consider the following:

(1) Whether the defective corporate act was originally approved or effectuated with the belief that the approval or effectuation was in compliance with the provisions of this title, the certificate of incorporation or bylaws of the corporation;

(2) Whether the corporation and board of directors has treated the defective corporate act as a valid act or transaction and whether any person has acted in reliance on the public record that such defective corporate act was valid;

(3) Whether any person will be or was harmed by the ratification or validation of the defective corporate act, excluding any harm that would have resulted if the defective corporate act had been valid when approved or effectuated;

(4) Whether any person will be harmed by the failure to ratify or validate the defective corporate act; and

(5) Any other factors or considerations the Court deems just and equitable.

(e) The Court of Chancery is hereby vested with exclusive jurisdiction to hear and determine all actions brought under this section.

(f) Notwithstanding any other provision of this section, no action asserting:

(1) That a defective corporate act or putative stock ratified in accordance with § 204 of this title is void or voidable due to a failure of authorization identified in the resolution adopted in accordance with 204(b) of this title; or

(2) That the Court of Chancery should declare in its discretion that a ratification in accordance with §204 of this title not be effective or be effective only on certain conditions,

may be brought after the expiration of 120 days from the later of (the validation effective time) and (the time notice, if any, that is required to be given pursuant to § 204(g) of this title is given with respect to such ratification), ◄except that this subsection shall not apply to an action asserting that a ratification was not accomplished in accordance with § 204 of this title or to any person to whom notice of the ratification was required to have been given pursuant to § 204(d) or (g) of this title, but to whom such notice was not given.►

Subchapter VII. Meetings, Elections, Voting and Notice

§ 211. Meetings of stockholders.

(a)(1) Meetings of stockholders may be held at such place, either within or without this State (as may be designated by or in the manner provided in the certificate of incorporation or bylaws,) or (if not so designated, as determined by the board of directors). ■ **If**, pursuant to this paragraph or the certificate of incorporation or the bylaws of the corporation, the board of directors is authorized to determine the place of a meeting of stockholders, **[then]** the board of directors may, in its sole discretion, determine that the meeting shall not be held at any place, but may instead be held solely by means of remote communication as authorized by paragraph (a)(2) of this section.

(2) If authorized by the board of directors in its sole discretion, and subject to such guidelines and procedures as the board of directors may adopt, stockholders and proxyholders not physically present at a meeting of stockholders may, by means of remote communication:

a. Participate in a meeting of stockholders; and

b. Be deemed present in person and vote at a meeting of stockholders, whether such meeting is to be held at a designated place or solely by means of remote communication, provided that **(i)** the corporation shall implement reasonable measures to verify that each person deemed present and permitted to vote at the meeting by means of remote communication is a stockholder or proxyholder, **(ii)** the corporation shall implement reasonable measures to provide such stockholders and proxyholders a reasonable opportunity to participate in the meeting and to vote on matters submitted to the stockholders, including an opportunity to read or hear the proceedings of the meeting substantially concurrently with such proceedings, and **(iii)** if any stockholder or proxyholder votes or takes other action at the meeting by means of remote communication, a record of such vote or other action shall be maintained by the corporation.

(b) Unless directors are elected by written consent in lieu of an annual meeting as permitted by this subsection, **[then]** an annual meeting of stockholders shall be held for the election of directors on a date and at a time designated by or in the manner provided in the bylaws. ■ Stockholders may, unless the certificate of incorporation otherwise provides, act by written consent to elect directors; [provided, however, that], **if** such consent is less than unanimous, **[then]** such action by written consent **may be** in lieu of holding an annual meeting **only if** all of the directorships to which directors could be elected at an annual meeting held at the effective time of such action are vacant [and] are filled by such action. ∎ Any other proper business may be transacted at the annual meeting.

(c) A failure to hold the annual meeting at the designated time or to elect a sufficient number of directors to conduct the business of the corporation shall not affect otherwise valid corporate acts [or] work a forfeiture or dissolution of the corporation (except as may be otherwise specifically provided in this chapter.) ∎ **If** the annual meeting for election of directors is not held on the date designated therefor [or] action by written consent to elect directors in lieu of an annual meeting has not been taken, **[then]** the directors shall cause the meeting to be held as soon as is convenient. ∎ **If** there be a failure to hold the annual meeting [or] to take action by written consent to elect directors in lieu of an annual meeting for a period of 30 days after the date designated for the annual meeting, [or] **if** no date has been designated, for a period of 13 months after the latest to occur of the organization of the corporation, its last annual meeting or the last action by written consent to elect directors in lieu of an annual meeting, **[then]** the Court of Chancery may summarily order a meeting to be held upon the application of any stockholder or director. ∎ The shares of stock represented at such meeting, either in person or by proxy, and entitled to vote thereat, shall constitute a quorum for the purpose of such meeting, notwithstanding any provision of the certificate of incorporation or bylaws to the contrary. ∎ The Court of Chancery may issue such orders as may be appropriate, including, without limitation, orders designating (the time and place of such meeting), (the record date or dates for determination of stockholders entitled to notice of the meeting and to vote thereat), [and] (the form of notice of such meeting).

(d) Special meetings of the stockholders may be called by the board of directors or by such person or persons as may be authorized by the certificate of incorporation or by the bylaws.

(e) All elections of directors shall be by written ballot unless otherwise provided in the certificate of incorporation; if authorized by the board of directors, such requirement of a written ballot shall be satisfied by a ballot submitted by electronic transmission, [provided that] any such electronic transmission must either set forth or be submitted with information from which it can be determined that the electronic transmission was authorized by the stockholder or proxy holder.

§ 212. Voting rights of stockholders; proxies; limitations.

(a) Unless otherwise provided in the certificate of incorporation and subject to § 213 of this title, each stockholder shall be entitled to 1 vote for each share of capital stock held by such stockholder. ∎ **If** the certificate of incorporation provides for more or less than 1 vote for any share, on any matter, **[then]** every reference in this chapter to a majority or other proportion of stock, voting stock or shares shall refer to such majority [or] other proportion of the votes of such stock, voting stock or shares.

(b) Each stockholder entitled to vote at a meeting of stockholders or to express consent or dissent to corporate action in writing without a meeting may authorize another person or persons to act for such stockholder by proxy, [but] [then] no such proxy shall be voted or acted upon after 3 years from its date, **unless** the proxy provides for a longer period.

(c) Without limiting the manner in which a stockholder may authorize another person or persons to act for such stockholder as proxy pursuant to subsection (b) of this section, the following shall constitute a valid means by which a stockholder may grant such authority:

(1) A stockholder, or such stockholder's authorized officer, director, employee or agent, may execute a document authorizing another person or persons to act for such stockholder as proxy.

(2) A stockholder may authorize another person or persons to act for such stockholder as proxy by transmitting or authorizing the transmission of an electronic transmission to the person who will be the holder of the proxy or to a proxy solicitation firm, proxy support service organization or like agent duly authorized by the person who will be the holder of the proxy to receive such transmission, [provided that] any such transmission must either set forth [or] be submitted with information from which it can be determined that the transmission was authorized by the stockholder. ■ **If** it is determined that such transmissions are valid, [then] the inspectors or, if there are no inspectors, such other persons making that determination shall specify the information upon which they relied.

(3) The authorization of a person to act as a proxy may be documented, signed and delivered in accordance with § 116 of this title, [provided that] such authorization shall set forth, or be delivered with information enabling the corporation to determine, the identity of the stockholder granting such authorization.

(d) Any copy, facsimile telecommunication or other reliable reproduction of the document (including any electronic transmission) created pursuant to subsection (c) of this section may be substituted [or] used in lieu of the original document for any and all purposes for which the original document could be used, [provided that] such copy, facsimile telecommunication or other reproduction shall be a complete reproduction of the entire original document.

(e) [Then] A duly executed proxy shall be irrevocable **if** it states that it is irrevocable [and] **if**, and only as long as, it is coupled with an interest sufficient in law to support an irrevocable power. ■ A proxy may be made irrevocable regardless of whether the interest with which it is coupled is **(**an interest in the stock itself**)** [or] **(**an interest in the corporation generally**)**.

§ 213. Fixing date for determination of stockholders of record.

(a) **In order that** the corporation may determine the stockholders entitled to notice of any meeting of stockholders or any adjournment thereof, [then] the board of directors may fix a record date, **which** record date shall not precede the date upon which the resolution fixing the record date is adopted by the board of directors, and **which** record date shall not be more than 60 nor less than 10 days before the date of such meeting. ■ **If** the board of directors so fixes a date, [then] such date shall also be the record date for determining the stockholders entitled to vote at such meeting **unless** the board of directors determines, at the time it fixes such record date, that a later date on or before the date of the meeting shall be the date for making such determination. ■ **If** no record date is fixed by the board of directors, [then] the record date for determining stockholders entitled to notice of and to vote at a meeting of stockholders shall be (at the close of business on the day next preceding the day on which notice is given), or, if notice is waived, (at the close of business on the day next preceding the day on which the meeting is held). ■ A determination of stockholders of record entitled to notice of or to vote at a meeting of stockholders shall apply to any adjournment of the meeting; provided, however, that the board of directors may fix a new record date for determination of stockholders entitled to vote at the adjourned meeting, and in such case shall also fix as the record date for stockholders entitled to notice of such adjourned meeting the same or an earlier date as (that fixed for determination of stockholders entitled to vote in accordance with the foregoing provisions of this subsection (a) at the adjourned meeting).

(b) In order that the corporation may determine the stockholders entitled to consent to corporate action without a meeting in accordance with § 228 of this title, the board of directors may fix a record date, (which record date shall not precede the date upon which the resolution fixing the record date is adopted by the board of directors), and (which date shall not be more than 10 days after the date upon which the resolution fixing the record date is adopted by the board of directors). ■ If no record date has been fixed by the board of directors, [then] the record date for determining stockholders entitled to consent to corporate action without a meeting, when no prior action by the board of directors is required by this chapter, shall be the first date on which a signed consent setting forth the action taken or proposed to be taken is delivered to the corporation in accordance with § 228(d) of this title. ■ If no record date has been fixed by the board of directors and prior action by the board of directors is required by this chapter, [then] the record date for determining stockholders entitled to consent to corporate action in writing without a meeting shall be at the close of business on the day on which the board of directors adopts the resolution taking such prior action.

(c) **In order that** the corporation may determine the stockholders entitled to receive payment of any dividend or other distribution or allotment of any rights or the stockholders entitled to exercise any rights in respect of any change, conversion or exchange of stock, or for the purpose of any other lawful action, [then] the board of directors may fix a record date, **which** record date shall not precede the date upon which the resolution fixing the record date is adopted, and **which** record date shall be not more than 60 days prior to such action. ■ If no record date is fixed, [then] the record date for determining stockholders for any such purpose shall be at the close of business on the day on which the board of directors adopts the resolution relating thereto.

§ 214. Cumulative voting.

The certificate of incorporation of any corporation may provide that (at all elections of directors of the corporation), or (at elections held under specified circumstances), each holder of stock or of any class or classes or of a series or series thereof shall be entitled to as many votes as shall equal (the number of votes which (except for such provision as to cumulative voting) such holder would be entitled to cast for the election of directors with respect to such holder's shares of stock) multiplied by (the number of directors to be elected by such holder), and that such holder may cast all of such votes for a single director or may distribute them among the number to be voted for, or for any 2 or more of them as such holder may see fit.

§ 215. Voting rights of members of nonstock corporations; quorum; proxies.

(a) Sections 211 through 214 and 216 of this title shall not apply to nonstock corporations, ◄except that § 211(a) and (d) of this title and § 212(c), (d), and (e) of this title shall apply to such corporations, and, when so applied, all references therein to stockholders and to the board of directors shall be deemed to refer to the members and the governing body of a nonstock corporation, respectively▶; [and] all references to stock, capital stock, or shares thereof shall be deemed to refer to memberships of a nonprofit nonstock corporation [and] to membership interests of any other nonstock corporation.

(b) Unless otherwise provided in the certificate of incorporation or the bylaws of a nonstock corporation, [and] subject to subsection (f) of this section, each member shall be entitled at every meeting of members to 1 vote on each matter submitted to a vote of members. ■ A member may exercise such voting rights in person or by proxy, [but] **[then]** no proxy shall be voted on after 3 years from its date, **unless** the proxy provides for a longer period.

(c) Unless otherwise provided in this chapter, the certificate of incorporation or bylaws of a nonstock corporation may specify the number of members having voting power who shall be present or represented by proxy at any meeting in order to constitute a quorum for, [and] the votes that shall be necessary for, the transaction of any business. ■ In the absence of such specification in the certificate of incorporation or bylaws of a nonstock corporation:

(1) One-third of the members of such corporation shall constitute a quorum at a meeting of such members;

(2) **[Then]** In all matters other than the election of the governing body of such corporation, the affirmative vote of a majority of such members **(**present in person or represented by proxy at the meeting**)** and **(**entitled to vote on the subject matter**)** shall be the act of the members, **unless** the vote of a greater number is required by this chapter;

(3) Members of the governing body shall be elected by a plurality of the votes of the members of the corporation present in person or represented by proxy at the meeting and entitled to vote thereon; [and]

(4) **Where** a separate vote by a class or group or classes or groups is required, **[then]** a majority of the members of such class or group or classes or groups, present in person or represented by proxy, shall constitute a quorum entitled to take action with respect to that vote on that matter [and], in all matters other than the election of members of the governing body, the affirmative vote of the majority of the members of such class or group or classes or groups present in person or represented by proxy at the meeting shall be the act of such class or group or classes or groups.

(d) If the election of the governing body of any nonstock corporation shall not be held on the day designated by the bylaws, **[then]** the governing body shall cause the election to be held as soon thereafter as convenient. ■ The failure to hold such an election at the designated time shall not work any forfeiture [or] dissolution of the corporation, [but] the Court of Chancery may summarily order such an election to be held upon the application of any member of the corporation. ■ At any election pursuant to such order the persons entitled to vote in such election who shall be present at such meeting, either in person or by proxy, shall constitute a quorum for such meeting, notwithstanding any provision of the certificate of incorporation or the bylaws of the corporation to the contrary.

(e) If authorized by the governing body, any requirement of a written ballot shall be satisfied by a ballot submitted by electronic transmission, `provided that` any such electronic transmission must either set forth `or` be submitted with information from which it can be determined that the electronic transmission was authorized by the member or proxy holder.

(f) ◀Except as otherwise provided in the certificate of incorporation, in the bylaws, or by resolution of the governing body,▶ the record date for any meeting or corporate action shall be deemed to be the date of such meeting or corporate action; `provided, however, that` no record date may precede any action by the governing body fixing such record date.

§ 216. Quorum and required vote for stock corporations.

Subject to this chapter in respect of the vote that shall be required for a specified action, the certificate of incorporation `or` bylaws of any corporation authorized to issue stock may specify the number of shares `and/or` the amount of other securities having voting power the holders of which shall be present or represented by proxy at any meeting in order to constitute a quorum for, and the votes that shall be necessary for, the transaction of any business, **(**but in no event shall a quorum consist of less than 1/3 of the shares entitled to vote at the meeting**)**, ◀except that, where a separate vote by a class or series or classes or series is required, a quorum shall consist of no less than 1/3 of the shares of such class or series or classes or series.▶ ■ In the absence of such specification in the certificate of incorporation or bylaws of the corporation:

> **(1)** A majority of the shares entitled to vote, present in person or represented by proxy, shall constitute a quorum at a meeting of stockholders;

> **(2)** In all matters other than the election of directors, the affirmative vote of the majority of shares **(**present in person or represented by proxy at the meeting**)** `and` **(**entitled to vote on the subject matter**)** shall be the act of the stockholders;

> **(3)** Directors shall be elected by a plurality of the votes of the shares **(**present in person or represented by proxy at the meeting**)** `and` **(**entitled to vote on the election of directors**)**; `and`

> **(4)** **Where** a separate vote by a class or series or classes or series is required, [then] a majority of the outstanding shares of such class or series or classes or series, present in person or represented by proxy, shall constitute a quorum entitled to take action with respect to that vote on that matter `and`, in all matters other than the election of directors, the affirmative vote of the majority of shares of such class or series or classes or series present in person or represented by proxy at the meeting shall be the act of such class or series or classes or series.

A bylaw amendment adopted by stockholders which specifies the votes that shall be necessary for the election of directors shall not be further amended or repealed by the board of directors.

§ 217. Voting rights of fiduciaries, pledgors and joint owners of stock.

(a) Persons holding stock in a fiduciary capacity shall be entitled to vote the shares so held. ■ [Then] Persons whose stock is pledged shall be entitled to vote, **unless** in the transfer by the pledgor on the books of the corporation such person has expressly empowered the pledgee to vote thereon, in which case only the pledgee, or such pledgee's proxy, may represent such stock and vote thereon.

(b) If shares or other securities having voting power stand of record in the names of 2 or more persons, whether fiduciaries, members of a partnership, joint tenants, tenants in common, tenants by the entirety or otherwise, or if 2 or more persons have the same fiduciary relationship respecting the same shares, **unless** the secretary of the corporation is given written notice to the contrary and is furnished with a copy of the instrument or order appointing them or creating the relationship wherein it is so provided, [then] their acts with respect to voting shall have the following effect:

(1) If only 1 votes, [then] such person's act binds all;

(2) If more than 1 vote, [then] the act of the majority so voting binds all;

(3) If more than 1 vote, but the vote is evenly split on any particular matter, [then] each faction may vote the securities in question proportionally, or any person voting the shares, or a beneficiary, if any, may apply to the Court of Chancery or such other court as may have jurisdiction to appoint an additional person to act with the persons so voting the shares, which shall then be voted as determined by a majority of such persons and the person appointed by the Court. ■ If the instrument so filed shows that any such tenancy is held in unequal interests, [then] a majority or even split for the purpose of this subsection shall be a majority or even split in interest.

§ 218. Voting trusts and other voting agreements.

(a) One stockholder or 2 or more stockholders may by agreement in writing deposit capital stock of an original issue with or transfer capital stock to any person or persons, or entity or entities authorized to act as trustee, for the purpose of vesting in such person or persons, entity or entities, who may be designated voting trustee, or voting trustees, the right to vote thereon for any period of time determined by such agreement, upon the terms and conditions stated in such agreement. ■ The agreement may contain any other lawful provisions not inconsistent with such purpose. ■ After delivery of a copy of the agreement to (the registered office of the corporation in this State) or (the principal place of business of the corporation), which copy shall be open to the inspection of any stockholder of the corporation or any beneficiary of the trust under the agreement daily during business hours, certificates of stock or uncertificated stock shall be issued to the voting trustee or trustees to represent any stock of an original issue so deposited with such voting trustee or trustees, and any certificates of stock or uncertificated stock so transferred to the voting trustee or trustees shall be surrendered and cancelled and new certificates or uncertificated stock shall be issued therefore to the voting trustee or trustees. ■ In the certificate so issued, if any, it shall be stated that it is issued pursuant to such agreement, and that fact shall also be stated in the stock ledger of the corporation. ■ The voting trustee or trustees may vote the stock so issued or transferred during the period specified in the agreement. ■ Stock standing in the name of the voting trustee or trustees may be voted either in person or by proxy, and in voting the stock, the voting trustee or trustees shall incur no responsibility as stockholder, trustee or otherwise, ◀except for their own individual malfeasance▶. ■ **In any case where** 2 or more persons or entities are designated as voting trustees, and the right and method of voting any stock standing in their names at any meeting of the corporation are not fixed by the agreement appointing the trustees, **[then]** the right to vote the stock and the manner of voting it at the meeting shall be determined by a majority of the trustees, or **if** they be equally divided as to the right and manner of voting the stock in any particular case, **[then]** the vote of the stock in such case shall be divided equally among the trustees.

(b) Any amendment to a voting trust agreement shall be made by a written agreement, a copy of which shall be delivered to the registered office of the corporation in this State or principal place of business of the corporation.

(c) An agreement between 2 or more stockholders, if in writing and signed by the parties thereto, may provide that in exercising any voting rights, the shares held by them shall be voted **(**as provided by the agreement**)**, or **(**as the parties may agree**)**, or **(**as determined in accordance with a procedure agreed upon by them**)**.

(d) This section shall not be deemed to invalidate any voting or other agreement among stockholders or any irrevocable proxy which is not otherwise illegal.

§ 219. List of stockholders entitled to vote; penalty for refusal to produce; stock ledger.

(a) The corporation shall prepare, at least 10 days before every meeting of stockholders, a complete list of the stockholders entitled to vote at the meeting; **provided, however, if** the record date for determining the stockholders entitled to vote is less than 10 days before the meeting date, **[then]** the list shall reflect the stockholders entitled to vote as of the tenth day before the meeting date, arranged in alphabetical order, and showing the address of each stockholder and the number of shares registered in the name of each stockholder. ■ Nothing contained in this section shall require the corporation to include electronic mail addresses or other electronic contact information on such list. ■ Such list shall be open to the examination of any stockholder for any purpose germane to the meeting for a period of at least 10 days prior to the meeting: **(i)** [then] on a reasonably accessible electronic network, provided that the information required to gain access to such list is provided with the notice of the meeting, or **(ii)** during ordinary business hours, at the principal place of business of the corporation. ■ **In the event that** the corporation determines to make the list available on an electronic network, **[then]** the corporation may take reasonable steps to ensure that such information is available only to stockholders of the corporation. ■ **If** the meeting is to be held at a place, **then** a list of stockholders entitled to vote at the meeting shall be produced and kept at the time and place of the meeting during the whole time thereof and may be examined by any stockholder who is present. ■ **If** the meeting is to be held solely by means of remote communication, **then** such list shall also be open to the examination of any stockholder during the whole time of the meeting on a reasonably accessible electronic network, and the information required to access such list shall be provided with the notice of the meeting.

(b) **If** the corporation, or an officer or agent thereof, refuses to permit examination of the list by a stockholder, [then] such stockholder may apply to the Court of Chancery for an order to compel the corporation to permit such examination. ■ The burden of proof shall be on the corporation to establish that the examination such stockholder seeks is for a purpose not germane to the meeting. ■ The Court may summarily order the corporation to permit examination of the list upon such conditions as the Court may deem appropriate, and may make such additional orders as may be appropriate, including, without limitation, postponing the meeting or voiding the results of the meeting.

(c) For purposes of this chapter, "stock ledger" means 1 or more records administered by or on behalf of the corporation in which the names of all of the corporation's stockholders of record, the address and number of shares registered in the name of each such stockholder, and all issuances and transfers of stock of the corporation are recorded in accordance with § 224 of this title. ■ The stock ledger shall be the only evidence as to who are the stockholders entitled by this section (to examine the list required by this section) or (to vote in person or by proxy at any meeting of stockholders).

§ 220. Inspection of books and records.

(a) As used in this section:

(1) "Stockholder" means a holder of record of stock in a stock corporation, or a person who is the beneficial owner of shares of such stock held either in a voting trust or by a nominee on behalf of such person.

(2) "Subsidiary" means any entity directly or indirectly owned, in whole or in part, by the corporation of which the stockholder is a stockholder and over the affairs of which the corporation directly or indirectly exercises control, and includes, without limitation, corporations, partnerships, limited partnerships, limited liability partnerships, limited liability companies, statutory trusts and/or joint ventures.

(3) "Under oath" includes statements the declarant affirms to be true under penalty of perjury under the laws of the United States or any state.

(b) Any stockholder, in person or by attorney or other agent, shall, upon written demand under oath stating the purpose thereof, have the right during the usual hours for business to inspect for any proper purpose, and to make copies and extracts from:

(1) The corporation's stock ledger, a list of its stockholders, and its other books and records; and

(2) [Then] A subsidiary's books and records, to the extent that:

a. The corporation has actual possession and control of such records of such subsidiary; or

b. The corporation could obtain such records through the exercise of control over such subsidiary, provided that as of the date of the making of the demand:

1. The stockholder inspection of such books and records of the subsidiary would not constitute a breach of an agreement between the corporation or the subsidiary and a person or persons not affiliated with the corporation; and

2. The subsidiary would not have the right under the law applicable to it to deny the corporation access to such books and records upon demand by the corporation.

In every instance **where** the stockholder is other than a record holder of stock in a stock corporation, [or] a member of a nonstock corporation, **[then]** the demand under oath shall state the person's status as a stockholder, be accompanied by documentary evidence of beneficial ownership of the stock, [and] state that such documentary evidence is a true and correct copy of what it purports to be. ■ A proper purpose shall mean a purpose reasonably related to such person's interest as a stockholder. ■ In every instance **where** an attorney [or] other agent shall be the person who seeks the right to inspection, **[then]** the demand under oath shall be accompanied by a power of attorney or such other writing which authorizes the attorney or other agent to so act on behalf of the stockholder. ■ The demand under oath shall be directed to the corporation (at its registered office in this State) or (at its principal place of business).

(c) If the corporation, or an officer or agent thereof, refuses to permit an inspection sought by a stockholder or attorney or other agent acting for the stockholder pursuant to subsection (b) of this section [or] does not reply to the demand within 5 business days after the demand has been made, **[then]** the stockholder may apply to the Court of Chancery for an order to compel such inspection. ■ The Court of Chancery is hereby vested with exclusive jurisdiction to determine whether or not the person seeking inspection is entitled to the inspection sought. ■ The Court may summarily order the corporation to permit the stockholder to inspect the corporation's stock ledger, an existing list of stockholders, and its other books and records, and to make copies or extracts therefrom; [or] the Court may order the corporation to furnish to the stockholder a list of its stockholders as of a specific date (on condition that the stockholder first pay to the corporation the reasonable cost of obtaining and furnishing such list) and (on such other conditions as the Court deems appropriate). ■ **Where** the stockholder seeks to inspect the corporation's books and records, other than its stock ledger or list of stockholders, **[then]** such stockholder shall first establish that:

(1) Such stockholder is a stockholder;

(2) Such stockholder has complied with this section respecting the form and manner of making demand for inspection of such documents; [and]

(3) The inspection such stockholder seeks is for a proper purpose.

Where the stockholder seeks to inspect the corporation's stock ledger or list of stockholders [and] establishes that such stockholder is a stockholder and has complied with this section respecting the form and manner of making demand for inspection of such documents, **[then]** the burden of proof shall be upon the corporation to establish that the inspection such stockholder seeks is for an improper purpose. ■ The Court may, in its discretion, prescribe any limitations or conditions with reference to the inspection, [or] award such other or further relief as the Court may deem just and proper. ■ The Court may order books, documents and records, pertinent extracts therefrom, [or] duly authenticated copies thereof, to be (brought within this State) [and] (kept in this State) upon such terms and conditions as the order may prescribe.

(d) Any director shall have the right to examine the corporation's stock ledger, a list of its stockholders and its other books and records for a purpose reasonably related to the director's position as a director. ■ The Court of Chancery is hereby vested with the exclusive jurisdiction to determine whether a director is entitled to the inspection sought. ■ The Court may summarily order the corporation to permit the director to inspect any and all books and records, the stock ledger and the list of stockholders and to make copies or extracts therefrom. ■ The burden of proof shall be upon the corporation to establish that the inspection such director seeks is for an improper purpose. ■ The Court may, in its discretion, prescribe any limitations or conditions with reference to the inspection, [or] award such other and further relief as the Court may deem just and proper.

§ 221. Voting, inspection and other rights of bondholders and debenture holders.

Every corporation may in its certificate of incorporation confer upon the holders of any bonds, debentures or other obligations issued or to be issued by the corporation the power to vote in respect to the corporate affairs and management of the corporation to the extent and in the manner provided in the certificate of incorporation and may confer upon such holders of bonds, debentures or other obligations the same right of inspection of its books, accounts and other records, [and] also any other rights, which the stockholders of the corporation have or may have by reason of this chapter or of its certificate of incorporation. ■ If the certificate of incorporation so provides, [then] such holders of bonds, debentures or other obligations shall be deemed to be stockholders, [and] their bonds, debentures or other obligations shall be deemed to be shares of stock, for the purpose of any provision of this chapter which requires the vote of stockholders as a prerequisite to any corporate action [and] the certificate of incorporation may divest the holders of capital stock, in whole or in part, of their right to vote on any corporate matter whatsoever, ◀except as set forth in § 242(b)(2) of this title▶.

§ 222. Notice of meetings and adjourned meetings.

(a) **Whenever** stockholders are required or permitted to take any action at a meeting, **[then]** a notice of the meeting in the form of a writing or electronic transmission shall be given which shall state (the place, if any, date and hour of the meeting), (the means of remote communications, if any, by which stockholders and proxy holders may be deemed to be present in person and vote at such meeting), (the record date for determining the stockholders entitled to vote at the meeting, if such date is different from the record date for determining stockholders entitled to notice of the meeting), [and], (in the case of a special meeting, the purpose or purposes for which the meeting is called).

(b) Unless otherwise provided in this chapter, the notice of any meeting shall be given not less than 10 nor more than 60 days before the date of the meeting to each stockholder entitled to vote at such meeting as of (the record date for determining the stockholders entitled to notice of the meeting).

(c) **When** a meeting is adjourned to another time or place, **unless** the bylaws otherwise require, **[then]** notice need not be given of the adjourned meeting **if** the time, place, if any, thereof, [and] the means of remote communications, if any, by which stockholders and proxy holders may be deemed to be present in person and vote at such adjourned meeting are announced at the meeting at which the adjournment is taken. ■ At the adjourned meeting the corporation may transact any business which might have been transacted at the original meeting. ■ **If** the adjournment is for more than 30 days, **[then]** a notice of the adjourned meeting shall be given to each stockholder of record entitled to vote at the meeting. ■ **If** after the adjournment a new record date for stockholders entitled to vote is fixed for the adjourned meeting, **[then]** the board of directors shall fix a new record date for notice of such adjourned meeting in accordance with § 213(a) of this title, and shall give notice of the adjourned meeting to (each stockholder of record entitled to vote at such adjourned meeting as of the record date fixed for notice of such adjourned meeting).

§ 223. Vacancies and newly created directorships.

(a) Unless otherwise provided in the certificate of incorporation or bylaws:

   (1) Vacancies and newly created directorships resulting from any increase in the authorized number of directors elected by all of the stockholders having the right to vote as a single class may be filled (by a majority of the directors then in office, although less than a quorum), or (by a sole remaining director);

   (2) Whenever the holders of any class or classes of stock or series thereof are entitled to elect 1 or more directors by the certificate of incorporation, **[then]** vacancies and newly created directorships of such class or classes or series may be filled (by a majority of the directors elected by such class or classes or series thereof then in office), or (by a sole remaining director so elected).

If at any time, by reason of death or resignation or other cause, a corporation should have no directors in office, **then** any officer or any stockholder or an executor, administrator, trustee or guardian of a stockholder, or other fiduciary entrusted with like responsibility for the person or estate of a stockholder, may call a special meeting of stockholders in accordance with the certificate of incorporation or the bylaws, or may apply to the Court of Chancery for a decree summarily ordering an election as provided in § 211 or § 215 of this title.

(b) In the case of a corporation the directors of which are divided into classes, any directors chosen under subsection (a) of this section shall hold office (until the next election of the class for which such directors shall have been chosen), and (until their successors shall be elected and qualified).

(c) If, at the time of filling any vacancy or any newly created directorship, the directors then in office shall constitute less than a majority of the whole board (as constituted immediately prior to any such increase), **[then]** the Court of Chancery may, upon application of any stockholder or stockholders holding at least 10 percent of the voting stock at the time outstanding having the right to vote for such directors, summarily order an election to be held (to fill any such vacancies or newly created directorships), or (to replace the directors chosen by the directors then in office as aforesaid), which election shall be governed by § 211 or § 215 of this title as far as applicable.

(d) Unless otherwise provided in the certificate of incorporation or bylaws, when 1 or more directors shall resign from the board, effective at a future date, **[then]** a majority of the directors then in office, including those who have so resigned, shall have power to fill such vacancy or vacancies, the vote thereon to take effect when such resignation or resignations shall become effective, and each director so chosen shall hold office as provided in this section in the filling of other vacancies.

§ 224. Form of records.

Any records administered by or on behalf of the corporation in the regular course of its business, including its stock ledger, books of account, and minute books, may be kept on, or by means of, or be in the form of, any information storage device, method, or 1 or more electronic networks or databases (including 1 or more distributed electronic networks or databases), provided that the records so kept can be converted into clearly legible paper form within a reasonable time, and, with respect to the stock ledger, that the records so kept **(i)** can be used to prepare the list of stockholders specified in §§ 219 and 220 of this title, **(ii)** record the information specified in §§ 156, 159, 217(a) and 218 of this title, and **(iii)** record transfers of stock as governed by Article 8 of subtitle I of Title 6. ■ Any corporation shall convert any records so kept into clearly legible paper form upon the request of any person entitled to inspect such records pursuant to any provision of this chapter. ■ When records are kept in such manner, [then] a clearly legible paper form prepared from or by means of the information storage device, method, or 1 or more electronic networks or databases (including 1 or more distributed electronic networks or databases) shall be valid and admissible in evidence, and accepted for all other purposes, to the same extent as an original paper record of the same information would have been, provided the paper form accurately portrays the record.

§ 225. Contested election of directors; proceedings to determine validity.

(a) Upon application of any stockholder or director, or any officer whose title to office is contested, the Court of Chancery may hear and determine the validity of any election, appointment, removal or resignation of any director or officer of any corporation, and the right of any person to hold or continue to hold such office, and, in case any such office is claimed by more than 1 person, may determine the person entitled thereto; and to that end make such order or decree in any such case as may be just and proper, with power to enforce the production of any books, papers and records of the corporation relating to the issue. ■ In case it should be determined that no valid election has been held, [then] the Court of Chancery may order an election to be held in accordance with § 211 or § 215 of this title. ■ In any such application, service of copies of the application upon the registered agent of the corporation shall be deemed to be service upon the corporation and upon the person whose title to office is contested and upon the person, if any, claiming such office; and the registered agent shall forward immediately a copy of the application **(**to the corporation**)** and **(**to the person whose title to office is contested**)** and **(**to the person, if any, claiming such office**)**, in a postpaid, sealed, registered letter addressed to such corporation and such person at their post-office addresses last known to the registered agent or furnished to the registered agent by the applicant stockholder. ■ The Court may make such order respecting further or other notice of such application as it deems proper under the circumstances.

(b) Upon application of any stockholder or upon application of the corporation itself, the Court of Chancery may hear and determine the result of any vote of stockholders upon matters other than the election of directors or officers. ■ Service of the application upon the registered agent of the corporation shall be deemed to be service upon the corporation, and no other party need be joined in order for the Court to adjudicate the result of the vote. ■ The Court may make such order respecting notice of the application as it deems proper under the circumstances.

(c) If 1 or more directors has been convicted of a felony in connection with the duties of such director or directors to the corporation, or if there has been a prior judgment on the merits by a court of competent jurisdiction that 1 or more directors has committed a breach of the duty of loyalty in connection with the duties of such director or directors to that corporation, **then**, upon application by the corporation, or derivatively in the right of the corporation by any stockholder, in a subsequent action brought for such purpose, the Court of Chancery may remove from office such director or directors if the Court determines that ❨the director or directors did not act in good faith in performing the acts resulting in the prior conviction or judgment❩ and ❨judicial removal is necessary to avoid irreparable harm to the corporation❩. ■ In connection with such removal, the Court may make such orders as are necessary to effect such removal. ■ In any such application, service of copies of the application upon the registered agent of the corporation shall be deemed to be service upon the corporation and upon the director or directors whose removal is sought; and the registered agent shall forward immediately a copy of the application to the corporation and to such director or directors, in a postpaid, sealed, registered letter addressed to such corporation and such director or directors at their post office addresses last known to the registered agent or furnished to the registered agent by the applicant. ■ The Court may make such order respecting further or other notice of such application as it deems proper under the circumstances.

§ 226. Appointment of custodian or receiver of corporation on deadlock or for other cause.

(a) **[Then]** The Court of Chancery, upon application of any stockholder, may appoint 1 or more persons to be custodians, and, if the corporation is insolvent, to be receivers, of and for any corporation **when**:

> (1) At any meeting held for the election of directors the stockholders are so divided that they have failed to elect successors to directors whose terms have expired or would have expired upon qualification of their successors; or

> (2) The business of the corporation is suffering or is threatened with irreparable injury because the directors are so divided respecting the management of the affairs of the corporation that the required vote for action by the board of directors cannot be obtained and the stockholders are unable to terminate this division; or

> (3) The corporation has abandoned its business and has failed within a reasonable time to take steps to dissolve, liquidate or distribute its assets.

(b) A custodian appointed under this section shall have all the powers and title of a receiver appointed under § 291 of this title, but the authority of the custodian is to continue the business of the corporation and not to liquidate its affairs and distribute its assets, ❨except when the Court shall otherwise order❩ and ❨except in cases arising under paragraph (a)(3) of this section or § 352(a)(2) of this title.❩

(c) In the case of a charitable nonstock corporation, the applicant shall provide a copy of any application referred to in subsection (a) of this section to the Attorney General of the State of Delaware within 1 week of its filing with the Court of Chancery.

§ 227. Powers of Court in elections of directors.

(a) The Court of Chancery, in any proceeding instituted under § 211, § 215 or § 225 of this title may determine the right and power of persons claiming to own stock to vote at any meeting of the stockholders.

(b) The Court of Chancery may appoint a Master to hold any election provided for in § 211, § 215 or § 225 of this title under such orders and powers as it deems proper; and it may punish any officer or director for contempt in case of disobedience of any order made by the Court; and, in case of disobedience by a corporation of any order made by the Court, may enter a decree against such corporation for a penalty of not more than $5,000.

§ 228. Consent of stockholders or members in lieu of meeting.

(a) **[Then]** Unless otherwise provided in the certificate of incorporation, any action required by this chapter to be taken at any annual or special meeting of stockholders of a corporation, or any action which may be taken at any annual or special meeting of such stockholders, may be taken without a meeting, without prior notice and without a vote, **if** a consent or consents in writing, setting forth the action so taken, shall be signed by the holders of outstanding stock having not less than the minimum number of votes that would be necessary to authorize or take such action at a meeting at which all shares entitled to vote thereon were present and voted and shall be delivered to the corporation in the manner required by this section.

(b) **[Then]** Unless otherwise provided in the certificate of incorporation, any action required by this chapter to be taken at a meeting of the members of a nonstock corporation, or any action which may be taken at any meeting of the members of a nonstock corporation, may be taken without a meeting, without prior notice and without a vote, **if** a consent or consents, setting forth the action so taken, shall be signed by members having not less than the minimum number of votes that would be necessary to authorize or take such action at a meeting at which all members having a right to vote thereon were present and voted and shall be delivered to the corporation in the manner required by this section.

(c) A consent must be set forth in writing or in an electronic transmission. ■ **[Then]** No consent shall be effective to take the corporate action referred to therein **unless** consents signed by a sufficient number of holders or members to take action are delivered to the corporation in the manner required by this section within 60 days of the first date on which a consent is so delivered to the corporation. **[Then]** Any person executing a consent may provide, whether through instruction to an agent or otherwise, that such a consent will be effective at a future time (including a time determined upon the happening of an event), no later than 60 days after such instruction is given or such provision is made, **if** evidence of such instruction or provision is provided to the corporation. ■ Unless otherwise provided, any such consent shall be revocable prior to its becoming effective. ■ All references to a consent in this section means a consent permitted by this section.

Subchapter VII. Meetings, Elections, Voting and Notice   § 229

(d)(1) A consent permitted by this section shall be delivered: **(i)** to the principal place of business of the corporation; **(ii)** to an officer or agent of the corporation having custody of the book in which proceedings of meetings of stockholders or members are recorded; **(iii)** to the registered office of the corporation in this State by hand or by certified or registered mail, return receipt requested; or **(iv)** subject to the next sentence, in accordance with § 116 of this title to an information processing system, if any, designated by the corporation for receiving such consents. ■ In the case of delivery pursuant to the foregoing clause (iv), such consent must set forth or be delivered with information that enables the corporation to determine the date of delivery of such consent and the identity of the person giving such consent, and, if such consent is given by a person authorized to act for a stockholder or member as proxy, such consent must comply with the applicable provisions of § 212(c)(2) & (3) of this title.

(2) Any copy, facsimile or other reliable reproduction of a consent in writing may be substituted or used in lieu of the original writing for any and all purposes for which the original writing could be used, provided that such copy, facsimile or other reproduction shall be a complete reproduction of the entire original writing. ■ A consent may be documented and signed in accordance with § 116 of this title, and when so documented or signed shall be deemed to be in writing for purposes of this title; provided that if such consent is delivered pursuant to clause (i), (ii) or (iii) of subsection (d)(1) of this section, such consent must be reproduced and delivered in paper form.

(e) Prompt notice of the taking of the corporate action without a meeting by less than unanimous consent shall be given to those stockholders or members (who have not consented) and (who, if the action had been taken at a meeting, would have been entitled to notice of the meeting) if the record date for notice of such meeting had been the date that consents signed by a sufficient number of holders or members to take the action were delivered to the corporation as provided in this section. ■ **In the event that** the action which is consented to is such as would have required the filing of a certificate under any other section of this title, if such action had been voted on by stockholders or by members at a meeting thereof, [then] the certificate filed under such other section shall state, in lieu of any statement required by such section concerning any vote of stockholders or members, that consent has been given in accordance with this section.

§ 229. Waiver of notice.

Whenever notice is required to be given under any provision of this chapter or the certificate of incorporation or bylaws, [then] a written waiver, signed by the person entitled to notice, or a waiver by electronic transmission by the person entitled to notice, whether before or after the time stated therein, shall be deemed equivalent to notice. ■ Attendance of a person at a meeting shall constitute a waiver of notice of such meeting, (except when the person attends a meeting for the express purpose of objecting at the beginning of the meeting, to the transaction of any business because the meeting is not lawfully called or convened). ■ [Then] Neither the business to be transacted at, nor the purpose of, any regular or special meeting of the stockholders, directors or members of a committee of directors need be specified in any written waiver of notice or any waiver by electronic transmission **unless** so required by the certificate of incorporation or the bylaws.

§ 230. Exception to requirements of notice.

(a) Whenever notice is required to be given, under any provision of this chapter or of the certificate of incorporation or bylaws of any corporation, to any person with whom communication is unlawful, **[then]** the giving of such notice to such person shall not be required and there shall be no duty to apply to any governmental authority or agency for a license or permit to give such notice to such person. ■ Any action or meeting which shall be taken or held without notice to any such person with whom communication is unlawful shall have the same force and effect as if such notice had been duly given. ■ **In the event that** the action taken by the corporation is such as to require the filing of a certificate under any of the other sections of this title, **[then]** the certificate shall state, if such is the fact and if notice is required, that (notice was given to all persons entitled to receive notice except such persons with whom communication is unlawful).

(b) Whenever notice is required to be given, under any provision of this title or the certificate of incorporation or bylaws of any corporation, to any stockholder or, if the corporation is a nonstock corporation, to any member, to whom ((1) notice of 2 consecutive annual meetings, and all notices of meetings or of the taking of action by written consent without a meeting to such person during the period between such 2 consecutive annual meetings), or ((2) all, and at least 2, payments (if sent by first-class mail) of dividends or interest on securities during a 12-month period), have been mailed addressed to such person at such person's address as shown on the records of the corporation and have been returned undeliverable, **[then]** the giving of such notice to such person shall not be required. ■ Any action or meeting which shall be taken or held without notice to such person shall have the same force and effect as if such notice had been duly given. ■ **If** any such person shall deliver to the corporation a written notice setting forth such person's then current address, **[then]** the requirement that notice be given to such person shall be reinstated. ■ **In the event that** the action taken by the corporation is such as to require the filing of a certificate under any of the other sections of this title, **[then]** the certificate need not state that notice was not given to persons to whom notice was not required to be given pursuant to this subsection.

(c) [Then] The exception in paragraph (b)(1) of this section to the requirement that notice be given shall not be applicable to any notice returned as undeliverable **if** the notice was given by electronic transmission. ■ The exception in paragraph (b)(1) of this section to the requirement that notice be given shall not be applicable to any stockholder or member whose electronic mail address appears on the records of the corporation and to whom notice by electronic transmission is not prohibited by Section 232 of this title.

§ 231. Voting procedures and inspectors of elections.

(a) The corporation shall, in advance of any meeting of stockholders, appoint 1 or more inspectors to act at the meeting and make a written report thereof. ■ The corporation may designate 1 or more persons as alternate inspectors to replace any inspector who fails to act. ■ **If** no inspector or alternate is able to act at a meeting of stockholders, **[then]** the person presiding at the meeting shall appoint 1 or more inspectors to act at the meeting. ■ Each inspector, before entering upon the discharge of the duties of inspector, shall take and sign an oath faithfully to execute the duties of inspector with strict impartiality and according to the best of such inspector's ability.

(b) The inspectors shall:

(1) Ascertain the number of shares outstanding and the voting power of each;

(2) Determine the shares represented at a meeting and the validity of proxies and ballots;

(3) Count all votes and ballots;

(4) Determine and retain for a reasonable period a record of the disposition of any challenges made to any determination by the inspectors; and

(5) Certify their determination of the number of shares represented at the meeting, and their count of all votes and ballots.

The inspectors may appoint or retain other persons or entities to assist the inspectors in the performance of the duties of the inspectors.

(c) The date and time of the opening and the closing of the polls for each matter upon which the stockholders will vote at a meeting shall be announced at the meeting. ■ **[Then]** No ballot, proxies or votes, nor any revocations thereof or changes thereto, shall be accepted by the inspectors after the closing of the polls **unless** the Court of Chancery upon application by a stockholder shall determine otherwise.

(d) In determining the validity and counting of proxies and ballots, the inspectors shall be limited to an examination of (the proxies), (any envelopes submitted with those proxies), (any information provided in accordance with § 211(e) or § 212(c)(2) of this title, or any information provided pursuant to § 211(a)(2)b.(i) or (iii) of this title), (ballots) and (the regular books and records of the corporation), (except that the inspectors may consider other reliable information for the limited purpose of reconciling proxies and ballots submitted by or on behalf of banks, brokers, their nominees or similar persons which represent more votes than the holder of a proxy is authorized by the record owner to cast or more votes than the stockholder holds of record). ■ If the inspectors consider other reliable information for the limited purpose permitted herein, **[then]** the inspectors at the time they make their certification pursuant to paragraph (b)(5) of this section shall specify the precise information considered by them including (the person or persons from whom they obtained the information), (when the information was obtained), (the means by which the information was obtained) and (the basis for the inspectors' belief that such information is accurate and reliable).

(e) Unless otherwise provided in the certificate of incorporation or bylaws, this section shall not apply to a corporation that does not have a class of voting stock that is:

(1) Listed on a national securities exchange;

(2) Authorized for quotation on an interdealer quotation system of a registered national securities association; or

(3) Held of record by more than 2,000 stockholders.

§ 232. Delivery of notice; notice by electronic transmission.

(a) **[Then]** Without limiting the manner by which notice otherwise may be given effectively to stockholders, any notice to stockholders given by the corporation under any provision of this chapter, the certificate of incorporation, or the bylaws may be given in writing directed to the stockholder's mailing address (or by electronic transmission directed to the stockholder's electronic mail address, as applicable) as it appears on the records of the corporation and shall be given **(1)** if mailed, when the notice is deposited in the U.S. mail, postage prepaid, **(2)** if delivered by courier service, the earlier of when the notice is received or left at such stockholder's address or **(3)** if given by electronic mail, when directed to such stockholder's electronic mail address **unless** the stockholder has notified the corporation in writing or by electronic transmission of an objection to receiving notice by electronic mail or such notice is prohibited by subsection (e) of this section. ■ A notice by electronic mail must include a prominent legend that the communication is an important notice regarding the corporation.

(b) Without limiting the manner by which notice otherwise may be given effectively to stockholders, but subject to subsection (e) of this section, any notice to stockholders given by the corporation under any provision of this chapter, the certificate of incorporation, or the bylaws shall be effective if given by a form of electronic transmission consented to by the stockholder to whom the notice is given. ■ Any such consent shall be revocable by the stockholder by written notice or electronic transmission to the corporation. ■ A corporation may give a notice by electronic mail in accordance with subsection (a) of this section without obtaining the consent required by this subsection (b).

(c) Notice given pursuant to subsection (b) of this section shall be deemed given:

(1) If by facsimile telecommunication, when directed to a number at which the stockholder has consented to receive notice;

(2) If by a posting on an electronic network together with separate notice to the stockholder of such specific posting, upon the later of (A) such posting and (B) the giving of such separate notice; and

(3) If by any other form of electronic transmission, when directed to the stockholder.

(d) For purposes of this chapter, **(1)** "electronic transmission" means any form of communication, not directly involving the physical transmission of paper, including the use of, or participation in, 1 or more electronic networks or databases (including 1 or more distributed electronic networks or databases), (that creates a record that may be retained, retrieved and reviewed by a recipient thereof), and (that may be directly reproduced in paper form by such a recipient through an automated process), **(2)** [then] "electronic mail" means an electronic transmission directed to a unique electronic mail address (which electronic mail shall be deemed to include any files attached thereto and any information hyperlinked to a website **if** such electronic mail includes the contact information of an officer or agent of the corporation who is available to assist with accessing such files and information) and **(3)** "electronic mail address" means a destination, commonly expressed as a string of characters, consisting of a unique user name or mailbox (commonly referred to as the "local part" of the address) and a reference to an internet domain (commonly referred to as the "domain part" of the address), whether or not displayed, to which electronic mail can be sent or delivered.

(e) Notwithstanding the foregoing, a notice may not be given by an electronic transmission from and after the time that **(1)** the corporation is unable to deliver by such electronic transmission 2 consecutive notices given by the corporation and **(2)** such inability becomes known to the secretary or an assistant secretary of the corporation or to the transfer agent, or other person responsible for the giving of notice, **provided, however**, the inadvertent failure to discover such inability shall not invalidate any meeting or other action.

(f) An affidavit of the secretary or an assistant secretary or of the transfer agent or other agent of the corporation that notice has been given shall, in the absence of fraud, be prima facie evidence of the facts stated therein.

(g) No provision of this section, except for paragraphs (a)(1), (d)(2) and (d)(3) of this section shall apply to § 164, § 296, § 311, § 312, or § 324 of this title.

§ 233. Notice to stockholders sharing an address.

(a) Without limiting the manner by which notice otherwise may be given effectively to stockholders, any notice to stockholders given by the corporation under any provision of this chapter, the certificate of incorporation, or the bylaws shall be effective if given by a single written notice to stockholders who share an address if consented to by the stockholders at that address to whom such notice is given. ■ Any such consent shall be revocable by the stockholder by written notice to the corporation.

(b) Any stockholder who fails to object in writing to the corporation, within 60 days of having been given written notice by the corporation of its intention to send the single notice permitted under subsection (a) of this section, shall be deemed to have consented to receiving such single written notice.

(c) [Repealed.]

(d) This section shall not apply to § 164, § 296, § 311, § 312 or § 324 of this title.

Subchapter VIII. Amendment of Certificate of Incorporation; Changes in Capital and Capital Stock

§ 241. Amendment of certificate of incorporation before receipt of payment for stock.

(a) [Then] Before a corporation has received any payment for any of its stock, it may amend its certificate of incorporation at any time or times, in any and as many respects as may be desired, **so long as** its certificate of incorporation as amended would contain only such provisions as it would be lawful and proper to insert in an original certificate of incorporation filed at the time of filing the amendment.

(b) [Then] The amendment of a certificate of incorporation authorized by this section shall be adopted by a majority of the incorporators, **if** directors were not named in the original certificate of incorporation [or] have not yet been elected, [or], **if** directors were named in the original certificate of incorporation [or] have been elected and have qualified, [then] by a majority of the directors. ■ A certificate setting forth the amendment and certifying that the corporation has not received any payment for any of its stock, or that the corporation has no members, as applicable, and that the amendment has been duly adopted in accordance with this section shall be executed, acknowledged and filed in accordance with § 103 of this title. ■ Upon such filing, the corporation's certificate of incorporation shall be deemed to be amended accordingly as of the date on which the original certificate of incorporation became effective, ◂except as to those persons who are substantially and adversely affected by the amendment and as to those persons the amendment shall be effective from the filing date.▸

(c) This section will apply to a nonstock corporation before such a corporation has any members; `provided, however, that` all references to directors shall be deemed to be references to members of the governing body of the corporation.

§ 242. Amendment of certificate of incorporation after receipt of payment for stock; nonstock corporations.

(a) [Then] After a corporation has received payment for any of its capital stock, or after a nonstock corporation has members, it may amend its certificate of incorporation, from time to time, in any and as many respects as may be desired, **so long as** its certificate of incorporation as amended would contain only such provisions as it would be lawful and proper to insert in an original certificate of incorporation filed at the time of the filing of the amendment; `and`, if a change in stock or the rights of stockholders, or an exchange, reclassification, subdivision, combination or cancellation of stock or rights of stockholders is to be made, [then] such provisions as may be necessary to effect such change, exchange, reclassification, subdivision, combination or cancellation. ■ In particular, and without limitation upon such general power of amendment, a corporation may amend its certificate of incorporation, from time to time, so as:

(1) To change its corporate name; `or`

(2) To change, substitute, enlarge or diminish the nature of its business or its corporate powers and purposes; `or`

(3) To increase or decrease its authorized capital stock or to reclassify the same, ❨by changing the number, par value, designations, preferences, or relative, participating, optional, or other special rights of the shares, or the qualifications, limitations or restrictions of such rights,❩ `or` ❨by changing shares with par value into shares without par value, or shares without par value into shares with par value either with or without increasing or decreasing the number of shares,❩ `or` ❨by subdividing or combining the outstanding shares of any class or series of a class of shares into a greater or lesser number of outstanding shares❩; `or`

(4) To cancel or otherwise affect the right of the holders of the shares of any class to receive dividends which have accrued but have not been declared; `or`

(5) To create new classes of stock having rights and preferences either prior and superior or subordinate and inferior to the stock of any class then authorized, whether issued or unissued; or

(6) To change the period of its duration; `or`

(7) To delete:

a. Such provisions of the original certificate of incorporation which named ❨the incorporator or incorporators❩, ❨the initial board of directors❩ and ❨the original subscribers for shares❩; `and`

b. [Then] Such provisions contained in any amendment to the certificate of incorporation as were necessary to effect a change, exchange, reclassification, subdivision, combination or cancellation of stock, if such change, exchange, reclassification, subdivision, combination or cancellation has become effective.

Any or all such changes or alterations may be effected by 1 certificate of amendment.

(b) Every amendment authorized by subsection (a) of this section shall be made and effected in the following manner:

(1) If the corporation has capital stock, **[then]** its board of directors shall adopt a resolution setting forth the amendment proposed, declaring its advisability, and either calling a special meeting of the stockholders entitled to vote in respect thereof for the consideration of such amendment or directing that the amendment proposed be considered at the next annual meeting of the stockholders; **provided, however, that** unless otherwise expressly required by the certificate of incorporation, no meeting or vote of stockholders shall be required to adopt an amendment that effects only changes described in paragraph (a)(1) or (7) of this section. ■ Such special or annual meeting shall be called and held upon notice in accordance with § 222 of this title. ■ **[Then]** The notice shall set forth such amendment in full or a brief summary of the changes to be effected thereby **unless** such notice constitutes a notice of internet availability of proxy materials under the rules promulgated under the Securities Exchange Act of 1934 [15 U.S.C. § 78a et seq.]. ■ At the meeting a vote of the stockholders entitled to vote thereon shall be taken for and against any proposed amendment that requires adoption by stockholders. ■ **If** no vote of stockholders is required to effect such amendment, or **if** a majority of the outstanding stock entitled to vote thereon, and a majority of the outstanding stock of each class entitled to vote thereon as a class has been voted in favor of the amendment, **[then]** a certificate setting forth the amendment and certifying that such amendment has been duly adopted in accordance with this section shall be executed, acknowledged and filed and shall become effective in accordance with § 103 of this title.

(2) [Then] The holders of the outstanding shares of a class shall be entitled to vote as a class upon a proposed amendment, whether or not entitled to vote thereon by the certificate of incorporation, **if** the amendment would increase or decrease the aggregate number of authorized shares of such class, increase or decrease the par value of the shares of such class, or alter or change the powers, preferences, or special rights of the shares of such class so as to affect them adversely. ■ **If** any proposed amendment would alter or change the powers, preferences, or special rights of 1 or more series of any class so as to affect them adversely, but shall not so affect the entire class, **then** only the shares of the series so affected by the amendment shall be considered a separate class for the purposes of this paragraph. ■ The number of authorized shares of any such class or classes of stock may be increased or decreased (but not below the number of shares thereof then outstanding) by the affirmative vote of the holders of a majority of the stock of the corporation entitled to vote irrespective of this subsection, if so provided **(**in the original certificate of incorporation**)**, **(**in any amendment thereto which created such class or classes of stock or which was adopted prior to the issuance of any shares of such class or classes of stock**)**, or **(**in any amendment thereto which was authorized by a resolution or resolutions adopted by the affirmative vote of the holders of a majority of such class or classes of stock**)**.

(3) If the corporation is a nonstock corporation, **then** the governing body thereof shall adopt a resolution setting forth the amendment proposed and declaring its advisability. ■ **If** a majority of all the members of the governing body shall vote in favor of such amendment, [then] a certificate thereof shall be executed, acknowledged and filed [and] shall become effective in accordance with § 103 of this title. ■ The certificate of incorporation of any nonstock corporation may contain a provision (requiring any amendment thereto to be approved by a specified number or percentage of the members or of any specified class of members of such corporation) [in which event] such proposed amendment shall be submitted to the members or to any specified class of members of such corporation in the same manner, so far as applicable, as is provided in this section for an amendment to the certificate of incorporation of a stock corporation; [and] in the event of the adoption thereof by such members, a certificate evidencing such amendment shall be executed, acknowledged and filed [and] shall become effective in accordance with § 103 of this title.

(4) Whenever the certificate of incorporation shall require for action (by the board of directors of a corporation other than a nonstock corporation) or (by the governing body of a nonstock corporation), by the holders of any class or series of shares or by the members, or by the holders of any other securities having voting power the vote of a greater number or proportion than is required by any section of this title, **[then]** the provision of the certificate of incorporation requiring such greater vote shall not be altered, amended [or] repealed ◄except by such greater vote.►

(c) The resolution authorizing a proposed amendment to the certificate of incorporation may provide that (at any time prior to the effectiveness of the filing of the amendment with the Secretary of State, notwithstanding authorization of the proposed amendment by the stockholders of the corporation or by the members of a nonstock corporation, the board of directors or governing body may abandon such proposed amendment without further action by the stockholders or members).

§ 243. Retirement of stock.

(a) A corporation, by resolution of its board of directors, may retire any shares of its capital stock that are issued but are not outstanding.

(b) Whenever any shares of the capital stock of a corporation are retired, **[then]** they shall resume the status of authorized and unissued shares of the class or series to which they belong **unless** the certificate of incorporation otherwise provides. ■ **If** the certificate of incorporation prohibits the reissuance of such shares, [or] prohibits the reissuance of such shares as a part of a specific series only, **[then]** a certificate stating that reissuance of the shares (as part of the class or series) is prohibited identifying the shares and reciting their retirement shall be executed, acknowledged and filed [and] shall become effective in accordance with § 103 of this title. ■ **When** such certificate becomes effective, **[then]** it shall have the effect (of amending the certificate of incorporation so as to reduce accordingly the number of authorized shares of the class or series to which such shares belong) or, if such retired shares constitute all of the authorized shares of the class or series to which they belong, (of eliminating from the certificate of incorporation all reference to such class or series of stock).

(c) **If** the capital of the corporation will be reduced by or in connection with the retirement of shares, **[then]** the reduction of capital shall be effected pursuant to § 244 of this title.

§ 244. Reduction of capital.

(a) A corporation, by resolution of its board of directors, may reduce its capital in any of the following ways:

(1) By reducing or eliminating the capital represented by shares of capital stock which have been retired;

(2) By applying to an otherwise authorized purchase or redemption of outstanding shares of its capital stock (some or all of the capital represented by the shares being purchased or redeemed), or (any capital that has not been allocated to any particular class of its capital stock);

(3) By applying to an otherwise authorized conversion or exchange of outstanding shares of its capital stock (some or all of the capital represented by the shares being converted or exchanged), or (some or all of any capital that has not been allocated to any particular class of its capital stock), or (both), to the extent that such capital in the aggregate exceeds the total aggregate par value or the stated capital of any previously unissued shares issuable upon such conversion or exchange; or

(4) By transferring to surplus **(i)** some or all of the capital not represented by any particular class of its capital stock; **(ii)** some or all of the capital represented by issued shares of its par value capital stock, which capital is in excess of the aggregate par value of such shares; or **(iii)** some of the capital represented by issued shares of its capital stock without par value.

(b) **[Then]** Notwithstanding the other provisions of this section, no reduction of capital shall be made or effected **unless** the assets of the corporation remaining after such reduction shall be sufficient to pay any debts of the corporation for which payment has not been otherwise provided. ■ No reduction of capital shall release any liability of any stockholder whose shares have not been fully paid.

(c) [Repealed.]

§ 245. Restated certificate of incorporation.

(a) A corporation may, whenever desired, integrate into a single instrument all of the provisions of its certificate of incorporation which are then in effect and operative as a result of there having theretofore been filed with the Secretary of State 1 or more certificates or other instruments pursuant to any of the sections referred to in § 104 of this title, and it may at the same time also further amend its certificate of incorporation by adopting a restated certificate of incorporation.

(b) **If** the restated certificate of incorporation merely restates and integrates but does not further amend the certificate of incorporation, as theretofore amended or supplemented by any instrument that was filed pursuant to any of the sections mentioned in § 104 of this title, **[then]** it may be adopted by the board of directors without a vote of the stockholders, or it may be proposed by the directors and submitted by them to the stockholders for adoption, **in which case** the procedure and vote required, if any, by § 242 of this title for amendment of the certificate of incorporation shall be applicable. ■ **If** the restated certificate of incorporation restates and integrates and also further amends in any respect the certificate of incorporation, as theretofore amended or supplemented, **[then]** it shall be proposed by the directors and adopted by the stockholders (in the manner and by the vote prescribed by § 242 of this title) or, if the corporation has not received any payment for any of its stock, (in the manner and by the vote prescribed by § 241 of this title).

(c) A restated certificate of incorporation shall be specifically designated as such in its heading. ■ It shall state, either in its heading or in an introductory paragraph, the corporation's present name, and, if it has been changed, the name under which it was originally incorporated, and the date of filing of its original certificate of incorporation with the Secretary of State. ■ A restated certificate shall also state that it was duly adopted in accordance with this section. ■ **If** it was adopted by the board of directors without a vote of the stockholders (unless it was adopted pursuant to § 241 of this title or without a vote of members pursuant to 242(b)(3) of this title), **[then]** it shall state (that it only restates and integrates and does not further amend (except, if applicable, as permitted under § 242(a)(1) and § 242(b)(1) of this title) the provisions of the corporation's certificate of incorporation as theretofore amended or supplemented), and (that there is no discrepancy between those provisions and the provisions of the restated certificate). ■ A restated certificate of incorporation may omit **(a)** such provisions of the original certificate of incorporation which named the incorporator or incorporators, the initial board of directors and the original subscribers for shares, and **(b)** such provisions contained in any amendment to the certificate of incorporation as were necessary to effect a change, exchange, reclassification, subdivision, combination or cancellation of stock, **if** such change, exchange, reclassification, subdivision, combination or cancellation has become effective. ■ Any such omissions shall not be deemed a further amendment.

(d) A restated certificate of incorporation shall be executed, acknowledged and filed in accordance with § 103 of this title. ■ Upon its filing with the Secretary of State, the original certificate of incorporation, as theretofore amended or supplemented, shall be superseded; **[and]** thenceforth, the restated certificate of incorporation, including any further amendments or changes made thereby, shall be the certificate of incorporation of the corporation, **but** the original date of incorporation shall remain unchanged.

(e) Any amendment or change effected in connection with the restatement and integration of the certificate of incorporation shall be subject to any other provision of this chapter, not inconsistent with this section, which would apply if a separate certificate of amendment were filed to effect such amendment or change.

§ 246. [Reserved.]

Subchapter IX. Merger, Consolidation or Conversion

§ 251. Merger or consolidation of domestic corporations.

(a) Any 2 or more corporations of this State may merge into a single surviving corporation, which may be any 1 of the constituent corporations or may consolidate into a new resulting corporation formed by the consolidation, pursuant to an agreement of merger or consolidation, as the case may be, complying and approved in accordance with this section.

(b) The board of directors of each corporation which desires to merge or consolidate shall adopt a resolution approving an agreement of merger or consolidation and declaring its advisability. ■ The agreement shall state:

(1) The terms and conditions of the merger or consolidation;

(2) The mode of carrying the same into effect;

(3) In the case of a merger, such amendments or changes in the certificate of incorporation of the surviving corporation as are desired to be effected by the merger (which amendments or changes may amend and restate the certificate of incorporation of the surviving corporation in its entirety), or, if no such amendments or changes are desired, a statement that the certificate of incorporation of the surviving corporation shall be its certificate of incorporation;

(4) In the case of a consolidation, that the certificate of incorporation of the resulting corporation shall be as is set forth in an attachment to the agreement;

(5) The manner, if any, of converting the shares of each of the constituent corporations into shares or other securities of the corporation surviving or resulting from the merger or consolidation, or of cancelling some or all of such shares, and, if any shares of any of the constituent corporations are not to remain outstanding, to be converted solely into shares or other securities of the surviving or resulting corporation or to be cancelled, the cash, property, rights or securities of any other corporation or entity which the holders of such shares are to receive in exchange for, or upon conversion of such shares and the surrender of any certificates evidencing them, which cash, property, rights or securities of any other corporation or entity may be in addition to or in lieu of shares or other securities of the surviving or resulting corporation; and

(6) Such other details or provisions as are deemed desirable, including, without limiting the generality of the foregoing, a provision for the payment of cash in lieu of the issuance or recognition of fractional shares, rights or other securities of the surviving or resulting corporation or of any other corporation or entity the shares, rights or other securities of which are to be received in the merger or consolidation, or for any other arrangement with respect thereto, consistent with § 155 of this title.

The agreement so adopted shall be executed by an authorized person, provided that if the agreement is filed, it shall be executed and acknowledged in accordance with § 103 of this title. ■ Any of the terms of the agreement of merger or consolidation may be made dependent upon facts ascertainable outside of such agreement, provided that the manner in which such facts shall operate upon the terms of the agreement is clearly and expressly set forth in the agreement of merger or consolidation. ■ The term "facts," as used in the preceding sentence, includes, but is not limited to, the occurrence of any event, including a determination or action by (any person or body, including the corporation).

(c) The agreement required by subsection (b) of this section shall be submitted to the stockholders of each constituent corporation at an annual or special meeting for the purpose of acting on the agreement. ■ Due notice of the time, place and purpose of the meeting shall be given to each holder of stock, whether voting or nonvoting, of the corporation at the stockholder's address as it appears on the records of the corporation, at least 20 days prior to the date of the meeting. ■ The notice shall contain a copy of the agreement or a brief summary thereof. ■ At the meeting, the agreement shall be considered and a vote taken for its adoption or rejection. ■ If a majority of the outstanding stock of the corporation entitled to vote thereon shall be voted for the adoption of the agreement, [then] that fact shall be certified on the agreement by the secretary or assistant secretary of the corporation, provided that [then] such certification on the agreement shall not be required if a certificate of merger or consolidation is filed in lieu of filing the agreement. ■ If the agreement shall be so adopted and certified by each constituent corporation, [then] it shall then be filed and shall become effective, in accordance with § 103 of this title. ■ In lieu of filing the agreement of merger or consolidation required by this section, the surviving or resulting corporation may file a certificate of merger or consolidation, executed in accordance with § 103 of this title, which states:

(1) The name and state of incorporation of each of the constituent corporations;

(2) That an agreement of merger or consolidation has been approved, adopted, executed and acknowledged by each of the constituent corporations in accordance with this section;

(3) The name of the surviving or resulting corporation;

(4) In the case of a merger, such amendments or changes in the certificate of incorporation of the surviving corporation as are desired to be effected by the merger (which amendments or changes may amend and restate the certificate of incorporation of the surviving corporation in its entirety), or, if no such amendments or changes are desired, [then] a statement that the certificate of incorporation of the surviving corporation shall be its certificate of incorporation;

(5) In the case of a consolidation, that the certificate of incorporation of the resulting corporation shall be as set forth in an attachment to the certificate;

(6) That the executed agreement of consolidation or merger is on file at an office of the surviving or resulting corporation, stating the address thereof; and

(7) That a copy of the agreement of consolidation or merger will be furnished by the surviving or resulting corporation, on request and without cost, to any stockholder of any constituent corporation.

(d) Any agreement of merger or consolidation may contain a provision that (at any time prior to the time that the agreement (or a certificate in lieu thereof) filed with the Secretary of State becomes effective in accordance with § 103 of this title, the agreement may be terminated by the board of directors of any constituent corporation notwithstanding approval of the agreement by the stockholders of all or any of the constituent corporations); [and] in the event the agreement of merger or consolidation is terminated after the filing of the agreement (or a certificate in lieu thereof) with the Secretary of State but before the agreement (or a certificate in lieu thereof) has become effective, [then] a certificate of termination or merger or consolidation shall be filed in accordance with § 103 of this title. ■ Any agreement of merger or consolidation may contain a provision that the boards of directors of the constituent corporations may amend the agreement at any time prior to the time that the agreement (or a certificate in lieu thereof) filed with the Secretary of State becomes effective in accordance with § 103 of this title, provided that [then] an amendment made subsequent to the adoption of the agreement by the stockholders of any constituent corporation shall not (1) alter or change the amount [or] kind of shares, securities, cash, property and/or rights to be received in exchange for or on conversion of all or any of the shares of any class or series thereof of such constituent corporation, (2) alter or change any term of the certificate of incorporation of the surviving corporation to be effected by the merger or consolidation, [or] (3) alter or change any of the terms and conditions of the agreement if such alteration or change would adversely affect the holders of any class or series thereof of such constituent corporation; [[and]] **in the event** the agreement of merger or consolidation is amended after the filing thereof with the Secretary of State but before the agreement has become effective, [then] a certificate of amendment of merger or consolidation shall be filed in accordance with § 103 of this title.

(e) [Then] In the case of a merger, the certificate of incorporation of the surviving corporation shall automatically be amended **to the extent**, if any, that changes in the certificate of incorporation are set forth in the agreement of merger.

(f) [Then] Notwithstanding the requirements of subsection (c) of this section, unless required by its certificate of incorporation, no vote of stockholders of a constituent corporation surviving a merger shall be necessary to authorize a merger **if** (1) the agreement of merger does not amend in any respect the certificate of incorporation of such constituent corporation, (2) each share of stock of such constituent corporation outstanding immediately prior to the effective date of the merger is to be an identical outstanding or treasury share of the surviving corporation after the effective date of the merger, [and] (3) either (no shares of common stock of the surviving corporation and no shares, securities or obligations convertible into such stock are to be issued or delivered under the plan of merger), [or] (the authorized unissued shares or the treasury shares of common stock of the surviving corporation to be issued or delivered under the plan of merger plus those initially issuable upon conversion of any other shares, securities or obligations to be issued or delivered under such plan do not exceed 20% of the shares of common stock of such constituent corporation outstanding immediately prior to the effective date of the merger).
■ [Then] No vote of stockholders of a constituent corporation shall be necessary to authorize a merger or consolidation if no shares of the stock of such corporation shall have been issued prior to the adoption by the board of directors of the resolution approving the agreement of merger or consolidation. ■ If an agreement of merger is adopted by the constituent corporation surviving the merger, by action of its board of directors and without any vote of its stockholders pursuant to this subsection, [then] the secretary or assistant secretary of that corporation shall certify on the agreement (that the agreement has been adopted pursuant to this subsection) and, (1) if it has been adopted pursuant to the first sentence of this subsection, (that the conditions specified in that sentence have been satisfied), or (2) if it has been adopted pursuant to the second sentence of this subsection, (that no shares of stock of such corporation were issued prior to the adoption by the board of directors of the resolution approving the agreement of merger or consolidation), [provided that] [then] such certification on the agreement shall not be required if a certificate of merger or consolidation is filed in lieu of filing the agreement. ■ The agreement so adopted and certified shall then be filed [and] shall become effective, in accordance with § 103 of this title. ■ Such filing shall constitute a representation by the

person who executes the agreement (that the facts stated in the certificate remain true immediately prior to such filing).

(g) [Then] Notwithstanding the requirements of subsection (c) of this section, unless expressly required by its certificate of incorporation, <u>no vote</u> of stockholders of a constituent corporation <u>shall be necessary</u> to authorize a merger with or into a single direct or indirect wholly-owned subsidiary of such constituent corporation **if**:

(1) <u>such constituent corporation</u> and the direct or indirect <u>wholly-owned subsidiary</u> of such constituent corporation <u>are the only constituent entities</u> to the merger;

(2) <u>each share</u> or fraction of a share of the capital stock of the constituent corporation <u>outstanding immediately prior</u> to the effective time of the merger <u>is converted</u> in the merger into (a share or equal fraction of share of capital stock of a holding company) having the same designations, rights, powers and preferences, and the qualifications, limitations and restrictions thereof, as (the share of stock of the constituent corporation being converted in the merger);

(3) <u>the holding company</u> and <u>the constituent corporation are corporations</u> of this State and the direct or indirect <u>wholly-owned subsidiary</u> that is the other constituent entity to the merger <u>is a corporation</u> or <u>limited liability company</u> of this State;

(4) <u>the certificate of incorporation and bylaws of the holding company immediately following the effective time of the merger</u> <u>contain provisions identical</u> to the certificate of incorporation and bylaws of the constituent corporation immediately prior to the effective time of the merger ((other than provisions, if any, regarding the incorporator or incorporators, the corporate name, the registered office and agent, the initial board of directors and the initial subscribers for shares and such provisions contained in any amendment to the certificate of incorporation as were necessary to effect a change, exchange, reclassification, subdivision, combination or cancellation of stock, if such change, exchange, reclassification, subdivision, combination, or cancellation has become effective));

(5) as a result of the merger <u>the constituent corporation</u> or its successor <u>becomes</u> or remains <u>a</u> direct or indirect <u>wholly-owned subsidiary</u> of the holding company;

(6) <u>the directors</u> of the constituent corporation <u>become</u> or remain <u>the directors</u> of the holding company upon the effective time of the merger;

(7) <u>the organizational documents</u> of the surviving entity immediately following the effective time of the merger <u>contain provisions</u> requiring that

(A) any act or transaction by or involving the surviving entity, ◄other than the election or removal of directors or managers, managing members or other members of the governing body of the surviving entity►, that, if taken by the constituent corporation immediately prior to the effective time of the merger, would require (for its adoption under this chapter or under the certificate of incorporation or bylaws of the constituent corporation) immediately prior to the effective time of the merger, the approval of the stockholders of the constituent corporation shall, by specific reference to this subsection, (require, in addition to approval of the stockholders or members of the surviving entity, the approval of the stockholders of the holding company (or any successor by merger), by the same vote as is required by this chapter and/or by the certificate of incorporation or bylaws of the constituent corporation immediately prior to the effective time of the merger; provided, however, that for purposes of this clause (A) any amendment of the organizational documents of a surviving entity that is not a corporation, (which amendment would, if adopted by a corporation subject to this chapter, be required to be included in the certificate of incorporation of such corporation), shall, by specific reference to this subsection, require, in addition, the approval of the stockholders of the holding company (or any successor by merger), by the same vote as is required by this chapter and/or by the certificate of incorporation or bylaws of the constituent corporation immediately prior to the effective time of the merger and

(B) the business and affairs of a surviving entity that is not a corporation shall be managed by or under the direction of (a board of directors, board of managers or other governing body) consisting of individuals who are subject to the same fiduciary duties applicable to, and who are liable for breach of such duties to the same extent as, (directors of a corporation subject to this chapter); and

(8) the stockholders of the constituent corporation do not recognize gain or loss for United States federal income tax purposes as determined by the board of directors of the constituent corporation. Neither paragraph (g)(7)(i) of this section nor any provision of a surviving entity's organizational documents required by paragraph (g)(7)(i) of this section shall be deemed or construed to require approval of the stockholders of the holding company to elect or remove directors or managers, managing members or other members of the governing body of the surviving entity. ■ The term "organizational documents", as used in paragraph (g)(7) of this section and in the preceding sentence, shall, when used in reference to a corporation, mean the certificate of incorporation of such corporation, and when used in reference to a limited liability company, mean the limited liability company agreement of such limited liability company.

As used in this subsection only, the term "holding company" means a corporation (which, from its incorporation until consummation of a merger governed by this subsection, was at all times a direct or indirect wholly-owned subsidiary of the constituent corporation) and (whose capital stock is issued in such merger). ■ From and after the effective time of a merger adopted by a constituent corporation by action of its board of directors and without any vote of stockholders pursuant to this subsection: (i) to the extent the restrictions of § 203 of this title applied to the constituent corporation and its stockholders at the effective time of the merger, such restrictions shall apply to the holding company and its stockholders immediately after the effective time of the merger as though it were the constituent corporation, and all shares of stock of the holding company acquired in the merger shall for purposes of § 203 of this title be deemed to have been acquired at the time that the shares of stock of the constituent corporation converted in the merger were acquired, and provided further that any stockholder who immediately prior to the effective time of the merger was not an interested stockholder within the meaning of § 203 of this title shall not solely by reason of the merger become an interested stockholder of the holding company, (ii) if the corporate name of the holding company immediately following the effective time of the merger is the same as the corporate name of the constituent corporation immediately prior to the effective time of the merger, [then] the shares of capital stock of the holding company into which the shares of capital stock of the constituent corporation are converted in the merger shall be represented by the stock certificates that previously represented shares of capital stock of the constituent corporation and (iii) to the extent a stockholder of the constituent corporation immediately prior to the merger had standing to institute or maintain derivative litigation on behalf of the constituent corporation, [then] nothing in this section shall be deemed to limit or extinguish such standing. If an agreement of merger is adopted by a constituent corporation by action of its board of directors and without any vote of stockholders pursuant to this subsection, [then] the secretary or assistant secretary of the constituent corporation shall certify on the agreement (that the agreement has been adopted pursuant to this subsection) and (that the conditions specified in the first sentence of this subsection have been satisfied), provided that [then] such certification on the agreement shall not be required if a certificate of merger or consolidation is filed in lieu of filing the agreement. ■ The agreement so adopted and certified shall then be filed and become effective, in accordance with § 103 of this title. ■ Such filing shall constitute a representation by the person who executes the agreement (that the facts stated in the certificate remain true immediately prior to such filing).

(h) [Then] Notwithstanding the requirements of subsection (c) of this section, unless expressly required by its certificate of incorporation, no vote of stockholders of a constituent corporation that has a class or series of stock that is (listed on a national securities exchange) or (held of record by more than 2,000 holders) immediately prior to the execution of the agreement of merger by such constituent corporation shall be necessary to authorize a merger if:

(1) The agreement of merger expressly:

a. Permits or requires such merger to be effected under this subsection; and

b. Provides that such merger shall be effected as soon as practicable following the consummation of the offer referred to in paragraph (h)(2) of this section if such merger is effected under this subsection;

(2) A corporation consummates an offer for all of the outstanding stock of such constituent corporation on the terms provided in such agreement of merger (that, absent this subsection, would be entitled to vote on the adoption or rejection of the agreement of merger); provided, however, that such offer may be conditioned on the tender of a minimum number or percentage of shares of the stock of such constituent corporation, or of any class or series thereof, and such offer may exclude any excluded stock and provided further that the corporation may consummate separate offers for separate classes or series of the stock of such constituent corporation;

(3) Immediately following the consummation of the offer referred to in paragraph (h)(2) of this section, the stock irrevocably accepted for purchase or exchange pursuant to such offer and received by the depository prior to expiration of such offer, together with the stock otherwise owned by the consummating corporation or its affiliates and any rollover stock, equals at least such percentage of the shares of stock of such constituent corporation, and of each class or series thereof, (that, absent this subsection, would be required to adopt the agreement of merger by this chapter and by the certificate of incorporation of such constituent corporation);

(4) The corporation consummating the offer referred to in paragraph (h)(2) of this section merges with or into such constituent corporation pursuant to such agreement; and

(5) Each outstanding share (other than shares of excluded stock) of each class or series of stock of such constituent corporation that is the subject of and is not irrevocably accepted for purchase or exchange in the offer referred to in paragraph (h)(2) of this section is to be converted in such merger into, or into the right to receive, (the same amount and kind of cash, property, rights or securities to be paid for shares of such class or series of stock of such constituent corporation irrevocably accepted for purchase or exchange in such offer). ■

(6) As used in this section only, the term:

a. "Affiliate" means, in respect of the corporation making the offer referred to in paragraph (h)(2) of this section, any person that **(i)** owns, directly or indirectly, all of the outstanding stock of such corporation or **(ii)** is a direct or indirect wholly-owned subsidiary of such corporation or of any person referred to in clause (i) of this definition;

b. "Consummates" (and with correlative meaning, "consummation" and "consummating") means irrevocably accepts for purchase or exchange stock tendered pursuant to an offer;

c. "Depository" means an agent, including a depository, appointed to facilitate consummation of the offer referred to in paragraph (h)(2) of this section;

d. "Excluded stock" means **(i)** stock of such constituent corporation that is owned at the commencement of the offer referred to in paragraph (h)(2) of this section by (such constituent corporation), (the corporation making the offer referred to in paragraph (h)(2) of this section), (any person that owns, directly or indirectly, all of the outstanding stock of the corporation making such offer), or (any direct or indirect wholly-owned subsidiary of any of the foregoing) and **(ii)** rollover stock;

e. "Person" means any individual, corporation, partnership, limited liability company, unincorporated association or other entity;

f. "Received" (solely for purposes of paragraph (h)(3) of this section) means **(a)** with respect to certificated shares, physical receipt of a stock certificate accompanied by an executed letter of transmittal, **(b)** with respect to uncertificated shares held of record by a clearing corporation as nominee, transfer into the depository's account by means of an agent's message, and **(c)** with respect to uncertificated shares held of record by a person other than a clearing corporation as nominee, physical receipt of an executed letter of transmittal by the depository; provided, however, that shares shall cease to be "received" **(i)** with respect to certificated shares, if the certificate representing such shares was canceled prior to consummation of the offer referred to in paragraph (h)(2) of this section, or **(ii)** with respect to uncertificated shares, to the extent such uncertificated shares have been reduced or eliminated due to any sale of such shares prior to consummation of the offer referred to in paragraph (h)(2) of this section; and

g. "Rollover stock" means any shares of stock of such constituent corporation that are the subject of a written agreement requiring such shares to be transferred, contributed or delivered to the consummating corporation or any of its affiliates in exchange for stock or other equity interests in such consummating corporation or an affiliate thereof; provided, however, that such shares of stock shall cease to be rollover stock for purposes of paragraph (h)(3) of this section if, immediately prior to the time the merger becomes effective under this chapter, such shares have not been transferred, contributed or delivered to the consummating corporation or any of its affiliates pursuant to such written agreement.

If an agreement of merger is adopted without the vote of stockholders of a corporation pursuant to this subsection, [then] the secretary or assistant secretary of the surviving corporation shall certify on the agreement (that the agreement has been adopted pursuant to this subsection) and (that the conditions specified in this subsection (other than the condition listed in paragraph (h)(4) of this section) have been satisfied); provided that [then] such certification on the agreement shall not be required if a certificate of merger is filed in lieu of filing the agreement. ■ The agreement so adopted and certified shall then be filed and shall become effective, in accordance with § 103 of this title. ■ Such filing shall constitute a representation by the person who executes the agreement that the facts stated in the certificate remain true immediately prior to such filing.

§ 252. Merger or consolidation of domestic and foreign corporations; service of process upon surviving or resulting corporation.

(a) [Then] Any 1 or more corporations of this State may merge or consolidate with 1 or more foreign corporations, unless the laws of the jurisdiction or jurisdictions under which such foreign corporation or corporations are organized prohibit such merger or consolidation. ■ The constituent corporations may merge into a single surviving corporation, which may be any 1 of the constituent corporations, or they may consolidate into (a new resulting corporation formed by the consolidation, which may be a corporation of the jurisdiction of organization of any 1 of the constituent corporations), (pursuant to an agreement of merger or consolidation, as the case may be, complying and approved in accordance with this section).

(b) All the constituent corporations shall enter into an agreement of merger or consolidation. ■ The agreement shall state:

(1) The terms and conditions of the merger or consolidation;

(2) The mode of carrying the same into effect;

(3) In the case of a merger in which the surviving corporation is a corporation of this State, such amendments or changes in the certificate of incorporation of the surviving corporation as are desired to be effected by the merger (which amendments or changes may amend and restate the certificate of incorporation of the surviving corporation in its entirety), or, if no such amendments or changes are desired, a statement that the certificate of incorporation of the surviving corporation shall be its certificate of incorporation;

(4) In the case of a consolidation in which the resulting corporation is a corporation of this State, that the certificate of incorporation of the resulting corporation shall be as is set forth in an attachment to the agreement;

(5) The manner, if any, of converting the shares of each of the constituent corporations into shares or other securities of the corporation surviving or resulting from the merger or consolidation, or of cancelling some or all of such shares, and, if any shares of any of the constituent corporations are not to remain outstanding, to be converted solely into shares or other securities of the surviving or resulting corporation or to be cancelled, [then] the cash, property, rights or securities of any other corporation or entity which the holders of such shares are to receive in exchange for, or upon conversion of, such shares and the surrender of any certificates evidencing them, (which cash, property, rights or securities of any other corporation or entity may be in addition to or in lieu of the shares or other securities of the surviving or resulting corporation);

(6) Such other details or provisions as are deemed desirable, including, without limiting the generality of the foregoing, a provision (for the payment of cash in lieu of the issuance or recognition of fractional shares, rights or other securities of the surviving or resulting corporation or of any other corporation or entity the shares, rights or other securities of which are to be received in the merger or consolidation), or (for some other arrangement with respect thereto, consistent with § 155 of this title); and

(7) Such other provisions or facts as shall be required to be set forth in an agreement of merger or consolidation (including any provision for amendment of the certificate of incorporation (or equivalent document) of a surviving or resulting foreign corporation) by the laws of each jurisdiction under which any of the foreign corporations are organized.

[Then] Any of the terms of the agreement of merger or consolidation may be made dependent upon facts ascertainable outside of such agreement, **provided** that the manner in which such facts shall operate upon the terms of the agreement is clearly and expressly set forth in the agreement of merger or consolidation. ■ The term "facts," as used in the preceding sentence, includes, but is not limited to, the occurrence of any event, including a determination or action by (any person or body, including the corporation).

(c) The agreement shall be adopted, approved, certified, executed and acknowledged (by each of the constituent corporations in accordance with the laws under which it is organized), and, (in the case of a corporation of this State, in the same manner as is provided in § 251 of this title). ■ The agreement shall be filed and shall become effective for all purposes of the laws of this State when and as provided in § 251 of this title with respect to the merger or consolidation of corporations of this State. ■ In lieu of filing the agreement of merger or consolidation, the surviving or resulting corporation may file a certificate of merger or consolidation, executed in accordance with § 103 of this title, which states:

(1) The name and jurisdiction of organization of each of the constituent corporations;

(2) That an agreement of merger or consolidation has been approved, adopted, certified, executed and acknowledged by each of the constituent corporations in accordance with this subsection;

(3) The name of the surviving or resulting corporation;

(4) In the case of a merger in which the surviving corporation is a corporation of this State such amendments or changes in the certificate of incorporation of the surviving corporation as are desired to be effected by the merger (which amendments or changes

may amend and restate the certificate of incorporation of the surviving corporation in its entirety), or, if no such amendments or changes are desired, a statement that the certificate of incorporation of the surviving corporation shall be its certificate of incorporation;

(5) In the case of a consolidation in which the resulting corporation is a corporation of this State, that the certificate of incorporation of the resulting corporation shall be as is set forth in an attachment to the certificate;

(6) That the executed agreement of consolidation or merger is on file at an office of the surviving or resulting corporation and the address thereof;

(7) That a copy of the agreement of consolidation or merger will be furnished by the surviving or resulting corporation, on request and without cost, to any stockholder of any constituent corporation;

(8) If the corporation surviving or resulting from the merger or consolidation is a corporation of this State, [then] the authorized capital stock of each constituent corporation which is not a corporation of this State; and

(9) The agreement, if any, required by subsection (d) of this section.

(d) **If** the corporation surviving or resulting from the merger or consolidation is a foreign corporation, **[then]** it shall agree that it may be served with process in this State in any proceeding for enforcement of any obligation of any constituent corporation of this State, as well as for enforcement of any obligation of the surviving or resulting corporation arising from the merger or consolidation, including any suit or other proceeding to enforce the right of any stockholders as determined in appraisal proceedings pursuant to § 262 of this title, and shall irrevocably appoint the Secretary of State as its agent to accept service of process in any such suit or other proceedings and shall specify the address to which a copy of such process shall be mailed by the Secretary of State. ■ Process may be served upon the Secretary of State under this subsection by means of electronic transmission but only as prescribed by the Secretary of State. ■ The Secretary of State is authorized to issue such rules and regulations with respect to such service as the Secretary of State deems necessary or appropriate. ■ **[Then]** In the event of such service upon the Secretary of State in accordance with this subsection, the Secretary of State shall forthwith notify such surviving or resulting corporation thereof by letter, directed to such surviving or resulting corporation at its address so specified, **unless** such surviving or resulting corporation shall have designated in writing to the Secretary of State a different address for such purpose, **in which case** it shall be mailed to the last address so designated. ■ Such letter shall be sent by a mail or courier service that includes **(**a record of mailing or deposit with the courier**)** and **(**a record of delivery evidenced by the signature of the recipient**)**. ■ Such letter shall enclose a copy of the process and any other papers served on the Secretary of State pursuant to this subsection. ■ It shall be the duty of the plaintiff in the event of such service to serve process and any other papers in duplicate, **(**to notify the Secretary of State that service is being effected pursuant to this subsection**)** and **(**to pay the Secretary of State the sum of $50 for the use of the State, which sum shall be taxed as part of the costs in the proceeding, if the plaintiff shall prevail therein**)**. ■ The Secretary of State shall maintain an alphabetical record of any such service setting forth the name of the plaintiff and the defendant, the title, docket number and nature of the proceeding in which process has been served, the fact that service has been effected pursuant to this subsection, the return date thereof, and the day and hour service was made. ■ The Secretary of State shall not be required to retain such information longer than 5 years from receipt of the service of process.

(e) Section 251(d) of this title shall apply to any merger or consolidation under this section; [and] § 251(e) of this title shall apply to a merger under this section in which the surviving corporation is a corporation of this State; and § 251(f) and (h) of this title shall apply to any merger under this section.

§ 253. Merger of parent corporation and subsidiary corporation or corporations.

(a) **In any case in which:** **(1)** at least 90% of the outstanding shares of each class of the stock of a corporation or corporations (other than a corporation which has in its certificate of incorporation the provision required by § 251(g)(7)(i) of this title), of which class there are outstanding shares that, absent this subsection, would be entitled to vote on such merger, is owned by a corporation of this State or a foreign corporation, and **(2)** 1 or more of such corporations is a corporation of this State, **unless** the laws of the jurisdiction or jurisdictions under which the foreign corporation or corporations are organized prohibit such merger, **[then]** the parent corporation may either merge the subsidiary corporation or corporations into itself and assume all of its or their obligations, or merge itself, or itself and 1 or more of such other subsidiary corporations, into 1 of the subsidiary corporations by executing, acknowledging and filing, in accordance with § 103 of this title, a certificate of such ownership and merger setting forth a copy of the resolution of its board of directors to so merge and the date of the adoption; provided, however, that in case the parent corporation shall not own all the outstanding stock of all the subsidiary corporations, parties to a merger as aforesaid, **[then]** the resolution of the board of directors of the parent corporation shall state the terms and conditions of the merger, including the securities, cash, property, or rights to be issued, paid, delivered or granted by the surviving corporation upon (surrender of each share of the subsidiary corporation or corporations not owned by the parent corporation), or (the cancellation of some or all of such shares). ■ Any of the terms of the resolution of the board of directors to so merge may be made dependent upon facts ascertainable outside of such resolution, provided that the manner in which such facts shall operate upon the terms of the resolution is clearly and expressly set forth in the resolution. ■ The term "facts," as used in the preceding sentence, includes, but is not limited to, the occurrence of any event, including a determination or action by (any person or body, including the corporation). ■ **If** the parent corporation be not the surviving corporation, **[then]** the resolution shall include provision for the pro rata issuance of stock of the surviving corporation to the holders of the stock of the parent corporation on surrender of any certificates therefor, and the certificate of ownership and merger shall state [then] that the proposed merger has been approved by a majority of the outstanding stock of the parent corporation entitled to vote thereon at a meeting duly called and held after 20 days' notice of the purpose of the meeting given to each such stockholder at the stockholder's address as it appears on the records of the corporation if the parent corporation is a corporation of this State or [then] state that the proposed merger has been adopted, approved, certified, executed and acknowledged by the parent corporation in accordance with the laws under which it is organized if the parent corporation is a foreign corporation. ■ **If** the surviving corporation is a foreign corporation: **[then]**

(1) Section 252(d) of this title or § 258(c) of this title, as applicable, shall also apply to a merger under this section; and

(2) The terms and conditions of the merger shall obligate the surviving corporation to provide the agreement, and take the actions, required by § 252(d) of this title or § 258(c) of this title, as applicable.

(b) If the surviving corporation is a Delaware corporation, [then] it may change its corporate name by the inclusion of a provision to that effect in the resolution of merger adopted by the directors of the parent corporation and set forth in the certificate of ownership and merger, and upon the effective date of the merger, the name of the corporation shall be so changed.

(c) Section § 251(d) of this title shall apply to a merger under this section, and § 251(e) of this title shall apply to a merger under this section in which the surviving corporation is the subsidiary corporation and is a corporation of this State. ■ References to "agreement of merger" in § 251(d) and (e) of this title shall mean for purposes of this subsection the resolution of merger adopted by the board of directors of the parent corporation. ■ Any merger which effects any changes other than those authorized by this section or made applicable by this subsection shall be accomplished under § 251, § 252, § 257, or § 258 of this title. ■ Section 262 of this title shall not apply to any merger effected under this section, ❰except as provided in subsection (d) of this section❱.

(d) In the event all of the stock of a subsidiary Delaware corporation party to a merger effected under this section is not owned by the parent corporation immediately prior to the merger, [then] the stockholders of the subsidiary Delaware corporation party to the merger shall have appraisal rights as set forth in § 262 of this title.

(e) [Then] This section shall apply to nonstock corporations if the parent corporation is such a corporation and is the surviving corporation of the merger; provided, however, that references to the directors of the parent corporation shall be deemed to be references to members of the governing body of the parent corporation, and references to the board of directors of the parent corporation shall be deemed to be references to the governing body of the parent corporation.

(f) [Then] Nothing in this section shall be deemed to authorize the merger of a corporation with a charitable nonstock corporation, if the charitable status of such charitable nonstock corporation would thereby be lost or impaired.

§ 254. Merger or consolidation of domestic corporations and joint-stock or other associations.

(a) The term "joint-stock association" as used in this section, includes any association of the kind commonly known as a joint-stock association or joint-stock company and any unincorporated association, trust or enterprise having members or having outstanding shares of stock or other evidences of financial or beneficial interest therein, whether formed or organized by agreement or under statutory authority or otherwise and whether formed or organized under the laws of this State or any other jurisdiction, but does not include a corporation, partnership or limited liability company. ■ The term "stockholder" as used in this section, <u>includes every member</u> of such joint-stock association ⟦or⟧ <u>holder</u> of a share of stock or other evidence of financial or beneficial interest therein.

(b) <u>Any 1 or more corporations</u> of this State <u>may merge or consolidate</u> with 1 or more joint-stock associations, ◀ unless the laws of the jurisdiction or jurisdictions under which such joint-stock association or associations are formed or organized prohibit such merger or consolidation▶. ■ <u>Such corporation or corporations</u> ⟦and⟧ <u>such 1 or more joint-stock associations may merge</u> into a single surviving corporation or joint-stock association, which may be any 1 of such corporations or joint-stock associations, ⟦or⟧ <u>they may consolidate</u> into a new resulting corporation of this State or a joint-stock association, pursuant to an agreement of merger or consolidation, as the case may be, complying and approved in accordance with this section. ■ <u>The surviving or resulting entity may be organized</u> for profit or not organized for profit, ⟦and⟧ **if** <u>the surviving or resulting entity is a corporation,</u> **[then]** <u>it may be a stock corporation of this State</u> ⟦or⟧ <u>a nonstock corporation of this State</u>.

(c) <u>Each such corporation</u> ⟦and⟧ <u>joint-stock association shall enter into a written agreement of merger or consolidation.</u> ■ <u>The agreement shall state:</u>

(1) <u>The terms and conditions</u> of the merger or consolidation;

(2) <u>The mode</u> of carrying the same into effect;

(3) In the case of a merger in which the surviving entity is a corporation of this State, <u>such amendments or changes</u> in the certificate of incorporation of the surviving corporation as are desired to be effected by the merger (which amendments or changes may amend and restate the certificate of incorporation of the surviving corporation in its entirety), ⟦or⟧, if no such amendments or changes are desired, <u>a statement</u> that the certificate of incorporation of the surviving corporation shall be its certificate of incorporation;

(4) In the case of a consolidation in which the resulting entity is a corporation of this State, that the certificate of incorporation of the resulting corporation shall be as is set forth in an attachment to the agreement;

(5) <u>The manner,</u> if any, **(**of converting the shares of stock of each stock corporation, the interest of members of each nonstock corporation, and the shares, membership or financial or beneficial interests in each of the joint-stock associations into shares or other securities of a stock corporation or membership interests of a nonstock corporation or into shares, memberships or financial or beneficial interests of the joint-stock association surviving or resulting from such merger or consolidation**)**, or **(**of cancelling some or all of such shares, memberships or financial or beneficial interests**)**, ⟦and⟧, **if** any shares of any such stock corporation, any membership interests of any such nonstock corporation or any shares, memberships or financial or beneficial interests in any such joint-stock association are not to remain outstanding, to be converted solely into shares or other securities of the stock corporation or membership interests of the nonstock corporation or into shares, memberships or financial or beneficial interests of the joint-stock association surviving or resulting from such merger or consolidation or to be cancelled, **[then]** <u>the cash, property, rights or securities</u> of any other corporation or entity **(**which the holders of shares of any such stock corporation, membership interests of any such nonstock corporation, or shares, memberships or financial or beneficial

interests of any such joint-stock association are to receive in exchange for, or upon conversion of such shares, membership interests or shares, memberships or financial or beneficial interests, and the surrender of any certificates evidencing them**)**, which cash, property, rights or securities of any other corporation or entity may be in addition to or in lieu of shares or other securities of the stock corporation or membership interests of the nonstock corporation or shares, memberships or financial or beneficial interests of the joint-stock association surviving or resulting from such merger or consolidation;

(6) Such other details or provisions as are deemed desirable, including, without limiting the generality of the foregoing, a provision for the payment of cash in lieu of the issuance or recognition of fractional shares, rights, other securities or interests of the surviving or resulting entity or of fractional shares, rights, other securities or interests of any other corporation or entity the securities of which are to be received in the merger or consolidation, or for some other arrangement with respect thereto, consistent with § 155 of this title; and

(7) Such other provisions or facts as shall be required to be set forth in an agreement of merger or consolidation (including any provision for amendment of the governing documents of a surviving joint-stock association) or required to establish and maintain a joint-stock association by the laws under which the joint-stock association is formed or organized.

Any of the terms of the agreement of merger or consolidation may be made dependent upon facts ascertainable outside of such agreement, `provided that` the manner in which such facts shall operate upon the terms of the agreement is clearly and expressly set forth in the agreement of merger or consolidation. ■ The term "facts," as used in the preceding sentence, includes, but is not limited to, the occurrence of any event, including a determination or action by **(**any person or body, including the corporation**)**.

(d) The agreement required by subsection (c) of this section shall be adopted, approved, certified, executed `and` acknowledged by each of the stock or nonstock corporations **(**in the same manner as is provided in § 251 or § 255 of this title, respectively**)**, and in the case of the joint-stock associations **(**in accordance with the laws of the jurisdiction under which they are formed**)** or organized. ■ The agreement shall be filed `and` shall become effective for all purposes of the laws of this State when and as provided in § 251 of this title **(**with respect to the merger or consolidation of corporations of this State**)**. ■ In lieu of filing the agreement of merger or consolidation, the surviving or resulting entity may file a certificate of merger or consolidation, executed in accordance with § 103 of this title, which states:

(1) The name, jurisdiction of formation or organization and type of entity of each of the constituent entities;

(2) That an agreement of merger or consolidation has been approved, adopted, certified, executed and acknowledged by each of the constituent entities in accordance with this subsection;

(3) The name of the surviving or resulting corporation or joint-stock association;

(4) In the case of a merger in which the surviving entity is a corporation of this State, such amendments or changes in the certificate of incorporation of the surviving corporation as are desired to be effected by the merger (which amendments or changes may amend and restate the certificate of incorporation of the surviving corporation in its entirety), or, if no such amendments or changes are desired, [then] a statement that the certificate of incorporation of the surviving corporation shall be its certificate of incorporation;

(5) In the case of a consolidation in which the resulting entity is a corporation of this State, that the certificate of incorporation of the resulting corporation shall be as is set forth in an attachment to the certificate;

(6) That the executed agreement of consolidation or merger is on file at an office of the surviving or resulting corporation or joint-stock association and the address thereof;

(7) That a copy of the agreement of consolidation or merger will be furnished by the surviving or resulting corporation or joint-stock association, on request and without cost, to any stockholder or member of any constituent entity; and

(8) The agreement, if any, required by § 252(d) of this title.

(e) Sections 251(d), 251(e) to the extent the surviving entity is a corporation of this State, §§ 251(f), 252(d), 259 through 262 and 328 of this title shall, insofar as they are applicable, apply to mergers or consolidations between corporations and joint-stock associations; the word "corporation" where applicable, as used in those sections, being deemed to include joint-stock associations as defined herein. ■ **Where** the surviving or resulting entity is a corporation, for purposes of the laws of this State, **[then]** the personal liability, if any, of any stockholder of a joint-stock association existing at the time of such merger or consolidation shall not thereby be extinguished, shall remain personal to such stockholder and shall not become the liability (of any subsequent transferee of any share of stock in such surviving or resulting corporation) or (of any other stockholder of such surviving or resulting corporation).

(f) **[Then]** Nothing in this section shall be deemed to authorize the merger of a charitable nonstock corporation or charitable joint-stock association into a stock corporation or joint-stock association **if** the charitable status of such nonstock corporation or joint-stock association would be thereby lost or impaired, but a stock corporation or a joint-stock association may be merged into a charitable nonstock corporation or charitable joint-stock association which shall continue as the surviving corporation or joint-stock association.

§ 255. Merger or consolidation of domestic nonstock corporations.

(a) Any 2 or more nonstock corporations of this State, whether or not organized for profit, may merge into a single surviving corporation, which may be any 1 of the constituent corporations, or they may consolidate into a new resulting nonstock corporation, whether or not organized for profit, formed by the consolidation, pursuant to an agreement of merger or consolidation, as the case may be, complying and approved in accordance with this section.

(b) Subject to subsection (d) of this section, the governing body of each corporation which desires to merge or consolidate shall adopt a resolution approving an agreement of merger or consolidation. ■ The agreement shall state:

(1) The terms and conditions of the merger or consolidation;

(2) The mode of carrying the same into effect;

(3) In the case of a merger, such amendments or changes in the certificate of incorporation of the surviving corporation as are desired to be effected by the merger (which amendments or changes may amend and restate the certificate of incorporation of the surviving corporation in its entirety), or, if no such amendments or changes are desired, a statement that the certificate of incorporation of the surviving corporation shall be its certificate of incorporation;

(4) In the case of a consolidation, that the certificate of incorporation of the resulting corporation shall be as is set forth in an attachment to the agreement;

(5) The manner, if any, (of converting the memberships or membership interests of each of the constituent corporations into memberships or membership interests of the corporation surviving or resulting from the merger or consolidation), or (of cancelling some or all of such memberships or membership interests), and, if (any memberships or membership interests of any of the constituent corporations are not to remain outstanding, to be converted solely into memberships or membership interests of the surviving or resulting corporation or to be cancelled,) (the cash, property, rights or securities of any other corporation or entity which the holders of such memberships or membership interests are to receive in exchange for, or upon conversion of, such memberships or membership interests,) which cash, property, rights or securities of any other corporation or entity may be in addition to or in lieu of memberships or membership interests of the surviving or resulting corporation; and

(6) Such other details or provisions as are deemed desirable, including, without limiting the generality of the foregoing, a provision for the payment of cash in lieu of the issuance or recognition of fractional shares, rights or other securities of any other corporation or entity the shares, rights or other securities of which are to be received in the merger or consolidation, or for some other arrangement with respect thereto, consistent with § 155 of this title.

The agreement so adopted shall be executed by an authorized person, provided that if the agreement is filed, it shall be executed and acknowledged in accordance with § 103 of this title. ■ Any of the terms of the agreement of merger or consolidation may be made dependent upon facts ascertainable outside of such agreement, provided that the manner in which such facts shall operate upon the terms of the agreement is clearly and expressly set forth in the agreement of merger or consolidation. ■ The term "facts," as used in the preceding sentence, includes, but is not limited to, the occurrence of any event, including a determination or action by (any person or body, including the corporation).

(c) Subject to subsection (d) of this section, the agreement shall be submitted to the members of each constituent corporation, at an annual or special meeting thereof for the purpose of acting on the agreement. ■ Due notice of the time, place and purpose of the meeting shall be given (to each member of each such corporation who has the right to vote for the election of the members of the governing body of the corporation) and (to each other member who is entitled to vote on the merger under the certificate of incorporation or the bylaws of such corporation), at the member's address as it appears on the records of the corporation, at least 20 days prior to the date of the meeting. ■ The notice shall contain a copy of the agreement or a brief summary thereof. ■ At the meeting the agreement shall be considered and a vote, in person or by proxy, taken for the adoption or rejection of the agreement. ■ If the agreement is adopted by a majority of (the members of each such corporation entitled to vote for the election of the members of the governing body of the corporation) and (any other members entitled to vote on the merger under the certificate of incorporation or the bylaws of such corporation), **then** that fact shall be certified on the agreement by the officer of each such corporation performing the duties ordinarily performed by the secretary or assistant secretary of a corporation, provided that [then] such certification on the agreement shall not be required **if** a certificate of merger or consolidation is filed in lieu of filing the agreement. ■ **If** the agreement shall be adopted and certified by each constituent corporation in accordance with this section, [then] it shall be filed and shall become effective in accordance with § 103 of this title. ■ The provisions set forth in the last sentence of § 251(c) of this title shall apply to a merger under this section, and the reference therein to "stockholder" shall be deemed to include "member" hereunder.

(d) Notwithstanding subsection (b) or (c) of this section, **if**, under the certificate of incorporation or the bylaws of any 1 or more of the constituent corporations, there shall be no members who have the right to vote for the election of the members of the governing body of the corporation, or for the merger, other than the members of the governing body themselves, [then] no further action by the governing body or the members of such corporation shall be necessary **if** the resolution approving an agreement of merger or consolidation has been adopted by a majority of all the members of the governing body thereof, and that fact shall be certified on the agreement in the same manner as is provided in the case of the adoption of the agreement by the vote of the members of a corporation, provided that [then] such certification on the agreement shall not be required **if** a certificate of merger or consolidation is filed in lieu of filing the agreement, and thereafter the same procedure shall be followed to consummate the merger or consolidation.

(e) Section 251(d) of this title shall apply to a merger under this section; provided, however, that references to the board of directors, to stockholders, and to shares of a constituent corporation shall be deemed to be references to the governing body of the corporation, to members of the corporation, and to memberships or membership interests, as applicable, respectively.

(f) Section 251(e) of this title shall apply to a merger under this section.

(g) [Then] Nothing in this section shall be deemed to authorize the merger of a charitable nonstock corporation into a nonstock corporation **if** such charitable nonstock corporation would thereby have its charitable status lost or impaired; but a nonstock corporation may be merged into a charitable nonstock corporation which shall continue as the surviving corporation.

§ 256. Merger or consolidation of domestic and foreign nonstock corporations; service of process upon surviving or resulting corporation.

(a) [Then] Any 1 or more nonstock corporations of this State may merge or consolidate with 1 or more foreign nonstock corporations, unless the laws of the jurisdiction or jurisdictions under which such foreign nonstock corporation or corporations are organized prohibit such merger or consolidation.■ The constituent corporations may merge into a single surviving corporation, which may be any 1 of the constituent corporations, or they may consolidate into a new resulting nonstock corporation formed by the consolidation, (which may be a corporation of the jurisdiction of organization of any 1 of the constituent corporations), pursuant to an agreement of merger or consolidation, as the case may be, complying and approved in accordance with this section. ■ [Then] The term "foreign nonstock corporation" means a nonstock corporation organized under the laws of any jurisdiction other than this State.

(b) All the constituent corporations shall enter into an agreement of merger or consolidation. ■ The agreement shall state:

(1) The terms and conditions of the merger or consolidation;

(2) The mode of carrying the same into effect;

(3) In the case of a merger in which the surviving corporation is a corporation of this State, such amendments or changes in the certificate of incorporation of the surviving corporation as are desired to be effected by the merger (which amendments or changes may amend and restate the certificate of incorporation of the surviving corporation in its entirety), or, if no such amendments or changes are desired, a statement that the certificate of incorporation of the surviving corporation shall be its certificate of incorporation;

(4) In the case of a consolidation in which the resulting corporation is a corporation of this State, that the certificate of incorporation of the resulting corporation shall be as is set forth in an attachment to the agreement;

(5) The manner, if any, (of converting the memberships or membership interests of each of the constituent corporations into memberships or membership interests of the corporation surviving or resulting from the merger or consolidation), or (of cancelling some or all of such memberships or membership interests), and, if (any memberships or membership interests of any of the constituent corporations are not to remain outstanding, to be converted solely into memberships or membership interests of the surviving or resulting corporation or to be cancelled,) (the cash, property, rights or securities of any other corporation or entity which the holders of such memberships or membership interests are to receive in exchange for, or upon conversion of, such memberships or membership interests,) which cash, property, rights or securities of any other corporation or entity may be in addition to or in lieu of memberships or membership interests of the surviving or resulting corporation;

(6) Such other details or provisions as are deemed desirable, including, without limiting the generality of the foregoing, a provision for the payment of cash in lieu of the issuance or recognition of fractional shares, rights or other securities of any other corporation or entity the shares, rights or other securities of which are to be received in the merger or consolidation, or for some other arrangement with respect thereto, consistent with § 155 of this title; and

(7) Such other provisions or facts (as shall be required to be set forth in an agreement of merger or consolidation (including any provision for amendment of the certificate of incorporation (or equivalent document) of a surviving foreign nonstock corporation) by the laws of each jurisdiction under which any of the foreign nonstock corporations are organized.

[Then] Any of the terms of the agreement of merger or consolidation may be made dependent upon facts ascertainable outside of such agreement, provided that the manner in which such facts shall operate upon the terms of the agreement <u>is clearly and expressly set forth</u> in the agreement of merger or consolidation. ■ The term "<u>facts</u>," as used in the preceding sentence, <u>includes</u>, but is not limited to, <u>the occurrence</u> of any event, including a determination or action by (any person or body, including the corporation).

(c) The agreement shall be adopted, approved, certified, executed [and] acknowledged by each of the constituent corporations (in accordance with the laws under which it is organized) and, in the case of a Delaware corporation, (in the same manner as is provided in § 255 of this title). ■ The agreement shall be filed [and] shall become effective for all purposes of the laws of this State when and as provided in § 255 of this title with respect to the merger of nonstock corporations of this State. ■ Insofar as they may be applicable, <u>the provisions set forth</u> in the last sentence of § 252(c) of this title <u>shall apply to a merger</u> under this section, [and] the reference therein to "stockholder" <u>shall be deemed to include "member"</u> hereunder.

(d) If <u>the corporation surviving or resulting</u> from the merger or consolidation is a foreign nonstock corporation, **[then]** it shall agree that it may be served with process in this State in any proceeding for enforcement of any obligation of any constituent corporation of this State, as well as for enforcement of any obligation of the surviving or resulting corporation arising from the merger or consolidation [and] <u>shall irrevocably appoint</u> the Secretary of State as its agent to accept service of process in any suit or other proceedings [and] <u>shall specify the address</u> to which a copy of such process shall be mailed by the Secretary of State. ■ <u>Process may be served</u> upon the Secretary of State under this subsection by means of electronic transmission but only as prescribed by the Secretary of State. ■ <u>The Secretary of State is authorized to issue such rules and regulations</u> with respect to such service as the Secretary of State deems necessary or appropriate. ■ **[Then]** In the event of such service upon the Secretary of State in accordance with this subsection, <u>the Secretary of State shall forthwith notify such surviving or resulting corporation</u> thereof by letter, directed to such corporation at its address so specified, **unless** such surviving or resulting corporation shall have designated in writing to the Secretary of State <u>a different address</u> for such purpose, in which case it shall be mailed to the last address so designated. ■ <u>Such letter shall be sent</u> by a mail or courier service that includes (a record of mailing or deposit with the courier) and (a record of delivery evidenced by the signature of the recipient). ■ <u>Such letter shall enclose a copy</u> of the process [and] <u>any other papers served</u> upon the Secretary of State. ■ <u>It shall be the duty</u> of the plaintiff in the event of such service (to serve process and any other papers in duplicate), (to notify the Secretary of State that service is being made pursuant to this subsection), and (to pay the Secretary of State the sum of $50 for the use of the State), which sum shall be taxed as a part of the costs in the proceeding if the plaintiff shall prevail therein. ■ <u>The Secretary of State shall maintain an alphabetical record</u> of any such service setting forth the name of the plaintiff and defendant, the title, docket number and nature of the proceeding in which process has been served upon the Secretary of State, the fact that service has been effected pursuant to this subsection, the return date thereof, and the day and hour when the service was made. ■ <u>The Secretary of State shall not be required to retain such information</u> for a period longer than 5 years from receipt of the service of process.

(e) [Then] Section § 251(e) of this title <u>shall apply to a merger</u> under this section **if** <u>the corporation surviving the merger is a corporation</u> of this State.

(f) Section 251(d) of this title shall apply to a merger under this section; provided, however, that references to the board of directors, to stockholders, and to shares of a constituent corporation shall be deemed to be references to the governing body of the corporation, to members of the corporation, and to memberships or membership interests, as applicable, respectively.

(g) [Then] Nothing in this section shall be deemed to authorize the merger of a charitable nonstock corporation into a nonstock corporation, if the charitable status of such charitable nonstock corporation would thereby be lost or impaired; but a nonstock corporation may be merged into a charitable nonstock corporation which shall continue as the surviving corporation.

§ 257. Merger or consolidation of domestic stock and nonstock corporations.

(a) Any 1 or more nonstock corporations of this State, whether or not organized for profit, may merge or consolidate with 1 or more stock corporations of this State, whether or not organized for profit. ■ The constituent corporations may merge into a single surviving corporation, which may be any 1 of the constituent corporations, or they may consolidate into a new resulting corporation formed by the consolidation, pursuant to an agreement of merger or consolidation, as the case may be, complying and approved in accordance with this section. ■ The surviving constituent corporation or the resulting corporation may be organized for profit or not organized for profit and may be a stock corporation or a nonstock corporation.

(b) The board of directors of each stock corporation which desires to merge or consolidate and the governing body of each nonstock corporation which desires to merge or consolidate shall adopt a resolution approving an agreement of merger or consolidation. ■ The agreement shall state:

(1) The terms and conditions of the merger or consolidation;

(2) The mode of carrying the same into effect;

(3) In the case of a merger, such amendments or changes in the certificate of incorporation of the surviving corporation as are desired to be effected by the merger (which amendments or changes may amend and restate the certificate of incorporation of the surviving corporation in its entirety), or, if no such amendments or changes are desired, a statement that the certificate of incorporation of the surviving corporation shall be its certificate of incorporation;

(4) In the case of a consolidation, that the certificate of incorporation of the resulting corporation shall be as is set forth in an attachment to the agreement;

(5) The manner, if any, (of converting the shares of stock of a stock corporation and the memberships or membership interests of a nonstock corporation into shares or other securities of a stock corporation or memberships or membership interests of a nonstock corporation surviving or resulting from such merger or consolidation) or (of cancelling some or all of such shares or memberships or membership interests), and, if any shares of any such stock corporation or memberships or membership interests of any such nonstock corporation are not to remain outstanding, to be converted solely into shares or other securities of the stock corporation or memberships or membership interests of the nonstock corporation surviving or resulting from such merger or consolidation or to

be cancelled, [then] the cash, property, rights or securities of any other corporation or entity (which the holders of shares of any such stock corporation or memberships or membership interests of any such nonstock corporation are to receive in exchange for, or upon conversion of such shares or memberships or membership interests, and the surrender of any certificates evidencing them), which cash, property, rights or securities of any other corporation or entity may be in addition to or in lieu of shares or other securities of any stock corporation or memberships or membership interests of any nonstock corporation surviving or resulting from such merger or consolidation; and

(6) Such other details or provisions as are deemed desirable, including, without limiting the generality of the foregoing, a provision for the payment of cash in lieu of the issuance or recognition of fractional shares, rights or other securities of the surviving or resulting corporation or of any other corporation or entity the shares, rights or other securities of which are to be received in the merger or consolidation, or for some other arrangement with respect thereto, consistent with § 155 of this title.

Any of the terms of the agreement of merger or consolidation may be made dependent upon facts ascertainable outside of such agreement, provided that the manner in which such facts shall operate upon the terms of the agreement is clearly and expressly set forth in the agreement of merger or consolidation. ■ The term "facts," as used in the preceding sentence, includes, but is not limited to, the occurrence of any event, including a determination or action by (any person or body, including the corporation).

(c) The agreement required by subsection (b) of this section, in the case of each constituent stock corporation, shall be adopted, approved, certified, executed and acknowledged by each constituent corporation in the same manner as is provided in § 251 of this title and, in the case of each constituent nonstock corporation, shall be adopted, approved, certified, executed and acknowledged by each of said constituent corporations in the same manner as is provided in § 255 of this title. ■ The agreement shall be filed and shall become effective for all purposes of the laws of this State when and as provided in § 251 of this title with respect to the merger of stock corporations of this State. ■ Insofar as they may be applicable, the provisions set forth in the last sentence of § 251(c) of this title shall apply to a merger under this section, and the reference therein to "stockholder" shall be deemed to include "member" hereunder.

(d) [Then] Section 251(e) of this title shall apply to a merger under this section; [and] § 251(d) of this title shall apply to any constituent stock corporation participating in a merger or consolidation under this section; and § 251(f) of this title shall apply to any constituent stock corporation participating in a merger under this section.

(e) Section 251(d) of this title shall apply to a merger under this section; provided, however, that, for purposes of a constituent nonstock corporation, references to the board of directors, to stockholders, and to shares of a constituent corporation shall be deemed to be references to the governing body of the corporation, to members of the corporation, and to memberships or membership interests, as applicable, respectively.

(f) [Then] Nothing in this section shall be deemed to authorize the merger of a charitable nonstock corporation into a stock corporation, if the charitable status of such nonstock corporation would thereby be lost or impaired; but a stock corporation may be merged into a charitable nonstock corporation which shall continue as the surviving corporation.

§ 258. Merger or consolidation of domestic and foreign stock and nonstock corporations.

(a) [Then] Any 1 or more corporations of this State, whether stock or nonstock corporations and whether or not organized for profit, may merge or consolidate with 1 or more foreign corporations, unless the laws of the jurisdiction or jurisdictions under which such foreign corporation or corporations are organized prohibit such merger or consolidation. ∎ The constituent corporations may merge into a single surviving corporation, which may be any 1 of the constituent corporations, [or] they may consolidate into a new resulting corporation formed by the consolidation, which may be a corporation of the jurisdiction of organization of any 1 of the constituent corporations, pursuant to an agreement of merger or consolidation, as the case may be, complying and approved in accordance with this section. ∎ The surviving or resulting corporation may be either a domestic or foreign stock corporation [or] a domestic or foreign nonstock corporation, as shall be specified in the agreement of merger or consolidation required by subsection (b) of this section. ∎ For purposes of this section, the term "foreign corporation" includes a nonstock corporation organized under the laws of any jurisdiction other than this State.

(b) The method and procedure to be followed by the constituent corporations so merging or consolidating shall be as prescribed in § 257 of this title in the case of Delaware corporations. ∎ The agreement of merger or consolidation shall be as provided in § 257 of this title and also set forth such other provisions or facts as shall be required to be set forth in an agreement of merger or consolidation (including any provision for amendment of the certificate of incorporation (or equivalent document) of a surviving foreign corporation) by the laws of the jurisdiction or jurisdictions which are stated in the agreement to be the laws under which the foreign corporation or corporations are organized. ∎ The agreement, in the case of foreign corporations, shall be adopted, approved, certified, executed [and] acknowledged in accordance with the laws under which each is organized.

(c) The requirements of § 252(d) of this title as to the appointment of the Secretary of State to receive process and the manner of serving the same in the event the surviving or resulting corporation is a foreign corporation shall also apply to mergers or consolidations effected under this section [and] such appointment, if any, shall be included in the certificate of merger or consolidation, if any, filed pursuant to subsection (b) of this section. ∎ [Then] Section 251(e) of this title shall apply to mergers effected under this section if the surviving corporation is a corporation of this State; [[and]] § 251(d) of this title shall apply to any constituent corporation participating in a merger or consolidation under this section (provided, however, that for purposes of a constituent nonstock corporation, references to the board of directors, to stockholders, and to shares shall be deemed to be references to the governing body of the corporation, to members of the corporation, and to memberships or membership interests of the corporation, as applicable, respectively); [and] § 251(f) of this title shall apply to any constituent stock corporation of this State participating in a merger under this section.

(d) [Then] Nothing in this section shall be deemed to authorize the merger of a charitable nonstock corporation into a stock corporation, if the charitable status of such nonstock corporation would thereby be lost or impaired; [but] a stock corporation may be merged into a charitable nonstock corporation which shall continue as the surviving corporation.

§ 259. Status, rights, liabilities, of constituent and surviving or resulting corporations following merger or consolidation.

(a) When any merger or consolidation shall have become effective under this chapter, [then] for all purposes of the laws of this State the separate existence of all the constituent corporations, or of all such constituent corporations except the one into which the other or others of such constituent corporations have been merged, as the case may be, shall cease and the constituent corporations shall become a new corporation, or be merged into 1 of such corporations, as the case may be, possessing all the rights, privileges, powers and franchises as well of a public as of a private nature, and being subject to all the restrictions, disabilities and duties of each of such corporations so merged or consolidated; and all and singular, the rights, privileges, powers and franchises of each of said corporations, and all property, real, personal and mixed, and all debts due to any of said constituent corporations on whatever account, as well for stock subscriptions as all other things in action or belonging to each of such corporations shall be vested in the corporation surviving or resulting from such merger or consolidation; and all property, rights, privileges, powers and franchises, and all and every other interest shall be thereafter as effectually the property of the surviving or resulting corporation as they were of the several and respective constituent corporations, and the title to any real estate vested by deed or otherwise, under the laws of this State, in any of such constituent corporations, shall not revert or be in any way impaired by reason of this chapter; but all rights of creditors and all liens upon any property of any of said constituent corporations shall be preserved unimpaired, and all debts, liabilities and duties of the respective constituent corporations shall thenceforth attach to said surviving or resulting corporation, and may be enforced against it to the same extent as if said debts, liabilities and duties had been incurred or contracted by it.

(b) In the case of a merger of banks or trust companies, without any order or action on the part of any court or otherwise, all appointments, designations, and nominations, and all other rights and interests as trustee, executor, administrator, registrar of stocks and bonds, guardian of estates, assignee, receiver, trustee of estates of persons mentally ill and in every other fiduciary capacity, shall be automatically vested in the corporation resulting from or surviving such merger; provided, however, that any party in interest shall have the right to apply to an appropriate court or tribunal for a determination as to (whether the surviving corporation shall continue to serve in the same fiduciary capacity as the merged corporation), or (whether a new and different fiduciary should be appointed).

§ 260. Powers of corporation surviving or resulting from merger or consolidation; issuance of stock, bonds or other indebtedness.

When 2 or more corporations are merged or consolidated, [then] the corporation surviving or resulting from the merger may issue bonds or other obligations, negotiable or otherwise, and with or without coupons or interest certificates thereto attached, to an amount sufficient with its capital stock to provide for all the payments it will be required to make, or obligations it will be required to assume, in order to effect the merger or consolidation. ■ For the purpose of securing the payment of any such bonds and obligations, it shall be lawful for the surviving or resulting corporation to mortgage its corporate franchise, rights, privileges and property, real, personal or mixed. ■ The surviving or resulting corporation may issue certificates (of its capital stock or uncertificated stock if authorized to do so and other securities) to the stockholders of the constituent corporations (in exchange or payment for the original shares), in such amount as shall be necessary in accordance with the terms of the agreement of merger or consolidation (in order to effect such merger or consolidation in the manner and on the terms specified in the agreement).

§ 261. Effect of merger upon pending actions.

Any action or proceeding, whether civil, criminal or administrative, pending by or against any corporation which is a party to a merger or consolidation shall be prosecuted as if such merger or consolidation had not taken place, or the corporation surviving or resulting from such merger or consolidation may be substituted in such action or proceeding.

§ 262. Appraisal rights.

(a) Any stockholder of a corporation of this State (who holds shares of stock on the date of the making of a demand pursuant to subsection (d) of this section with respect to such shares), (who continuously holds such shares through the effective date of the merger or consolidation), (who has otherwise complied with subsection (d) of this section) and (who has neither voted in favor of the merger or consolidation nor consented thereto in writing pursuant to § 228 of this title) shall be entitled to an appraisal by the Court of Chancery of the fair value of the stockholder's shares of stock under the circumstances described in subsections (b) and (c) of this section. ■ As used in this section, the word "stockholder" means a holder of record of stock in a corporation; the words "stock" and "share" mean and include what is ordinarily meant by those words; and the words "depository receipt" mean a receipt or other instrument issued by a depository representing an interest in 1 or more shares, or fractions thereof, solely of stock of a corporation, which stock is deposited with the depository.

(b) Appraisal rights shall be available for the shares of any class or series of stock of a constituent corporation in a merger or consolidation to be effected pursuant to § 251 (other than a merger effected pursuant to § 251(g) of this title), § 252, § 254, § 255, § 256, § 257, § 258, § 263 or § 264 of this title:

(1) `Provided, however, that` no appraisal rights under this section shall be available for the shares of any class or series of stock, (which stock, or depository receipts in respect thereof, at the record date fixed to determine the stockholders entitled to receive notice of the meeting of stockholders to act upon the agreement of merger or consolidation (or, in the case of a merger pursuant to § 251(h), as of immediately prior to the execution of the agreement of merger), were either: **(i)** listed on a national securities exchange or **(ii)** held of record by more than 2,000 holders;) `and further provided that` **[then]** no appraisal rights shall be available for any shares of stock of the constituent corporation surviving a merger **if** the merger did not require for its approval the vote of the stockholders of the surviving corporation as provided in § 251(f) of this title.

(2) [Then] Notwithstanding paragraph (b)(1) of this section, appraisal rights under this section shall be available for the shares of any class or series of stock of a constituent corporation **if** the holders thereof are required by the terms of an agreement of merger or consolidation pursuant to §§ 251, 252, 254, 255, 256, 257, 258, 263 and 264 of this title to accept for such stock anything ◀except:

a. Shares of stock of the corporation surviving or resulting from such merger or consolidation, or depository receipts in respect thereof;

b. Shares of stock of any other corporation, or depository receipts in respect thereof, which shares of stock (or depository receipts in respect thereof) or depository receipts at the effective date of the merger or consolidation will be either listed on a national securities exchange or held of record by more than 2,000 holders;

c. Cash in lieu of fractional shares or fractional depository receipts described in the foregoing paragraphs (b)(2)a. and b. of this section; or

d. Any combination of the shares of stock, depository receipts and cash in lieu of fractional shares or fractional depository receipts described in the foregoing paragraphs (b)(2)a., b. and c. of this section.▶

(3) In the event all of the stock of a subsidiary Delaware corporation party to a merger effected under § 253 or § 267 of this title is not owned by the parent immediately prior to the merger, [then] appraisal rights shall be available for the shares of the subsidiary Delaware corporation.

(c) Any corporation may provide in its certificate of incorporation that appraisal rights under this section shall be available for the shares of any class or series of its stock as a result of (an amendment to its certificate of incorporation), (any merger or consolidation in which the corporation is a constituent corporation) or (the sale of all or substantially all of the assets of the corporation). ■ If the certificate of incorporation contains such a provision, [then] the provisions of this section, including those set forth in subsections (d), (e), and (g) of this section, shall apply as nearly as is practicable.

(d) Appraisal rights shall be perfected as follows:

(1) If a proposed merger or consolidation for which appraisal rights are provided under this section is to be submitted for approval at a meeting of stockholders, [then] the corporation, not less than 20 days prior to the meeting, shall notify each of its stockholders who was such on the record date for notice of such meeting (or such members who received notice in accordance with § 255(c) of this title) with respect to shares for which appraisal rights are available pursuant to subsection (b) or (c) of this section that appraisal rights are available for any or all of the shares of the constituent corporations, and shall include in such notice a copy of this section and, if 1 of the constituent corporations is a nonstock corporation, [then] a copy of § 114 of this title. ■ Each stockholder electing to demand the appraisal of such stockholder's shares shall deliver to the corporation, before the taking of the vote on the merger or consolidation, a written demand for appraisal of such stockholder's shares; provided that a demand may be delivered to the corporation by electronic transmission if directed to an information processing system (if any) expressly designated for that purpose in such notice. ■ [Then] Such demand will be sufficient if it reasonably informs the corporation (of the identity of the stockholder) and (that the stockholder intends thereby to demand the appraisal of such stockholder's shares). ■ A proxy or vote against the merger or consolidation shall not constitute such a demand. ■ A stockholder electing to take such action must do so by a separate written demand as herein provided. ■ Within 10 days after the effective date of such merger or consolidation, the surviving or resulting corporation shall notify each stockholder of each constituent corporation who has complied with this subsection and has not voted in favor of or consented to the merger or consolidation of the date that the merger or consolidation has become effective; or

(2) If the merger or consolidation was approved pursuant to § 228, § 251(h), § 253, or § 267 of this title, **then** either a constituent corporation before the effective date of the merger or consolidation [or] the surviving or resulting corporation within 10 days thereafter shall notify each of the holders of any class or series of stock of such constituent corporation who are entitled to appraisal rights of the approval of the merger or consolidation and that appraisal rights are available for any or all shares of such class or series of stock of such constituent corporation, [and] shall include in such notice a copy of this section [and], if 1 of the constituent corporations is a nonstock corporation, a copy of § 114 of this title. ∎ Such notice may, [and], if given on or after the effective date of the merger or consolidation, shall, also notify such stockholders of the effective date of the merger or consolidation. ∎ Any stockholder entitled to appraisal rights may, within 20 days after the date of giving such notice or, in the case of a merger approved pursuant to § 251(h) of this title, within the later of the consummation of the offer contemplated by § 251(h) of this title and 20 days after the date of giving such notice, demand in writing from the surviving or resulting corporation the appraisal of such holder's shares; [provided that] a demand may be delivered to the corporation by electronic transmission if directed to an information processing system (if any) expressly designated for that purpose in such notice. ∎ **[Then]** Such demand will be sufficient **if** it reasonably informs the corporation **(**of the identity of the stockholder**)** [and] **(**that the stockholder intends thereby to demand the appraisal of such holder's shares**)**. ∎ **If** such notice did not notify stockholders of the effective date of the merger or consolidation, **[then]** either **(i)** each such constituent corporation shall send a second notice before the effective date of the merger or consolidation notifying each of the holders of any class or series of stock of such constituent corporation that are entitled to appraisal rights of the effective date of the merger or consolidation [or] **(ii)** the surviving or resulting corporation shall send such a second notice to all such holders on or within 10 days after such effective date; [provided, however, that] **if** such second notice is sent more than 20 days following the sending of the first notice or, in the case of a merger approved pursuant to § 251(h) of this title, later than the later of the consummation of the offer contemplated by § 251(h) of this title and 20 days following the sending of the first notice, **[then]** such second notice need only be sent to each stockholder **(**who is entitled to appraisal rights**)** and **(**who has demanded appraisal of such holder's shares in accordance with this subsection**)**. ∎ An affidavit of the secretary or assistant secretary or of the transfer agent of the corporation that is required to give either notice **(**that such notice has been given**)** shall, in the absence of fraud, be prima facie evidence of the facts stated therein. ∎ For purposes of determining the stockholders entitled to receive either notice, each constituent corporation may fix, in advance, a record date that shall be not more than 10 days prior to the date the notice is given, [provided, that] **if** the notice is given on or after the effective date of the merger or consolidation, **[then]** the record date shall be such effective date. ∎ **If** no record date is fixed [and] the notice is given prior to the effective date, **[then]** the record date shall be the close of business on the day next preceding the day on which the notice is given.

(e) Within 120 days after the effective date of the merger or consolidation, the surviving or resulting corporation or any stockholder (who has complied with subsections (a) and (d) of this section hereof) and (who is otherwise entitled to appraisal rights), may commence an appraisal proceeding by filing a petition in the Court of Chancery demanding a determination of the value of the stock of all such stockholders. ■ Notwithstanding the foregoing, at any time within 60 days after the effective date of the merger or consolidation, any stockholder who has not commenced an appraisal proceeding or joined that proceeding as a named party shall have the right (to withdraw such stockholder's demand for appraisal) and (to accept the terms offered upon the merger or consolidation). ■ Within 120 days after the effective date of the merger or consolidation, any stockholder who has complied with the requirements of subsections (a) and (d) of this section hereof, upon request, given in writing (or by electronic transmission directed to an information processing system (if any) expressly designated for that purpose in the notice of appraisal), shall be entitled to receive from the corporation surviving the merger or resulting from the consolidation a statement setting forth (the aggregate number of shares not voted in favor of the merger or consolidation (or, in the case of a merger approved pursuant to § 251(h) of this title, the aggregate number of shares (other than any excluded stock (as defined in § 251(h)(6)d. of this title)) that were the subject of, and were not tendered into, and accepted for purchase or exchange in, the offer referred to in § 251(h)(2)), and, in either case, with respect to which demands for appraisal have been received) and (the aggregate number of holders of such shares). ■ Such statement shall be given to the stockholder (within 10 days after such stockholder's request for such a statement is received by the surviving or resulting corporation) or (within 10 days after expiration of the period for delivery of demands for appraisal under subsection (d) of this section hereof), whichever is later. ■ Notwithstanding subsection (a) of this section, a person who is the beneficial owner of shares of such stock held either in a voting trust or by a nominee on behalf of such person may, in such person's own name, file a petition or request from the corporation the statement described in this subsection.

(f) Upon the filing of any such petition by a stockholder, service of a copy thereof shall be made upon the surviving or resulting corporation, which shall within 20 days after such service file in the office of the Register in Chancery in which the petition was filed a duly verified list containing the names and addresses of all stockholders (who have demanded payment for their shares) and (with whom agreements as to the value of their shares have not been reached by the surviving or resulting corporation). ■ If the petition shall be filed by the surviving or resulting corporation, [then] the petition shall be accompanied by such a duly verified list. ■ The Register in Chancery, if so ordered by the Court, shall give notice of the time and place fixed for the hearing of such petition by registered or certified mail to the surviving or resulting corporation and to the stockholders shown on the list at the addresses therein stated. ■ Such notice shall also be given by 1 or more publications at least 1 week before the day of the hearing, in a newspaper of general circulation published in the City of Wilmington, Delaware or such publication as the Court deems advisable. ■ The forms of the notices by mail and by publication shall be approved by the Court, and the costs thereof shall be borne by the surviving or resulting corporation.

(g) At the hearing on such petition, the Court shall determine the stockholders (who have complied with this section) and (who have become entitled to appraisal rights). ■ The

Court may require the stockholders who have demanded an appraisal for their shares and who hold stock represented by certificates to submit their certificates of stock to the Register in Chancery for notation thereon of the pendency of the appraisal proceedings; [and] if any stockholder fails to comply with such direction, [then] the Court may dismiss the proceedings as to such stockholder. ■ If immediately before the merger or consolidation the shares of the class or series of stock of the constituent corporation as to which appraisal rights are available were listed on a national securities exchange, [then] the Court shall dismiss the proceedings as to all holders of such shares who are otherwise entitled to appraisal rights **unless** (1) the total number of shares entitled to appraisal exceeds 1% of the outstanding shares of the class or series eligible for appraisal, (2) the value of the consideration provided in the merger or consolidation for such total number of shares exceeds $1 million, or (3) the merger was approved pursuant to § 253 or § 267 of this title.

(h) **After** the Court determines the stockholders entitled to an appraisal, [then] the appraisal proceeding shall be conducted in accordance with the rules of the Court of Chancery, including any rules specifically governing appraisal proceedings. ■ Through such proceeding the Court shall determine the fair value of the shares exclusive of any element of value arising from the accomplishment or expectation of the merger or consolidation, together with interest, if any, to be paid upon the amount determined to be the fair value. ■ In determining such fair value, the Court shall take into account all relevant factors. ■ **Unless** the Court in its discretion determines otherwise for good cause shown, and ◄except as provided in this subsection►, [then] interest from the effective date of the merger through the date of payment of the judgment shall be compounded quarterly [and] shall accrue at 5% over the Federal Reserve discount rate (including any surcharge) as established from time to time during the period between the effective date of the merger and the date of payment of the judgment. ■ At any time before the entry of judgment in the proceedings, the surviving corporation may pay to each stockholder entitled to appraisal an amount in cash, in which case interest shall accrue thereafter as provided herein only upon the sum of (1) the difference, if any, between the amount so paid and the fair value of the shares as determined by the Court, and (2) interest theretofore accrued, unless paid at that time. ■ Upon application by the surviving or resulting corporation or by any stockholder entitled to participate in the appraisal proceeding, the Court may, in its discretion, proceed to trial upon the appraisal prior to the final determination of the stockholders entitled to an appraisal. ■ Any stockholder (whose name appears on the list filed by the surviving or resulting corporation pursuant to subsection (f) of this section) and (who has submitted such stockholder's certificates of stock to the Register in Chancery, if such is required), may participate fully in all proceedings **until** it is finally determined that such stockholder is not entitled to appraisal rights under this section.

(i) The Court shall direct the payment of the fair value of the shares, together with interest, if any, by the surviving or resulting corporation to the stockholders entitled thereto. ■ Payment shall be so made to each such stockholder, in (the case of holders of uncertificated stock forthwith), [and] (the case of holders of shares represented by certificates upon the surrender to the corporation of the certificates representing such stock). ■ The Court's decree may be enforced as other decrees in the Court of Chancery may be enforced,

(j) The costs of the proceeding may be determined by the Court and taxed upon the parties as the Court deems equitable in the circumstances. ■ Upon application of a stockholder, the Court may order all or a portion of (the expenses incurred by any stockholder in connection with the appraisal proceeding, including, without limitation, reasonable attorney's fees and the fees and expenses of experts), to be charged pro rata against the value of all the shares entitled to an appraisal.

(k) From and after the effective date of the merger or consolidation, no stockholder who has demanded appraisal rights as provided in subsection (d) of this section shall be entitled to vote such stock for any purpose or to receive payment of dividends or other distributions on the stock (except dividends or other distributions payable to stockholders of record at a date which is prior to the effective date of the merger or consolidation); provided, however, that if no petition for an appraisal shall be filed within the time provided in subsection (e) of this section, or if such stockholder shall deliver to the surviving or resulting corporation a written withdrawal of such stockholder's demand for an appraisal and an acceptance of the merger or consolidation, either (within 60 days after the effective date of the merger or consolidation as provided in subsection (e) of this section) or (thereafter with the written approval of the corporation), **then** the right of such stockholder to an appraisal shall cease. ■ Notwithstanding the foregoing, no appraisal proceeding in the Court of Chancery shall be dismissed as to any stockholder without the approval of the Court, and such approval may be conditioned upon such terms as the Court deems just; provided, however that this provision shall not affect the right of any stockholder who has not commenced an appraisal proceeding or joined that proceeding as a named party (to withdraw such stockholder's demand for appraisal) and (to accept the terms offered upon the merger or consolidation) within 60 days after the effective date of the merger or consolidation, as set forth in subsection (e) of this section.

(l) The shares of the surviving or resulting corporation to which the shares of such objecting stockholders would have been converted had they assented to the merger or consolidation shall have the status of authorized and unissued shares of the surviving or resulting corporation.

§ 263. Merger or consolidation of domestic corporations and partnerships; service of process upon surviving or resulting corporation or partnership.

(a) [Then] Any 1 or more corporations of this State may merge or consolidate with 1 or more partnerships (whether general (including a limited liability partnership) or limited (including a limited liability limited partnership)), **unless** the laws of the jurisdiction or jurisdictions under which such partnership or partnerships are formed prohibit such merger or consolidation. ■ Such corporation or corporations and such 1 or more partnerships may merge with or into a surviving corporation, which may be any 1 of such corporations, or they may merge with or into a surviving partnership, which may be any 1 of such partnerships, or they may consolidate into a new resulting corporation, which corporation shall be a corporation of this State, or a partnership formed pursuant to an agreement of merger or consolidation, as the case may be, complying and approved in accordance with this section. ■ The term "partnership" as used in this section includes any partnership (whether general (including a limited liability partnership) or limited (including a limited liability limited partnership)) formed under the laws of this State or the laws of any other jurisdiction.

(b) Each such corporation and partnership shall enter into a written agreement of merger or consolidation. ■ The agreement shall state:

(1) The terms and conditions of the merger or consolidation;

(2) The mode of carrying the same into effect;

(3) In the case of a merger in which the surviving entity is a corporation of this State, such amendments or changes in the certificate of incorporation of the surviving corporation as are desired to be effected by the merger (which amendments or changes may amend and restate the certificate of incorporation of the surviving corporation in its entirety), or, if no such amendments or changes are desired, a statement that the certificate of incorporation of the surviving corporation shall be its certificate of incorporation;

(4) In the case of a consolidation in which the resulting entity is a corporation of this State, that the certificate of incorporation of the resulting corporation shall be as is set forth in an attachment to the agreement;

(5) The manner, if any, (of converting the shares of stock of each such corporation and the partnership interests of each such partnership into shares, partnership interests or other securities of the entity surviving or resulting from such merger or consolidation) or (of cancelling some or all of such shares or interests, and if any shares of any such corporation or any partnership interests of any such partnership are not to remain outstanding, to be converted solely into shares, partnership interests or other securities of the entity surviving or resulting from such merger or consolidation or to be cancelled, [then] the cash, property, rights or securities of any other corporation or entity which the holders of such shares or partnership interests are to receive in exchange for, or upon conversion of such shares or partnership interests and the surrender of any certificates evidencing them, (which cash, property, rights or securities of any other corporation or entity may be in addition to or in lieu of shares, partnership interests or other securities of the entity surviving or resulting from such merger or consolidation);

(6) Such other details or provisions as are deemed desirable, including, without limiting the generality of the foregoing, a provision for the payment of cash in lieu of the issuance or recognition of fractional shares, rights, other securities or interests of the surviving or resulting corporation or partnership or of any other corporation or entity the shares, rights, other securities or interests of which are to be received in the merger or consolidation, or for some other arrangement with respect thereto, consistent with § 155 of this title; and

(7) Such other provisions or facts as shall be required to be set forth in an agreement of merger or consolidation (including any provision for amendment of the partnership agreement and statement of partnership existence or certificate of limited partnership (or equivalent documents) of the surviving partnership) by the laws of each jurisdiction under which any of the partnerships are formed.

Any of the terms of the agreement of merger or consolidation may be made dependent upon facts ascertainable outside of such agreement, provided that the manner in which such facts shall operate upon the terms of the agreement <u>is clearly and expressly set forth</u> in the agreement of merger or consolidation. ■ The term "<u>facts</u>," as used in the preceding sentence, <u>includes</u>, but is not limited to, <u>the occurrence</u> of any event, including a determination or action by (any person or body, including the corporation).

(c) <u>The agreement required</u> by subsection (b) of this section <u>shall be adopted, approved, certified, executed</u> and <u>acknowledged</u> by each of the corporations (in the same manner as is provided in § 251 or § 255 of this title) and, in the case of the partnerships, (in accordance with their partnership agreements and in accordance with the laws of the jurisdiction under which they are formed). ■ **If** <u>the surviving or resulting entity is a partnership,</u> **[then]** in addition to any other approvals, <u>each stockholder</u> of a merging corporation who will become a general partner of the surviving or resulting partnership <u>must approve the agreement</u> of merger or consolidation. ■ <u>The agreement shall be filed</u> and <u>shall become effective</u> for all purposes of the laws of this State when and as provided in § 251 or § 255 of this title with respect to the merger or consolidation of corporations of this State. ■ In lieu of filing the agreement of merger or consolidation, <u>the surviving or resulting corporation</u> or <u>partnership may file a certificate</u> of merger or consolidation, executed (in accordance with § 103 of this title, if the surviving or resulting entity is a corporation), or (by a general partner, if the surviving or resulting entity is a partnership), which states:

(1) The name, jurisdiction of formation or organization and type of entity of each of the constituent entities;

(2) That an agreement of merger or consolidation has been approved, adopted, certified, executed and acknowledged by each of the constituent entities in accordance with this subsection;

(3) The name of the surviving or resulting corporation or partnership;

(4) In the case of a merger in which a corporation is the surviving entity, (such amendments or changes in the certificate of incorporation of the surviving corporation as are desired to be effected by the merger (which amendments or changes may amend and restate the certificate of incorporation of the surviving corporation in its entirety)), or, if no such amendments or changes are desired, (a statement that the certificate of incorporation of the surviving corporation shall be its certificate of incorporation);

(5) In the case of a consolidation in which a corporation is the resulting entity, that the certificate of incorporation of the resulting corporation shall be as is set forth in an attachment to the certificate;

(6) That the executed agreement of consolidation or merger is on file at an office of the surviving or resulting corporation or partnership and the address thereof;

(7) That a copy of the agreement of consolidation or merger will be furnished by the surviving or resulting entity, on request and without cost, to any stockholder of any constituent corporation or any partner of any constituent partnership; and

(8) The agreement, if any, required by subsection (d) of this section.

(d) If <u>the entity surviving or resulting</u> from the merger or consolidation <u>is</u> a partnership formed under the laws of a jurisdiction other than this State, **[then]** <u>it shall agree</u> that it may be served with process in this State in any proceeding for enforcement of any obligation of any constituent corporation or partnership of this State, as well as for enforcement of any obligation of the surviving or resulting corporation or partnership arising from the merger or consolidation, including any suit or other proceeding to enforce the right of any stockholders as determined in appraisal proceedings pursuant to § 262 of this title, [and] shall irrevocably appoint the Secretary of State as its agent to accept service of process in any such suit or other proceedings [and] shall specify the address to which a copy of such process shall be mailed by the Secretary of State. ■ Process may be served upon the Secretary of State under this subsection by means of electronic transmission but only as prescribed by the Secretary of State. ■ The Secretary of State is authorized to issue such rules and regulations with respect to such service as the Secretary of State deems necessary or appropriate. ■ [Then] In the event of such service upon the Secretary of State in accordance with this subsection, the Secretary of State shall forthwith notify such surviving or resulting corporation [or] partnership thereof by letter, directed to such surviving or resulting corporation or partnership at its address so specified, **unless** such surviving or resulting corporation [or] partnership shall have designated in writing to the Secretary of State a different address for such purpose, **in which case** it shall be mailed to the last address so designated. ■ Such letter shall be sent by a mail or courier service that includes (a record of mailing or deposit with the courier) and (a record of delivery evidenced by the signature of the recipient). ■ Such letter shall enclose a copy of the process [and] any other papers served on the Secretary of State pursuant to this subsection. ■ It shall be the duty of the plaintiff in the event of such service to serve process and any other papers in duplicate, (to notify the Secretary of State that service is being effected pursuant to this subsection) and (to pay the Secretary of State the sum of $50 for the use of the State), which sum shall be taxed as part of the costs in the proceeding, if the plaintiff shall prevail therein. ■ The Secretary of State shall maintain an alphabetical record of any such service setting forth the name of the plaintiff and the defendant, the title, docket number and nature of the proceeding in which process has been served upon the Secretary of State, the fact that service has been effected pursuant to this subsection, the return date thereof, and the day and hour service was made. ■ The Secretary of State shall not be required to retain such information longer than 5 years from receipt of the service of process.

(e) Sections 251 (d)-(f), 255(c) (second sentence) and (d)-(f), 259-261 and 328 of this title shall, insofar as they are applicable, apply to mergers or consolidations between corporations and partnerships.

(f) [Then] Nothing in this section shall be deemed to authorize the merger of a charitable nonstock corporation into a partnership, **if** the charitable status of such nonstock corporation would thereby be lost or impaired; [but] a partnership may be merged into a charitable nonstock corporation which shall continue as the surviving corporation.

§ 264. Merger or consolidation of domestic corporations and limited liability companies; service of process upon surviving or resulting corporation or limited liability company.

(a) [Then] Any 1 or more corporations of this State may merge [or] consolidate with 1 or more limited liability companies, **unless** the laws of the jurisdiction or jurisdictions under which such limited liability company or limited liability companies are formed prohibit such merger [or] consolidation. ■ Such corporation or corporations and such 1 or more limited liability companies may merge with or into a surviving corporation, which may be any 1 of such corporations, or they may merge with or into a surviving limited liability company, which may be any 1 of such limited liability companies, or they may consolidate into a new resulting corporation, which corporation shall be a corporation of this State, or a limited liability company formed pursuant to an agreement of merger or consolidation, as the case may be, complying and approved in accordance with this section. ■ The term "limited liability company" as used in this section includes any limited liability company formed under the laws of this State or the laws of any other jurisdiction.

(b) Each such corporation and limited liability company shall enter into a written agreement of merger or consolidation. ■ The agreement shall state:

(1) The terms and conditions of the merger or consolidation;

(2) The mode of carrying the same into effect;

(3) In the case of a merger in which the surviving entity is a corporation of this State, [then] such amendments or changes in the certificate of incorporation of the surviving corporation as are desired to be effected by the merger (which amendments or changes may amend and restate the certificate of incorporation of the surviving corporation in its entirety), or, if no such amendments or changes are desired, [then] a statement that the certificate of incorporation of the surviving corporation shall be its certificate of incorporation;

(4) In the case of a consolidation in which the resulting entity is a corporation of this State, [then] that the certificate of incorporation of the resulting corporation shall be as is set forth in an attachment to the agreement;

(5) The manner, if any, **(** of converting the shares of stock of each such corporation and the limited liability company interests of each such limited liability company into shares, limited liability company interests or other securities of the entity surviving or resulting from such merger or consolidation**)** or **(** of cancelling some or all of such shares or interests**)**, and if any shares of any such corporation or any limited liability company interests of any such limited liability company are not to remain outstanding, to be converted solely into shares, limited liability company interests or other securities of the entity surviving or resulting from such merger or consolidation or to be cancelled, [then] the cash, property, rights or securities of any other corporation or entity which the holders of such shares or limited liability company interests are to receive in exchange for, or upon conversion of such shares or limited liability company interests and the surrender of any certificates evidencing them, **(** which cash, property, rights or securities of any other corporation or entity may be in addition to or in lieu of shares, limited liability company interests or other securities of the entity surviving or resulting from such merger or consolidation**)**;

(6) Such other details or provisions as are deemed desirable, including, without limiting the generality of the foregoing, a provision for the payment of cash in lieu of the issuance or recognition of fractional shares, rights, other securities or interests of the surviving or resulting corporation or limited liability company or of any other corporation or entity the shares, rights, other securities or interests of which are to be received in the merger or consolidation, or for some other arrangement with respect thereto, consistent with § 155 of this title; and

(7) Such other provisions or facts as shall be required to be set forth in an agreement of merger or consolidation (including any provision for amendment of the limited liability company agreement and certificate of formation (or equivalent documents) of the surviving limited liability company) by the laws of each jurisdiction under which any of the limited liability companies are formed.

Any of the terms of the agreement of merger or consolidation may be made dependent upon facts ascertainable outside of such agreement, provided that the manner in which such facts shall operate upon the terms of the agreement is clearly and expressly set forth in the agreement of merger or consolidation. ■ The term "facts," as used in the preceding sentence, includes, but is not limited to, the occurrence of any event, including a determination or action by (any person or body, including the corporation).

(c) The agreement required by subsection (b) of this section shall be adopted, approved, certified, executed and acknowledged by each of the corporations (in the same manner as is provided in § 251 or § 255 of this title) and, in the case of the limited liability companies, (in accordance with their limited liability company agreements and in accordance with the laws of the jurisdiction under which they are formed). ■ The agreement shall be filed and shall become effective for all purposes of the laws of this State when and as provided in § 251 or § 255 of this title with respect to the merger or consolidation of corporations of this State. ■ In lieu of filing the agreement of merger or consolidation, the surviving or resulting corporation or limited liability company may file a certificate of merger or consolidation, executed (in accordance with § 103 of this title, if the surviving or resulting entity is a corporation), or (by an authorized person, if the surviving or resulting entity is a limited liability company), which states:

(1) The name and jurisdiction of formation or organization of each of the constituent entities;

(2) That an agreement of merger or consolidation has been approved, adopted, certified, executed and acknowledged by each of the constituent entities in accordance with this subsection;

(3) The name of the surviving or resulting corporation or limited liability company;

(4) In the case of a merger in which a corporation is the surviving entity, [then] such amendments or changes in the certificate of incorporation of the surviving corporation as are desired to be effected by the merger (which amendments or changes may amend and restate the certificate of incorporation of the surviving corporation in its entirety), or, if no such amendments or changes are desired, [then] a statement that the certificate of incorporation of the surviving corporation shall be its certificate of incorporation;

(5) In the case of a consolidation in which a corporation is the resulting entity, [then] that the certificate of incorporation of the resulting corporation shall be as is set forth in an attachment to the certificate;

(6) That the executed agreement of consolidation or merger is on file at an office of the surviving or resulting corporation or limited liability company and the address thereof;

(7) That a copy of the agreement of consolidation or merger will be furnished by the surviving or resulting entity, on request and without cost, to any stockholder of any constituent corporation or any member of any constituent limited liability company; and

(8) The agreement, if any, required by subsection (d) of this section.

(d) **If** the entity surviving or resulting from the merger or consolidation is a limited liability company formed under the laws of a jurisdiction other than this State, [then] it shall agree that it may be served with process in this State in any proceeding for enforcement of any obligation of any constituent corporation or limited liability company of this State, as well as for enforcement of any obligation of the surviving or resulting corporation or limited liability company arising from the merger or consolidation, including any suit or other proceeding to enforce the right of any stockholders as determined in appraisal proceedings pursuant to the provisions of § 262 of this title, [and] shall irrevocably appoint the Secretary of State as its agent to accept service of process in any such suit or other proceedings [and] shall specify the address to which a copy of such process shall be mailed by the Secretary of State. ■ Process may be served upon the Secretary of State under this subsection by means of electronic transmission but only as prescribed by the Secretary of State. ■ The Secretary of State is authorized to issue such rules and regulations with respect to such service as the Secretary of State deems necessary or appropriate. ■ In the event of such service upon the Secretary of State in accordance with this subsection, the Secretary of State shall forthwith notify such surviving or resulting corporation [or] limited liability company thereof by letter, directed to such surviving or resulting corporation or limited liability company at its address so specified, **unless** such surviving or resulting corporation [or] limited liability company shall have designated in writing to the Secretary of State a different address for such purpose, **in which case** it shall be mailed to the last address so designated. ■ Such letter shall be sent by a mail or courier service that includes **(**a record of mailing or deposit with the courier**)** and **(**a record of delivery evidenced by the signature of the recipient**)**. ■ Such letter shall enclose a copy of the process [and] any other papers served on the Secretary of State pursuant to this subsection. ■ It shall be the duty of the plaintiff in the event of such service to serve process and any other papers in duplicate, **(**to notify the Secretary of State that service is being effected pursuant to this subsection**)** and **(**to pay the Secretary of State the sum of $50 for the use of the State, which sum shall be taxed as part of the costs in the proceeding, if the plaintiff shall prevail therein**)**. ■ The Secretary of State shall maintain an alphabetical record of any such service setting forth the name of the plaintiff and the defendant, the title, docket number and nature of the proceeding in which process has been served upon the Secretary of State, the fact that service has been effected pursuant to this subsection, the return date thereof, and the day and hour service was made. ■ The Secretary of State shall not be required to retain such information longer than 5 years from receipt of the service of process.

(e) Sections 251 (d)-(f), 255(c) (second sentence) and (d)-(f), 259-261 and 328 of this title shall, insofar as they are applicable, apply to mergers or consolidations between corporations and limited liability companies.

(f) [Then] Nothing in this section shall be deemed to authorize the merger of a charitable nonstock corporation into a limited liability company, **if** the charitable status of such nonstock corporation would thereby be lost or impaired; [but] a limited liability company may be merged into a charitable nonstock corporation which shall continue as the surviving corporation.

§ 265. Conversion of other entities to a domestic corporation.

(a) As used in this section, the term "other entity" means a limited liability company, statutory trust, business trust or association, real estate investment trust, common-law trust or any other unincorporated business including a partnership (whether general (including a limited liability partnership) or limited (including a limited liability limited partnership)), or a foreign corporation.

(b) Any other entity may convert to a corporation of this State by complying with subsection (h) of this section and filing in the office of the Secretary of State:

   (1) A certificate of conversion to corporation that has been executed in accordance with subsection (i) of this section and filed in accordance with § 103 of this title; and

   (2) A certificate of incorporation that has been executed, acknowledged and filed in accordance with § 103 of this title.

Each of the certificates required by this subsection (b) shall be filed simultaneously in the office of the Secretary of State and, if such certificates are not to become effective upon their filing as permitted by § 103(d) of this title, then each such certificate shall provide for the same effective date or time in accordance with § 103(d) of this title.

(c) The certificate of conversion to corporation shall state:

   (1) The date on which and jurisdiction where the other entity was first created, incorporated, formed or otherwise came into being and, if it has changed, its jurisdiction immediately prior to its conversion to a domestic corporation;

   (2) The name and type of entity of the other entity immediately prior to the filing of the certificate of conversion to corporation; and

   (3) The name of the corporation as set forth in its certificate of incorporation filed in accordance with subsection (b) of this section.

   (4) [Repealed.]

(d) Upon the effective time of the certificate of conversion to corporation and the certificate of incorporation, the other entity shall be converted to a corporation of this State and the corporation shall thereafter be subject to all of the provisions of this title, ◂except that notwithstanding § 106 of this title, the existence of the corporation shall be deemed to have commenced on the date the other entity commenced its existence in the jurisdiction in which the other entity was first created, formed, incorporated or otherwise came into being▸.

(e) The conversion of any other entity to a corporation of this State shall not be deemed to affect any obligations or liabilities of the other entity incurred prior to its conversion to a corporation of this State or the personal liability of any person incurred prior to such conversion.

(f) When an other entity has been converted to a corporation of this State pursuant to this section, [then] the corporation of this State shall, for all purposes of the laws of the State of Delaware, be deemed to be the same entity as the converting other entity. ■ When any conversion shall have become effective under this section, for all purposes of the laws of the State of Delaware, [then] all of the rights, privileges and powers of the other entity that has converted, and all property, real, personal and mixed, and all debts due to such other entity, as well as all other things and causes of action belonging to such other entity, shall remain vested in the domestic corporation to which such other entity has converted and shall be the property of such domestic corporation and the title to any real property vested by deed or otherwise in such other entity shall not revert or be in any way impaired by reason of this chapter; but all rights of creditors and all liens upon any property of such other entity shall be preserved unimpaired, and all debts, liabilities and duties of the other entity that has converted shall remain attached to the corporation of this State to which such other entity has converted, and may be enforced against it (to the same extent as if said debts, liabilities and duties had originally been incurred or contracted by it in its capacity as a corporation of this State). ■ The rights, privileges, powers and interests in property of the other entity, as well as the debts, liabilities and duties of the other entity, shall not be deemed, as a consequence of the conversion, to have been transferred to the domestic corporation to which such other entity has converted for any purpose of the laws of the State of Delaware.

(g) Unless otherwise agreed for all purposes of the laws of the State of Delaware or as required under applicable non-Delaware law, the converting other entity shall not be required to wind up its affairs or pay its liabilities and distribute its assets, and the conversion shall not be deemed to constitute a dissolution of such other entity and shall constitute a continuation of the existence of the converting other entity in the form of a corporation of this State.

(h) Prior to filing a certificate of conversion to corporation with the office of the Secretary of State, the conversion shall be approved in the manner provided for by the document, instrument, agreement or other writing, as the case may be, governing the internal affairs of the other entity and the conduct of its business or by applicable law, as appropriate, and a certificate of incorporation shall be approved by the same authorization required to approve the conversion.

(i) The certificate of conversion to corporation shall be signed by any person who is authorized to sign the certificate of conversion to corporation on behalf of the other entity.

(j) In connection with a conversion hereunder, rights or securities of, or interests in, the other entity which is to be converted to a corporation of this State may be exchanged for or converted into cash, property, or shares of stock, rights or securities of such corporation of this State or, in addition to or in lieu thereof, may be exchanged for or converted into cash, property, or shares of stock, rights or securities of or interests in another domestic corporation or other entity or may be cancelled.

§ 266. Conversion of a domestic corporation to other entities.

(a) A corporation of this State may, upon the authorization of such conversion in accordance with this section, convert to a limited liability company, statutory trust, business trust or association, real estate investment trust, common-law trust or any other unincorporated business including a partnership (whether general (including a limited liability partnership) or limited (including a limited liability limited partnership)) or a foreign corporation.

(b) The board of directors of the corporation which desires to convert under this section shall adopt a resolution approving such conversion, specifying the type of entity into which the corporation shall be converted and recommending the approval of such conversion by the stockholders of the corporation. ■ Such resolution shall be submitted to the stockholders of the corporation at an annual or special meeting. ■ Due notice of the time, and purpose of the meeting shall be given to each holder of stock, whether voting or nonvoting, of the corporation at the address of the stockholder as it appears on the records of the corporation, at least 20 days prior to the date of the meeting. ■ At the meeting, the resolution shall be considered and a vote taken for its adoption or rejection. ■ If all outstanding shares of stock of the corporation, whether voting or nonvoting, shall be voted for the adoption of the resolution, [then] the conversion shall be authorized.

(c) If a corporation shall convert in accordance with this section to another entity organized, formed or created under the laws of a jurisdiction other than the State of Delaware, [then] the corporation shall file with the Secretary of State a certificate of conversion executed in accordance with § 103 of this title, which certifies:

(1) The name of the corporation, and if it has been changed, [then] the name under which it was originally incorporated;

(2) The date of filing of its original certificate of incorporation with the Secretary of State;

(3) The name and jurisdiction of the entity to which the corporation shall be converted;

(4) That the conversion has been approved in accordance with the provisions of this section;

(5) The agreement of the corporation (that it may be served with process in the State of Delaware in any action, suit or proceeding for enforcement of any obligation of the corporation arising while it was a corporation of this State), and (that it irrevocably appoints the Secretary of State as its agent to accept service of process in any such action, suit or proceeding); and

(6) The address to which a copy of the process referred to in paragraph (c)(5) of this section shall be mailed to it by the Secretary of State. ■ Process may be served upon the Secretary of State in accordance with paragraph (c)(5) of this section by means of electronic transmission but only as prescribed by the Secretary of State. ■ The Secretary of State is authorized to issue such rules and regulations with respect to such service as the Secretary of State deems necessary or appropriate. ■ In the event of such service upon the Secretary of State in accordance with paragraph (c)(5) of this section, the Secretary of State shall forthwith notify such corporation that has converted out of the State of Delaware by letter, directed to such corporation that has converted out of the State of Delaware at the address so specified, ◄unless such corporation shall have designated in writing to the Secretary of State a different address for such purpose, in which case it shall be mailed to the last address designated►. ■ Such letter shall be sent by a mail or courier service that includes (a record of mailing or deposit with the courier) and (a record of delivery evidenced by the signature of the recipient). ■ Such letter shall enclose a copy of the process and any other papers served on the Secretary of State pursuant to this subsection. ■ It shall be the duty of the plaintiff in the event of such service (to serve process and any other papers in duplicate), (to notify the Secretary of State that service is being effected pursuant to this subsection) and (to pay the Secretary of State the sum of $50 for the use of the State, which sum shall be taxed as part of the

Subchapter IX. Merger, Consolidation or Conversion § 266

costs in the proceeding, if the plaintiff shall prevail therein). ■ The Secretary of State shall maintain an alphabetical record of any such service setting forth the name of the plaintiff and the defendant, the title, docket number and nature of the proceeding in which process has been served, the fact that service has been effected pursuant to this subsection, the return date thereof, and the day and hour service was made. ■ The Secretary of State shall not be required to retain such information longer than 5 years from receipt of the service of process.

(d) (Upon the filing in the Office of the Secretary of State of a certificate of conversion to non-Delaware entity in accordance with subsection (c) of this section) or (upon the future effective date or time of the certificate of conversion to non-Delaware entity and payment to the Secretary of State of all fees prescribed under this title), the corporation shall cease to exist as a corporation of this State at the time the certificate of conversion becomes effective in accordance with § 103 of this title. ■ A copy of the certificate of conversion to non-Delaware entity certified by the Secretary of State shall be prima facie evidence of the conversion by such corporation out of the State of Delaware.

(e) The conversion of a corporation out of the State of Delaware in accordance with this section and the resulting cessation of its existence as a corporation of this State pursuant to a certificate of conversion to non-Delaware entity shall not be deemed to affect any obligations or liabilities of the corporation incurred prior to such conversion or the personal liability of any person incurred prior to such conversion, nor shall it be deemed to affect the choice of law applicable to the corporation with respect to matters arising prior to such conversion.

(f) Unless otherwise provided in a resolution of conversion adopted in accordance with this section, the converting corporation shall not be required to wind up its affairs or pay its liabilities and distribute its assets, and the conversion shall not constitute a dissolution of such corporation.

(g) In connection with a conversion of a domestic corporation to another entity pursuant to this section, shares of stock, of the corporation of this State which is to be converted may be exchanged for or converted into cash, property, rights or securities of, or interests in, the entity to which the corporation of this State is being converted or, in addition to or in lieu thereof, may be exchanged for or converted into cash, property, shares of stock, rights or securities of, or interests in, another domestic corporation or other entity or may be cancelled.

(h) When a corporation has been converted to another entity or business form pursuant to this section, [then] the other entity or business form shall, for all purposes of the laws of the State of Delaware, be deemed to be the same entity as the corporation. ■ When any conversion shall have become effective under this section, for all purposes of the laws of the State of Delaware, [then] all of the rights, privileges and powers of the corporation that has converted, and all property, real, personal and mixed, and all debts due to such corporation, as well as all other things and causes of action belonging to such corporation, shall remain vested in the other entity or business form to which such corporation has converted and shall be the property of such other entity or business form, and the title to any real property vested by deed or otherwise in such corporation shall not revert or be in any way impaired by reason of this chapter; but all rights of creditors and all liens upon any property of such corporation shall be preserved unimpaired, and all debts, liabilities and duties of the corporation that has converted shall remain attached to the other entity or business form to which such corporation has converted, and may be enforced against it (to the same extent as if said debts, liabilities and duties had originally been incurred or contracted by it in its capacity as such other entity or business form). ■ The rights, privileges, powers and interest in property of the corporation that has converted, as well as the debts, liabilities and duties of such corporation, shall not be deemed, as a consequence of the conversion, to have been transferred to the other entity or business form to which such corporation has converted for any purpose of the laws of the State of Delaware.

(i) No vote of stockholders of a corporation shall be necessary to authorize a conversion if no shares of the stock of such corporation shall have been issued prior to the adoption by the board of directors of the resolution approving the conversion.

(j) [Then] Nothing in this section shall be deemed to authorize the conversion of a charitable nonstock corporation into another entity, if the charitable status of such charitable nonstock corporation would thereby be lost or impaired.

§ 267. Merger of parent entity and subsidiary corporation or corporations.

(a) In any case in which: (1) at least 90% of the outstanding shares of each class of the stock of a corporation or corporations (other than a corporation which has in its certificate of incorporation the provision required by § 251(g)(7)(i) of this title), of which class there are outstanding shares that, absent this subsection, would be entitled to vote on such merger, is owned by an entity, and (2) 1 or more of such corporations is a corporation of this State, unless the laws of the jurisdiction or jurisdictions under which such entity or such foreign corporations are formed or organized prohibit such merger, [then] the entity having such stock ownership may either merge the corporation or corporations into itself and assume all of its or their obligations, or merge itself, or itself and 1 or more of such corporations, into 1 of the other corporations by (a) authorizing such merger in accordance with such entity's governing documents and the laws of the jurisdiction under which such entity is formed or organized and (b) acknowledging and filing with the Secretary of State, in accordance with § 103 of this title, a certificate of such ownership and merger certifying (i) that such merger was authorized in accordance with such entity's governing documents and the laws of the jurisdiction under which such entity is formed or organized, such certificate executed in accordance with such entity's governing documents and in accordance with the laws of the jurisdiction under which such entity is formed or organized and (ii) the type of entity of each constituent entity to the merger; provided, however, that in case the entity shall not own all the outstanding stock of all the corporations, parties to a merger as aforesaid, [then] (A) the certificate of ownership and merger shall state the terms and conditions of the merger, including the securities, cash, property, or rights to be issued, paid, delivered or granted by the surviving constituent party upon surrender of each share of the corporation or corporations not owned by the entity, or the cancellation of some or all of such shares and (B) such terms and conditions of the merger may not result in a holder of stock in a corporation becoming a general partner in a surviving entity that is a partnership (other than a limited liability partnership or a limited liability limited partnership). ■ Any of the terms of the merger may be made dependent upon facts ascertainable outside of the certificate of ownership and merger, provided that the manner in which such facts shall operate upon the terms of the merger is clearly and expressly set forth in the certificate of ownership and merger. ■ The term "facts," as used in the preceding sentence, includes, but is not limited to, the occurrence of any event, including a determination or action by any person or body, including the entity. ■ **If** the surviving constituent party is an entity formed or organized under the laws of a jurisdiction other than this State, **[then] (1)** § 252(d) of this title shall also apply to a merger under this section; [and] **if** the surviving constituent party is the entity, **[then]** the word "corporation" where applicable, as used in § 252(d) of this title, shall be deemed to include an entity as defined herein; and **(2)** the terms and conditions of the merger shall obligate the surviving constituent party to provide the agreement, and take the actions, required by § 252(d) of this title.

(b) Sections 259, 261, and 328 of this title shall, insofar as they are applicable, apply to a merger under this section, and §§ 260 and 251(e) of this title shall apply to a merger under this section in which the surviving constituent party is a corporation of this State. ■ For purposes of this subsection, references to "agreement of merger" in § 251(e) of this title shall mean the terms and conditions of the merger set forth in the certificate of ownership and merger, and references to "corporation" in §§ 259-261 of this title, and § 328 of this title shall be deemed to include the entity, as applicable. ■ Section 262 of this title shall not apply to any merger effected under this section, ◄except as provided in subsection (c) of this section►.

(c) In the event all of the stock of a Delaware corporation party to a merger effected under this section is not owned by the entity immediately prior to the merger, **[then]** the stockholders of such Delaware corporation party to the merger shall have appraisal rights as set forth in § 262 of this title.

(d) As used in this section only, the term:

(1) "Constituent party" means an entity or corporation to be merged pursuant to this section;

(2) "Entity" means a partnership (whether general (including a limited liability partnership) or limited (including a limited liability limited partnership)), limited liability company, any association of the kind commonly known as a joint-stock association or joint-stock company and any unincorporated association, trust or enterprise having members or having outstanding shares of stock or other evidences of financial or beneficial interest therein, whether formed or organized by agreement or under statutory authority or otherwise and whether formed or organized under the laws of this State or the laws of any other jurisdiction; and

(3) "Governing documents" means a partnership agreement, limited liability company agreement, articles of association or any other instrument containing the provisions by which an entity is formed or organized.

Subchapter X. Sale of Assets, Dissolution and Winding Up

§ 271. Sale, lease or exchange of assets; consideration; procedure.

(a) Every corporation may at any meeting of its board of directors or governing body sell, lease or exchange all or substantially all of its property and assets, including its goodwill and its corporate franchises, upon such terms and conditions and for such consideration, which may consist in whole or in part of money or other property, (including shares of stock in, and/or other securities of, any other corporation or corporations, as its board of directors or governing body deems expedient and for the best interests of the corporation), when and as authorized by a resolution adopted (by the holders of a majority of the outstanding stock of the corporation entitled to vote thereon) or, if the corporation is a nonstock corporation, (by a majority of the members having the right to vote for the election of the members of the governing body and any other members entitled to vote thereon under the certificate of incorporation or the bylaws of such corporation), at a meeting duly called upon at least 20 days' notice. ■ The notice of the meeting shall state that such a resolution will be considered.

(b) Notwithstanding authorization or consent to a proposed sale, lease or exchange of a corporation's property and assets by the stockholders or members, the board of directors or governing body may abandon such proposed sale, lease or exchange without further action by the stockholders or members, (subject to the rights, if any, of third parties under any contract relating thereto).

(c) For purposes of this section only, the property and assets of the corporation include the property and assets of any subsidiary of the corporation. ■ As used in this subsection, "subsidiary" means any entity wholly-owned and controlled, directly or indirectly, by the corporation and includes, without limitation, corporations, partnerships, limited partnerships, limited liability partnerships, limited liability companies, and/or statutory trusts. ■ Notwithstanding subsection (a) of this section, ◄except to the extent the certificate of incorporation otherwise provides►, no resolution by stockholders or members shall be required for a sale, lease or exchange of property and assets of the corporation to a subsidiary.

§ 272. Mortgage or pledge of assets.

The authorization or consent of stockholders to the mortgage or pledge of a corporation's property and assets shall not be necessary, ◄except to the extent that the certificate of incorporation otherwise provides►.

§ 273. Dissolution of joint venture corporation having 2 stockholders.

(a) If the stockholders of a corporation of this State, having only 2 stockholders each of which own 50% of the stock therein, shall be engaged in the prosecution of a joint venture and if such stockholders shall be unable to agree upon the desirability of discontinuing such joint venture and disposing of the assets used in such venture, **[then]** either stockholder may, unless otherwise provided in the certificate of incorporation of the corporation or in a written agreement between the stockholders, file with the Court of Chancery a petition stating (that it desires to discontinue such joint venture and to dispose of the assets used in such venture in accordance with a plan to be agreed upon by both stockholders) or (that, if no such plan shall be agreed upon by both stockholders, the corporation be dissolved). ■ Such petition shall have attached thereto a copy of (the proposed plan of discontinuance and distribution) and (a certificate stating that copies of such petition and plan have been transmitted in writing to the other stockholder and to the directors and officers of such corporation). ■ The petition and certificate shall be executed and acknowledged in accordance with § 103 of this title.

(b) Unless both stockholders file with the Court of Chancery:

(1) Within 3 months of the date of the filing of such petition, a certificate similarly executed and acknowledged stating that they have agreed on such plan, or a modification thereof, and

(2) Within 1 year from the date of the filing of such petition, a certificate similarly executed and acknowledged stating that the distribution provided by such plan had been completed,

[then] the Court of Chancery may dissolve such corporation and may by appointment of 1 or more trustees or receivers with all the powers and title of a trustee or receiver appointed under § 279 of this title, administer and wind up its affairs. ■ Either or both of the above periods may be extended by agreement of the stockholders, evidenced by a certificate similarly executed, acknowledged and filed with the Court of Chancery prior to the expiration of such period.

(c) In the case of a charitable nonstock corporation, the petitioner shall provide a copy of any petition referred to in subsection (a) of this section to the Attorney General of the State of Delaware within 1 week of its filing with the Court of Chancery.

§ 274. Dissolution before issuance of shares or beginning of business; procedure.

If a corporation has not issued shares or has not commenced the business for which the corporation was organized, **[then]** a majority of the incorporators, or, if directors were named in the certificate of incorporation or have been elected, a majority of the directors, may surrender all of the corporation's rights and franchises by filing in the office of the Secretary of State a certificate, executed and acknowledged by a majority of the incorporators or directors, stating: (that no shares of stock have been issued or that the business or activity for which the corporation was organized has not been begun;) (the date of filing of the corporation's original certificate of incorporation with the Secretary of State;) (that no part of the capital of the corporation has been paid, or, if some capital has been paid, that the amount actually paid in for the corporation's shares, less any part thereof disbursed for necessary expenses, has been returned to those entitled thereto;) (that if the corporation has begun business but it has not issued shares, all debts of the corporation have been paid;) (that if the corporation has not begun business but has issued stock certificates, all issued stock certificates, if any, have been surrendered and cancelled;) and (that all rights and franchises of the corporation are surrendered). ■ Upon such certificate becoming effective in accordance with § 103 of this title, the corporation shall be dissolved.

§ 275. Dissolution generally; procedure.

(a) **If** it should be deemed advisable in the judgment of the board of directors of any corporation that it should be dissolved, [then] the board, after the adoption of a resolution to that effect by a majority of the whole board at any meeting called for that purpose, shall cause notice of the adoption of the resolution and of a meeting of stockholders to take action upon the resolution to be given to each stockholder entitled to vote thereon as of (the record date for determining the stockholders entitled to notice of the meeting).

(b) At the meeting a vote shall be taken upon the proposed dissolution. ■ **If** a majority of the outstanding stock of the corporation entitled to vote thereon shall vote for the proposed dissolution, [then] a certification of dissolution shall be filed with the Secretary of State pursuant to subsection (d) of this section.

(c) [Then] Dissolution of a corporation may also be authorized without action of the directors **if** all the stockholders entitled to vote thereon shall consent in writing and a certificate of dissolution shall be filed with the Secretary of State pursuant to subsection (d) of this section.

(d) **If** dissolution is authorized in accordance with this section, [then] a certificate of dissolution shall be executed, acknowledged and filed, and shall become effective, in accordance with § 103 of this title. ■ Such certificate of dissolution shall set forth:

(1) The name of the corporation;

(2) The date dissolution was authorized;

(3) (That the dissolution has been authorized by the board of directors and stockholders of the corporation, in accordance with subsections (a) and (b) of this section), or (that the dissolution has been authorized by all of the stockholders of the corporation entitled to vote on a dissolution, in accordance with subsection (c) of this section);

(4) The names and addresses of the directors and officers of the corporation; and

(5) The date of filing of the corporation's original certificate of incorporation with the Secretary of State.

(e) The resolution authorizing a proposed dissolution may provide that notwithstanding authorization or consent to the proposed dissolution by the stockholders, or the members of a nonstock corporation pursuant to § 276 of this title, (the board of directors or governing body may abandon such proposed dissolution without further action by the stockholders or members).

(f) Upon a certificate of dissolution becoming effective in accordance with § 103 of this title, the corporation shall be dissolved.

§ 276. Dissolution of nonstock corporation; procedure.

(a) **Whenever** it shall be desired to dissolve any nonstock corporation, [then] the governing body shall perform all the acts necessary for dissolution which are required by § 275 of this title to be performed by the board of directors of a corporation having capital stock. ■ **If** any members of a nonstock corporation are entitled to vote for the election of members of its governing body or are entitled to vote for dissolution under the certificate of incorporation or the bylaws of such corporation, [then] such members shall perform all the acts necessary for dissolution which are contemplated by § 275 of this title to be performed by the stockholders of a corporation having capital stock, [then] including dissolution without action of the members of the governing body if all the members of the corporation entitled to vote thereon shall consent in writing and a certificate of dissolution shall be filed with the Secretary of State pursuant to § 275(d) of this title. ■ If there is no member entitled to vote thereon, [then] the dissolution of the corporation shall be authorized at a meeting of the governing body, (upon the adoption of a resolution to dissolve by the vote of a majority of members of its governing body then in office). ■ In all other respects, the method and proceedings for the dissolution of a nonstock corporation shall conform as nearly as may be to the proceedings prescribed by § 275 of this title for the dissolution of corporations having capital stock.

(b) If a nonstock corporation has not commenced the business for which the corporation was organized, [then] a majority of the governing body or, if none, a majority of the incorporators may surrender all of the corporation rights and franchises by filing in the office of the Secretary of State a certificate, (executed and acknowledged by a majority of the incorporators or governing body, conforming as nearly as may be to the certificate prescribed by § 274 of this title).

§ 277. Payment of franchise taxes before dissolution, merger, transfer or conversion.

[Then] No corporation shall be dissolved, merged, transferred (without continuing its existence as a corporation of this State) or converted under this chapter **until**:

(1) All franchise taxes due to or assessable by the State including all franchise taxes due or which would be due or assessable for the entire calendar month during which such dissolution, merger, transfer or conversion becomes effective have been paid by the corporation; and

(2) All annual franchise tax reports including a final annual franchise tax report for the year in which such dissolution, merger, transfer or conversion becomes effective have been filed by the corporation;

notwithstanding the foregoing, if the Secretary of State certifies that an instrument to effect a dissolution, merger, transfer or conversion has been filed in the Secretary of State's office, [then] such corporation shall be dissolved, merged, transferred or converted at the effective time of such instrument.

§ 278. Continuation of corporation after dissolution for purposes of suit and winding up affairs.

All corporations, whether they expire by their own limitation or are otherwise dissolved, shall nevertheless be continued, for the term of 3 years from such expiration or dissolution or for such longer period as the Court of Chancery shall in its discretion direct, bodies corporate (for the purpose of prosecuting and defending suits, whether civil, criminal or administrative, by or against them, and of enabling them gradually to settle and close their business, to dispose of and convey their property, to discharge their liabilities and to distribute to their stockholders any remaining assets), but not (for the purpose of continuing the business for which the corporation was organized). ■ With respect to any action, suit or proceeding begun by or against the corporation either prior to or within 3 years after the date of its expiration or dissolution, the action shall not abate by reason of the dissolution of the corporation; [and] the corporation shall, solely for the purpose of such action, suit or proceeding, be continued as a body corporate beyond the 3-year period and until any judgments, orders or decrees therein shall be fully executed, without the necessity for any special direction to that effect by the Court of Chancery.

Sections 279 through 282 of this title shall apply to any corporation that has expired by its own limitation, and when so applied, all references in those sections to a dissolved corporation or dissolution shall include a corporation that has expired by its own limitation and to such expiration, respectively.

§ 279. Trustees or receivers for dissolved corporations; appointment; powers; duties.

When any corporation organized under this chapter shall be dissolved in any manner whatever, **[then]** the Court of Chancery, on application of any creditor, stockholder or director of the corporation, or any other person who shows good cause therefor, at any time, may either appoint 1 or more of the directors of the corporation to be trustees, or appoint 1 or more persons (to be receivers, of and for the corporation), (to take charge of the corporation's property), and (to collect the debts and property due and belonging to the corporation), with power to prosecute and defend, in the name of the corporation, or otherwise, all such suits as may be necessary or proper for the purposes aforesaid, and (to appoint an agent or agents under them), and (to do all other acts which might be done by the corporation, if in being, that may be necessary for the final settlement of the unfinished business of the corporation). ■ The powers of the trustees or receivers may be continued as long as the Court of Chancery shall think necessary for the purposes aforesaid.

§ 280. Notice to claimants; filing of claims.

(a)(1) After a corporation has been dissolved in accordance with the procedures set forth in this chapter, **[then]** the corporation or any successor entity may give notice of the dissolution, requiring all persons having a claim against the corporation other than a claim against the corporation in a pending action, suit or proceeding to which the corporation is a party to present their claims against the corporation in accordance with such notice. ■ Such notice shall state:

a. That all such claims (must be presented in writing) and (must contain sufficient information reasonably to inform the corporation or successor entity of the identity of the claimant and the substance of the claim);

b. The mailing address to which such a claim must be sent;

c. The date by which such a claim must be received by the corporation or successor entity, which date shall be no earlier than 60 days from the date thereof; and

d. That such claim will be barred if not received by the date referred to in paragraph (a)(1)c. of this section; and

e. That the corporation or a successor entity may make distributions to other claimants and the corporation's stockholders or persons interested as having been such without further notice to the claimant; and

f. The aggregate amount, on an annual basis, of all distributions made by the corporation to its stockholders for each of the 3 years prior to the date the corporation dissolved.

Such notice shall also be published at least once a week for 2 consecutive weeks in a newspaper of general circulation (in the county in which the office of the corporation's last registered agent in this State is located) and (in the corporation's principal place of business) and, (in the case of a corporation having $10,000,000 or more in total assets at the time of its dissolution, at least once in all editions of a daily newspaper with a national circulation). ■ On or before the date of the first publication of such notice, the corporation or successor entity shall mail a copy of such notice by certified or registered mail, return receipt requested, to each known claimant of the corporation (including persons with claims asserted against the corporation in a pending action, suit or proceeding to which the corporation is a party).

(2) [Then] Any claim against the corporation required to be presented pursuant to this subsection is barred if a claimant who was given actual notice under this subsection does not present the claim to the dissolved corporation or successor entity by the date referred to in paragraph (a)(1)c. of this section.

(3) A corporation or successor entity may reject, in whole or in part, any claim made by a claimant pursuant to this subsection by mailing notice of such rejection by certified or registered mail, return receipt requested, to the claimant (within 90 days after receipt of such claim) and, in all events, (at least 150 days before the expiration of the period described in § 278 of this title); provided however, that in the case of a claim filed pursuant to § 295 of this title against a corporation or successor entity for which a receiver or trustee has been appointed by the Court of Chancery the time period shall be as provided in § 296 of this title, and the 30-day appeal period provided for in § 296 of this title shall be applicable. ■ A notice sent by a corporation or successor entity pursuant to this subsection shall state that any claim rejected therein will be barred if an action, suit or proceeding with respect to the claim is not commenced within 120 days of the date thereof, and shall be accompanied by (a copy of §§ 278-283 of this title) and, (in the case of a notice sent by a court-appointed receiver or trustee and as to which a claim has been filed pursuant to § 295 of this title, copies of §§ 295 and 296 of this title).

(4) [Then] A claim against a corporation is barred if a claimant whose claim is rejected pursuant to paragraph (a)(3) of this section does not commence an action, suit or proceeding with respect to the claim no later than 120 days after the mailing of the rejection notice.

(b)(1) A corporation or successor entity electing to follow the procedures described in subsection (a) of this section shall also give notice of the dissolution of the corporation to persons with contractual claims (contingent upon the occurrence or nonoccurrence of future events) or (otherwise conditional or unmatured, and request that such persons present such claims in accordance with the terms of such notice. ■ Provided however, that as used in this section and in § 281 of this title, the term "contractual claims" shall not include any implied warranty as to any product manufactured, sold, distributed or handled by the dissolved corporation. ■ Such notice shall be in substantially the form, and sent and published in the same manner, as described in paragraph (a)(1) of this section.

(2) The corporation or successor entity shall offer any claimant on a contract whose claim is contingent, conditional or unmatured such security as the corporation or

successor entity determines is sufficient to provide compensation to the claimant if the claim matures. ■ The corporation [or] successor entity shall mail such offer to the claimant by certified or registered mail, return receipt requested, (within 90 days of receipt of such claim) and, (in all events, at least 150 days before the expiration of the period described in § 278 of this title). ■ If the claimant offered such security does not deliver in writing to the corporation or successor entity a notice rejecting the offer within 120 days after receipt of such offer for security, [then] the claimant shall be deemed to have accepted such security as the sole source from which to satisfy the claim against the corporation.

(c)(1) A corporation [or] successor entity which has given notice in accordance with subsection (a) of this section shall petition the Court of Chancery to determine the amount and form of security that will be reasonably likely to be sufficient to provide compensation for (any claim against the corporation which is the subject of a pending action, suit or proceeding to which the corporation is a party) ◄other than a claim barred pursuant to subsection (a) of this section▶.

(2) A corporation [or] successor entity which has given notice in accordance with subsections (a) and (b) of this section shall petition the Court of Chancery to determine the amount and form of security that will be sufficient to provide compensation to (any claimant who has rejected the offer for security made pursuant to paragraph (b)(2) of this section).

(3) A corporation [or] successor entity which has given notice in accordance with subsection (a) of this section shall petition the Court of Chancery to determine the amount and form of security which will be reasonably likely to be sufficient to provide compensation for claims (that have not been made known to the corporation) [or] (that have not arisen) but that, based on facts known to the corporation or successor entity, are likely to arise or to become known to the corporation or successor entity within (5 years after the date of dissolution) [or] (such longer period of time as the Court of Chancery may determine not to exceed 10 years after the date of dissolution). ■ The Court of Chancery may appoint a guardian ad litem in respect of any such proceeding brought under this subsection. ■ The reasonable fees and expenses of such guardian, including all reasonable expert witness fees, shall be paid by the petitioner in such proceeding.

(d) The giving of any notice or making of any offer pursuant to this section shall not revive any claim then barred [or] constitute acknowledgment by the corporation or successor entity that any person to whom such notice is sent is a proper claimant [and] shall not operate as a waiver of any defense or counterclaim in respect of any claim asserted by any person to whom such notice is sent.

(e) As used in this section, the term "successor entity" shall include any trust, receivership or other legal entity governed by the laws of this State to which the remaining assets and liabilities of a dissolved corporation are transferred and which exists solely (for the purposes of prosecuting and defending suits, by or against the dissolved corporation, enabling the dissolved corporation to settle and close the business of the dissolved corporation, to dispose of and convey the property of the dissolved corporation, to discharge the liabilities of the dissolved corporation and to distribute to the dissolved corporation's stockholders any remaining assets), but not (for the purpose of continuing the business for which the dissolved corporation was organized).

(f) The time periods and notice requirements of this section shall, in the case of a corporation or successor entity for which a receiver or trustee has been appointed by the Court of Chancery, be subject to variation by, or in the manner provided in, the Rules of the Court of Chancery.

(g) In the case of a nonstock corporation, any notice referred to in the last sentence of paragraph (a)(3) of this section shall include a copy of § 114 of this title. ■ In the case of a nonprofit nonstock corporation, provisions of this section regarding distributions to members shall not apply to the extent that those provisions conflict (with any other applicable law) or (with that corporation's certificate of incorporation or bylaws).

§ 281. Payment and distribution to claimants and stockholders.

(a) A dissolved corporation or successor entity which has followed the procedures described in § 280 of this title:

(1) Shall pay the claims made and not rejected in accordance with § 280(a) of this title,

(2) Shall post the security offered and not rejected pursuant to § 280(b)(2) of this title,

(3) Shall post any security ordered by the Court of Chancery in any proceeding under § 280(c) of this title, and

(4) Shall pay or make provision for all other claims that are mature, known and uncontested or that have been finally determined to be owing by the corporation or such successor entity.

Such claims or obligations shall be paid in full and any such provision for payment shall be made in full if there are sufficient assets. ■ If there are insufficient assets, [then] such claims and obligations shall be paid or provided for (according to their priority), and, (among claims of equal priority, ratably) to the extent of assets legally available therefor. ■ Any remaining assets shall be distributed to the stockholders of the dissolved corporation; provided, however, that such distribution shall not be made before the expiration of 150 days from the date of the last notice of rejections given pursuant to § 280(a)(3) of this title. ■ In the absence of actual fraud, the judgment of (the directors of the dissolved corporation) or (the governing persons of such successor entity) as to the provision made for the payment of all obligations under paragraph (a)(4) of this section shall be conclusive.

(b) A dissolved corporation or successor entity which has not followed the procedures described in § 280 of this title shall, prior to the expiration of the period described in § 278 of this title, adopt a plan of distribution pursuant to which the dissolved corporation or successor entity **(i)** shall pay or make reasonable provision to pay all claims and obligations, including all contingent, conditional or unmatured contractual claims known to the corporation or such successor entity, **(ii)** shall make such provision as will be reasonably likely to be sufficient to provide compensation for any claim against the corporation which is the subject of a pending action, suit or proceeding to which the corporation is a party and **(iii)** shall make such provision as will be reasonably likely to be sufficient to provide compensation for claims that have not been made known to the corporation or that have not arisen but that, based on facts known to the corporation or successor entity, are likely to arise or to become known to the corporation or successor entity within 10 years after the date of dissolution. ∎ **[Then]** The plan of distribution <u>shall provide</u> that such claims shall be paid in full and any such provision for payment made shall be made in full **if** <u>there are sufficient assets</u>. ∎ **If** <u>there are insufficient assets,</u> **[then]** <u>such plan shall provide</u> that such claims and obligations shall be paid or provided for (according to their priority) and, (among claims of equal priority, ratably) to the extent of assets legally available therefor. ∎ <u>Any remaining assets shall be distributed</u> to the stockholders of the dissolved corporation.

(c) <u>Directors</u> of a dissolved corporation or <u>governing persons</u> of a successor entity which has complied with subsection (a) or (b) of this section <u>shall not be personally liable</u> to the claimants of the dissolved corporation.

(d) As used in this section, the term "<u>successor entity" has the meaning set forth</u> in § 280(e) of this title.

(e) The term "<u>priority,</u>" as used in this section, <u>does not refer</u> either (to the order of payments set forth in paragraph (a)(1)-(4) of this section) or (to the relative times at which any claims mature or are reduced to judgment).

(f) In the case of a nonprofit nonstock corporation, <u>provisions</u> of this section regarding distributions to members <u>shall not apply</u> to the extent that those provisions conflict (with any other applicable law) or (with that corporation's certificate of incorporation or bylaws).

§ 282. Liability of stockholders of dissolved corporations.

(a) <u>A stockholder</u> of a dissolved corporation the assets of which were distributed pursuant to § 281(a) or (b) of this title <u>shall not be liable</u> for any claim against the corporation in an amount in excess of (such stockholder's pro rata share of the claim) or (the amount so distributed to such stockholder), whichever is less.

(b) <u>A stockholder</u> of a dissolved corporation the assets of which were distributed pursuant to § 281(a) of this title <u>shall not be liable</u> for any claim against the corporation on which (an action, suit or proceeding is not begun prior to the expiration of the period described in § 278 of this title).

(c) <u>The aggregate liability</u> of any stockholder of a dissolved corporation for claims against the dissolved corporation <u>shall not exceed the amount distributed</u> to such stockholder in dissolution.

§ 283. Jurisdiction.

<u>The Court of Chancery shall have jurisdiction</u> of any application prescribed in this subchapter and of all questions arising in the proceedings thereon, and <u>may make such orders and decrees and issue injunctions</u> therein as justice and equity shall require.

§ 284. Revocation or forfeiture of charter; proceedings.

(a) Upon motion by the Attorney General, the <u>Court of Chancery shall have jurisdiction</u> to revoke or forfeit the charter of any corporation for abuse, misuse or nonuse of its corporate powers, privileges or franchises. ■ The Attorney General shall proceed for this purpose by complaint in the Court of Chancery.

(b) The Court of Chancery shall have power, by appointment of trustees, receivers or otherwise, to administer and wind up the affairs of any corporation whose charter shall be revoked or forfeited by the Court of Chancery under this section, [and] to make such orders and decrees with respect thereto as shall be just and equitable respecting its affairs and assets and the rights of its stockholders and creditors.

(c) No proceeding shall be instituted under this section for nonuse of any corporation's powers, privileges or franchises during the first 2 years after its incorporation.

§ 285. Dissolution or forfeiture of charter by decree of court; filing.

Whenever any corporation is dissolved [or] its charter forfeited by decree or judgment of the Court of Chancery, **[then]** the decree or judgment shall be forthwith filed by the Register in Chancery of the county in which the decree or judgment was entered, in the office of the Secretary of State, [and] a note thereof shall be made by the Secretary of State on the corporation's charter or certificate of incorporation and on the index thereof.

Subchapter XI. Insolvency; Receivers and Trustees

§ 291. Receivers for insolvent corporations; appointment and powers.

Whenever a corporation shall be insolvent, **[then]** the Court of Chancery, on the application of any creditor or stockholder thereof, may, at any time, appoint 1 or more persons **(**to be receivers of and for the corporation**)**, **(**to take charge of its assets, estate, effects, business and affairs, and to collect the outstanding debts, claims, and property due and belonging to the corporation, with power to prosecute and defend, in the name of the corporation or otherwise, all claims or suits**)**, **(**to appoint an agent or agents under them**)**, and **(**to do all other acts which might be done by the corporation and which may be necessary or proper**)**. ■ The powers of the receivers shall be such [and] shall continue so long as the Court shall deem necessary.

§ 292. Title to property; filing order of appointment; exception.

(a) Trustees or receivers appointed by the Court of Chancery of and for any corporation, [and] their respective survivors and successors, shall, upon their appointment and qualification or upon the death, resignation or discharge of any co-trustee or co-receiver, be vested by operation of law and without any act or deed, with the title of the corporation to **(**all of its property, real, personal or mixed of whatsoever nature, kind, class or description, and wheresoever situate**)**, ◀except real estate situate outside this State▶.

(b) Trustees or receivers appointed by the Court of Chancery shall, within 20 days from the date of their qualification, file in the office of the recorder in each county in this State, in which any real estate belonging to the corporation may be situated, a certified copy of the order of their appointment [and] evidence of their qualification.

(c) This section shall not apply to receivers appointed pendente lite.

§ 293. Notices to stockholders and creditors.

All notices required to be given to stockholders and creditors in any action in which a receiver or trustee for a corporation was appointed shall be given by the Register in Chancery, ◂unless otherwise ordered by the Court of Chancery▸.

§ 294. Receivers or trustees; inventory; list of debts and report.

Trustees or receivers shall, as soon as convenient, file in the office of the Register in Chancery of the county in which the proceeding is pending, a full and complete itemized inventory of all the assets of the corporation which shall show (their nature and probable value), and (an account of all debts due from and to it), as nearly as the same can be ascertained. ■ They shall make a report to the Court of their proceedings, whenever and as often as the Court shall direct.

§ 295. Creditors' proofs of claims; when barred; notice.

All creditors shall make proof under oath of their respective claims against the corporation, and cause the same to be filed in the office of the Register in Chancery of the county in which the proceeding is pending (within the time fixed by) and (in accordance with) the procedure established by the rules of the Court of Chancery. ■ All creditors and claimants failing to do so, within the time limited by this section, or the time prescribed by the order of the Court, may, by direction of the Court, be barred from participating in the distribution of the assets of the corporation. ■ The Court may also prescribe what notice, by publication or otherwise, shall be given to the creditors of the time fixed for the filing and making proof of claims.

§ 296. Adjudication of claims; appeal.

(a) The Register in Chancery, immediately upon the expiration of the time fixed for the filing of claims, in compliance with § 295 of this title, shall notify the trustee or receiver of the filing of the claims, and the trustee or receiver, within 30 days after receiving the notice, shall inspect the claims, and **if** the trustee or receiver or any creditor shall not be satisfied with the validity or correctness of the same, or any of them, **[then]** the trustee or receiver shall forthwith notify the creditors whose claims are disputed of such trustee's or receiver's decision. ■ The trustee or receiver shall require all creditors whose claims are disputed to submit themselves to such examination in relation to their claims as the trustee or receiver shall direct, and the creditors shall produce such books and papers relating to their claims as shall be required. ■ The trustee or receiver shall have power to examine, under oath or affirmation, all witnesses produced before such trustee or receiver touching the claims, and shall pass upon and allow or disallow the claims, or any part thereof, and notify the claimants of such trustee's or receiver's determination.

(b) Every creditor or claimant who shall have received notice from the receiver or trustee that such creditor's or claimant's claim has been disallowed in whole or in part may appeal to the Court of Chancery within 30 days thereafter. ■ The Court, after hearing, shall determine the rights of the parties.

Subchapter XI. Insolvency; Receivers and Trustees   § 297

§ 297. Sale of perishable or deteriorating property.

Whenever the property of a corporation is at the time of the appointment of a receiver or trustee encumbered with liens of any character, [and] the validity, extent [or] legality of any lien is disputed [or] brought in question, [and] the property of the corporation is of a character which will deteriorate in value pending the litigation respecting the lien, **[then]** the Court of Chancery may order the receiver or trustee to (sell the property of the corporation, clear of all encumbrances, at public or private sale, for the best price that can be obtained therefor), and (pay the net proceeds arising from the sale thereof after deducting the costs of the sale into the Court), there to remain subject to the order of the Court, and to be disposed of as the Court shall direct.

§ 298. Compensation, costs and expenses of receiver or trustee.

The Court of Chancery, before making distribution of the assets of a corporation among the creditors or stockholders thereof, shall allow a reasonable compensation to the receiver or trustee for such receiver's or trustee's services, [and] the costs and expenses incurred in and about the execution of such receiver's or trustee's trust, [and] the costs of the proceedings in the Court, to be first paid out of the assets.

§ 299. Substitution of trustee or receiver as party; abatement of actions.

A trustee or receiver, upon application by such receiver or trustee in the court in which any suit is pending, shall be substituted as party plaintiff (in the place of the corporation) (in any suit or proceeding which was so pending at the time of such receiver's or trustee's appointment). ■ No action against a trustee or receiver of a corporation shall abate by reason of such receiver's or trustee's death, [but], upon suggestion of the facts on the record, shall be continued against (such receiver's or trustee's successor) or (against the corporation in case no new trustee or receiver is appointed).

§ 300. Employee's lien for wages when corporation insolvent.

Whenever any corporation of this State, or any foreign corporation doing business in this State, shall become insolvent, **[then]** the employees doing labor or service of whatever character in the regular employ of the corporation, shall have a lien upon the assets thereof for the amount of the wages due to them, not exceeding 2 months' wages respectively, which shall be paid prior to any other debt or debts of the corporation. ■ The word "employee" shall not be construed to include any of the officers of the corporation.

§ 301. Discontinuance of liquidation.

[Then] The liquidation of the assets and business of an insolvent corporation may be discontinued at any time during the liquidation proceedings [when] it is established that cause for liquidation no longer exists. ■ In such event the Court of Chancery in its discretion, and subject to such condition as it may deem appropriate, may dismiss the proceedings [and] direct the receiver or trustee to redeliver to the corporation all of its remaining property and assets.

§ 302. Compromise or arrangement between corporation and creditors or stockholders.

(a) **Whenever** the provision permitted by § 102(b)(2) of this title is included in the original certificate of incorporation of any corporation, [then] all persons who become creditors or stockholders thereof shall be deemed to have become such creditors or stockholders subject in all respects to that provision and the same shall be absolutely binding upon them. ∎ **Whenever** that provision is inserted in the certificate of incorporation of any such corporation by an amendment of its certificate [then] all persons who become creditors or stockholders of such corporation after such amendment shall be deemed to have become such creditors or stockholders subject in all respects to that provision and the same shall be absolutely binding upon them.

(b) The Court of Chancery may administer and enforce any compromise or arrangement made pursuant to the provision contained in § 102(b)(2) of this title and may restrain, pendente lite, all actions and proceedings against any corporation with respect to which the Court shall have begun the administration and enforcement of that provision and may appoint a temporary receiver for such corporation and may grant the receiver such powers as it deems proper, and may make and enforce such rules as it deems necessary for the exercise of such jurisdiction.

§ 303. Proceeding under the Federal Bankruptcy Code of the United States; effectuation.

(a) Any corporation of this State, an order for relief with respect to which has been entered pursuant to the Federal Bankruptcy Code, 11 U.S.C. § 101 et seq., or any successor statute, may put into effect and carry out any decrees and orders of the court or judge in such bankruptcy proceeding and may take any corporate action provided or directed by such decrees and orders, without further action by its directors or stockholders. ∎ Such power and authority may be exercised, and such corporate action may be taken, as may be directed by such decrees or orders, **(**by the trustee or trustees of such corporation appointed or elected in the bankruptcy proceeding (or a majority thereof)**)**, or if none be appointed or elected and acting, **(**by designated officers of the corporation**)**, or **(**by a representative appointed by the court or judge**)**, with like effect as if exercised and taken by unanimous action of the directors and stockholders of the corporation.

(b) Such corporation may, in the manner provided in subsection (a) of this section, but without limiting the generality or effect of the foregoing, alter, amend or repeal its bylaws; [and] constitute or reconstitute and classify or reclassify its board of directors, and name, constitute or appoint directors and officers in place of or in addition to all or some of the directors or officers then in office; [and] amend its certificate of incorporation, and make any change in its capital or capital stock, or any other amendment, change, or alteration, or provision, authorized by this chapter; [and] be dissolved, transfer all or part of its assets, merge or consolidate as permitted by this chapter, in which case, however, no stockholder shall have any statutory right of appraisal of such stockholder's stock; [and] change the location of its registered office, [and] change its registered agent, and remove or appoint any agent to receive service of process; [and] authorize and fix the terms, manner and conditions of, the issuance of bonds, debentures or other obligations, whether or not convertible into stock of any class, or bearing warrants or other evidences of optional rights to purchase or subscribe for stock of any class; or lease its property and franchises to any corporation, if permitted by law.

(c) A certificate of any amendment, change or alteration, or of dissolution, or any agreement of merger or consolidation, made by such corporation pursuant to the foregoing provisions, shall be filed with the Secretary of State in accordance with § 103 of this title, and, subject to § 103(d) of this title, shall thereupon become effective in accordance with its terms and the provisions hereof. ■ Such certificate, agreement of merger or other instrument shall be made, executed and acknowledged, as may be directed by such decrees or orders, by the trustee or trustees appointed or elected in the bankruptcy proceeding (or a majority thereof), or, if none be appointed or elected and acting, by the officers of the corporation, or by a representative appointed by the court or judge, and shall certify that provision for the making of such certificate, agreement or instrument is contained in a decree or order of a court or judge having jurisdiction of a proceeding under such Federal Bankruptcy Code or successor statute.

(d) This section shall cease to apply to such corporation upon the entry of a final decree in the bankruptcy proceeding closing the case and discharging the trustee or trustees, if any; provided however, that the closing of a case and discharge of trustee or trustees, if any, will not affect the validity of any act previously performed pursuant to subsections (a) through (c) of this section.

(e) On filing any certificate, agreement, report or other paper made or executed pursuant to this section, there shall be paid to the Secretary of State for the use of the State the same fees as are payable by corporations not in bankruptcy upon the filing of like certificates, agreements, reports or other papers.

Subchapter XII. Renewal, Revival, Extension and Restoration of Certificate of Incorporation or Charter

§ 311. Revocation of voluntary dissolution; restoration of expired certificate of incorporation.

(a) (At any time prior to the expiration of 3 years following the dissolution of a corporation pursuant to § 275 of this title or such longer period as the Court of Chancery may have directed pursuant to § 278 of this title**)**, or **(**at any time prior to the expiration of 3 years following the expiration of the time limited for the corporation's existence as provided in its certificate of incorporation or such longer period as the Court of Chancery may have directed pursuant to § 278 of this title**)**, a corporation may revoke the dissolution theretofore effected by it or restore its certificate of incorporation after it has expired by its own limitation in the following manner:

  (1) For purposes of this section, the term "stockholders" shall mean the stockholders of record on the date the dissolution became effective or the date of expiration by limitation.

  (2) The board of directors shall adopt a resolution **(**recommending that the dissolution be revoked in the case of a dissolution or that the certificate of incorporation be restored in the case of an expiration by limitation**)** and **(**directing that the question of the revocation or restoration be submitted to a vote at a special meeting of stockholders**)**.

(3) Notice of the special meeting of stockholders shall be given in accordance with § 222 of this title to each of the stockholders.

(4) At the meeting a vote of the stockholders shall be taken on a resolution to revoke the dissolution in the case of a dissolution or to restore the certificate of incorporation in the case of an expiration by limitation. ∎ **If** a majority of the stock of the corporation which was outstanding and entitled to vote upon a dissolution at the time of its dissolution , in the case of a revocation of dissolution, or which was outstanding and entitled to vote upon an amendment to the certificate of incorporation to change the period of the corporation's duration at the time of its expiration by limitation, in the case of a restoration, shall be voted for the resolution, **[then]** a certificate of revocation of dissolution or a certificate of restoration shall be executed, acknowledged and filed in accordance with § 103 of this title, which shall be specifically designated as a certificate of revocation of dissolution or a certificate of restoration in its heading and shall state:

    a. The name of the corporation;

    b. The address (which shall be stated in accordance with § 131(c) of this title) of the corporation's registered office in this State, and the name of its registered agent at such address;

    c. The names and respective addresses of its officers;

    d. The names and respective addresses of its directors;

    e. **(**That a majority of the stock of the corporation which was outstanding and entitled to vote upon a dissolution at the time of its dissolution have voted in favor of a resolution to revoke the dissolution, in the case of a revocation of dissolution**)**, or **(**that a majority of the stock of the corporation which was outstanding and entitled to vote upon an amendment to the certificate of incorporation to change the period of the corporation's duration at the time of its expiration by limitation, in the case of a restoration, have voted in favor of a resolution to restore the certificate of incorporation**)**; or, if it be the fact, **(**that, in lieu of a meeting and vote of stockholders, the stockholders have given their written consent to the revocation or restoration in accordance with § 228 of this title**)**; and

    f. In the case of a restoration, the new specified date limiting the duration of the corporation's existence or that the corporation shall have perpetual existence.

(b) Upon the effective time of the filing in the office of the Secretary of State of the certificate of revocation of dissolution or the certificate of restoration, the revocation of the dissolution or the restoration of the corporation shall become effective and the corporation may again carry on its business.

(c) Upon the effectiveness of the revocation of the dissolution or the restoration of the corporation as provided in subsection (b) of this section, the provisions of § 211(c) of this title shall govern, and the period of time the corporation was in dissolution or was expired by limitation shall be included within the calculation of the 30-day and 13-month periods to which § 211(c) of this title refers. ∎ An election of directors, however, may be held at the special meeting of stockholders to which subsection (a) of this section refers, and in that event, that meeting of stockholders shall be deemed an annual meeting of stockholders for purposes of § 211(c) of this title.

(d) If after the dissolution became effective or after the expiration by limitation any other corporation organized under the laws of this State shall have adopted the same name as the corporation, or shall have adopted a name so nearly similar thereto as not to distinguish it from the corporation, or any foreign corporation shall have qualified to do business in this State under the same name as the corporation or under a name so nearly similar thereto as not to distinguish it from the corporation, **then**, in such case, the corporation shall not be reinstated under the same name which it bore when its dissolution became effective or it expired by limitation, but shall adopt and be reinstated or restored under some other name, and in such case the certificate to be filed under this section shall set forth the name borne by the corporation at the time its dissolution became effective or it expired by limitation and the new name under which the corporation is to be reinstated or restored.

(e) Nothing in this section shall be construed to affect the jurisdiction or power of the Court of Chancery under § 279 or § 280 of this title.

(f) (At any time prior to the expiration of 3 years following the dissolution of a nonstock corporation pursuant to § 276 of this title or such longer period as the Court of Chancery may have directed pursuant to § 278 of this title**)**, or **(**at any time prior to the expiration of 3 years following the expiration of the time limited for a nonstock corporation's existence as provided in its certificate of incorporation or such longer period as the Court of Chancery may have directed pursuant to § 278 of this title**)**, a nonstock corporation may revoke the dissolution theretofore effected by it or restore its certificate of incorporation after it has expired by limitation **(**in a manner analogous to that by which the dissolution was authorized**)** or, in the case of a restoration, **(**in the manner in which an amendment to the certificate of incorporation to change the period of the corporation's duration would have been authorized at the time of its expiration by limitation**)** including **(i)** if applicable, a vote of the members entitled to vote, if any, on the dissolution or the amendment and **(ii)** the filing of a certificate of revocation of dissolution or a certificate of restoration containing information comparable to that required by paragraph (a)(4) of this section. ■ Notwithstanding the foregoing, only subsections (b), (d), and (e) of this section shall apply to nonstock corporations.

(g) Any corporation that revokes its dissolution or restores its certificate of incorporation pursuant to this section shall file all annual franchise tax reports that the corporation would have had to file if it had not dissolved or expired and shall pay all franchise taxes that the corporation would have had to pay if it had not dissolved or expired. ■ No payment made pursuant to this subsection shall reduce the amount of franchise tax due under Chapter 5 of this title for the year in which such revocation or restoration is effected.

§ 312. Revival of certificate of incorporation.

(a) As used in this section, the term "certificate of incorporation" includes the charter of a corporation organized under any special act or any law of this State.

(b) Any corporation whose certificate of incorporation has become forfeited or void pursuant to this title or whose certificate of incorporation has been revived, but, through failure to comply strictly with the provisions of this chapter, the validity of whose revival

§ 312 Subchapter XII. Renewal, Revival, Extension and Restoration of Certificate of Incorporation or Charter

has been brought into question, <u>may</u> at any time <u>procure a revival</u> of its certificate of incorporation, together with all the rights, franchises, privileges and immunities and subject to all of its duties, debts and liabilities which had been secured or imposed by its original certificate of incorporation and all amendments thereto, by complying with the requirements of this section. ■ Notwithstanding the foregoing, <u>this section shall not be applicable</u> to a corporation whose certificate of incorporation has been revoked or forfeited pursuant to § 284 of this title.

(c) <u>The revival</u> of the certificate of incorporation <u>may be procured</u> **(**as authorized by the board of directors or members of the governing body of the corporation in accordance with subsection(h) of this section**)** and **(**by executing, acknowledging and filing a certificate of revival in accordance with § 103 of this title**)**.

(d) <u>The certificate required</u> by subsection (c) of this section <u>shall state</u>:

>**(1)** <u>The date</u> of filing of the corporation's original certificate of incorporation; <u>the name</u> under which the corporation was originally incorporated; <u>the name</u> of the corporation at the time its certificate of incorporation became forfeited or void pursuant to this title; [and] the new name under which the corporation is to be revived to the extent required by subsection (f) of this section;

>**(2)** <u>The address</u> (which shall be stated in accordance with § 131(c) of this title) of the corporation's registered office in this State and the name of its registered agent at such address;

>**(3)** That the corporation desiring to be revived and so reviving its certificate of incorporation was organized under the laws of this State;

>**(4)** <u>The date</u> when the certificate of incorporation became forfeited or void pursuant to this title, or that the validity of any revival has been brought into question; [and]

>**(5)** That the certificate of revival is filed by authority of the board of directors or members of the governing body of the corporation in accordance with subsection (h) of this section.

(e) Upon the filing of the certificate in accordance with § 103 of this title <u>the corporation shall be revived</u> with the same force and effect as if its certificate of incorporation **(**had not been forfeited or void pursuant to this title**)**. ■ <u>Such revival shall validate all contracts, acts, matters and things made, done and performed</u> within the scope of its certificate of incorporation by the corporation, its directors or members of its governing body, officers, agents and stockholders or members **(**during the time when its certificate of incorporation was forfeited or void pursuant to this title**)**, with the same force and effect and to all intents and purposes as if the certificate of incorporation had at all times remained in full force and effect. ■ <u>All real and personal property, rights and credits</u>, which belonged to the corporation at the time its certificate of incorporation became forfeited or void pursuant to this title and which were not disposed of prior to the time of its revival, [and] <u>all real and personal property, rights and credits</u> acquired by the corporation after its certificate of incorporation became forfeited or void pursuant to this title <u>shall be vested</u> in the corporation, after its revival, as if its certificate of incorporation had at all times remained in full force and effect, [and] <u>the corporation</u> after its revival <u>shall be as exclusively liable</u> for all contracts, acts, matters and things made, done or performed in its name and on its behalf by its directors or members of its governing body, officers, agents and stockholders or members prior to its revival, as if its certificate of incorporation had at all times remained in full force and effect.

(f) If, since the certificate of incorporation became forfeited or void pursuant to this title, any other corporation organized under the laws of this State shall have adopted the same name as the corporation sought to be revived or shall have adopted a name so nearly similar thereto as not to distinguish it from the corporation to be revived or any foreign corporation qualified in accordance with § 371 of this title shall have adopted the same name as the corporation sought to be revived or shall have adopted a name so nearly similar thereto as not to distinguish it from the corporation to be revived, **then** in such case the corporation to be revived shall not be revived under the same name which it bore when its certificate of incorporation became forfeited or void pursuant to this title, but shall be revived under some other name as set forth in the certificate to be filed pursuant to subsection (c) of this section.

(g) Any corporation that revives its certificate of incorporation under this chapter shall pay to this State a sum equal to (all franchise taxes, penalties and interest thereon due at the time its certificate of incorporation became forfeited or void pursuant to this title; provided, however, that any corporation that revives its certificate of incorporation under this chapter whose certificate of incorporation has been forfeited or void for more than 5 years shall, in lieu of the payment of the franchise taxes and penalties otherwise required by this subsection, pay a sum equal to (3 times the amount of the annual franchise tax that would be due and payable by such corporation for the year in which the revival is effected, computed at the then current rate of taxation). ■ No payment made pursuant to this subsection shall reduce the amount of franchise tax due under Chapter 5 of this title for the year in which the revival is effected.

(h) For purposes of this section and § 502(a) of this title, the board of directors or governing body of the corporation shall be comprised of the persons, who, but for the certificate of incorporation having become forfeited or void pursuant to this title, would be the duly elected or appointed directors or members of the governing body of the corporation. ■ **[Then]** The requirement for authorization by the board of directors under subsection (c) of this section shall be satisfied if a majority of the directors or members of the governing body then in office, even though less than a quorum, or the sole director or member of the governing body then in office, authorizes the revival of the certificate of incorporation of the corporation and the filing of the certificate required by subsection (c) of this section. ■ **In any case where** there shall be no directors of the corporation available for the purposes aforesaid, **[then]** the stockholders may elect a full board of directors, as provided by the bylaws of the corporation, and the board so elected may then authorize the revival of the certificate of incorporation of the corporation and the filing of the certificate required by subsection (c) of this section. ■ A special meeting of the stockholders for the purpose of electing directors may be called by any officer or stockholder upon notice given in accordance with § 222 of this title. ■ For purposes of this section, the bylaws shall be the bylaws of the corporation that, but for the certificate of incorporation having become forfeited or void pursuant to this title, would be the duly adopted bylaws of the corporation.

(i) After a revival of the certificate of incorporation of the corporation shall have been effected, **[then]** the provisions of § 211(c) of this title shall govern and the period of time during which the certificate of incorporation of the corporation was forfeited or void

§ 313 Subchapter XII. Renewal, Revival, Extension and Restoration of Certificate of Incorporation or Charter

pursuant to this title shall be included within the calculation of the 30-day and 13-month periods to which § 211(c) of this title refers. ■ A special meeting of stockholders held in accordance with subsection (h) of this section shall be deemed an annual meeting of stockholders for purposes of § 211(c) of this title.

(j) ❨Except as otherwise provided in § 313 of this title❩, **whenever** it shall be desired to revive the certificate of incorporation of any nonstock corporation, **[then]** the governing body shall perform all the acts necessary for the revival of the certificate of incorporation of the corporation which are performed by the board of directors in the case of a corporation having capital stock, and the members of any nonstock corporation who are entitled to vote for the election of members of its governing body and any other members entitled to vote for dissolution under the certificate of incorporation or the bylaws of such corporation, shall perform all the acts necessary for the revival of the certificate of incorporation of the corporation which are performed by the stockholders in the case of a corporation having capital stock. ■ ❨Except as otherwise provided in § 313 of this title❩, in all other respects, the procedure for the revival of the certificate of incorporation of a nonstock corporation shall conform, as nearly as may be applicable, to the procedure prescribed in this section for the revival of the certificate of incorporation of a corporation having capital stock; provided, however, that subsection (i) of this section shall not apply to nonstock corporations.

§ 313. Revival of certificate of incorporation or charter of exempt corporations.

(a) Every exempt corporation whose certificate of incorporation or charter has become forfeited, pursuant to § 136 (b) of this title for failure to obtain a registered agent, or inoperative and void, by operation of § 510 of this title for failure to file annual franchise tax reports required, and for failure to pay taxes or penalties from which it would have been exempt if the reports had been filed, shall be deemed to have filed all the reports and be relieved of all the taxes and penalties, ❨upon satisfactory proof submitted to the Secretary of State of its right to be classified as an exempt corporation pursuant to § 501(b) of this title❩, and ❨upon filing with the Secretary of State a certificate of revival in manner and form as required by § 312 of this title❩.

(b) Upon ❨the filing by the corporation of the proof of classification as required by subsection (a) of this section❩, ❨the filing of the certificate of revival❩ and ❨payment of the required filing fees❩, the corporation shall be revived with the same force and effect as provided in § 312(e) of this title for other corporations.

(c) As used in this section, the term "exempt corporation" shall have the meaning given to it in § 501(b) of this title. ■ Nothing contained in this section relieves any exempt corporation from filing the annual report required by § 502 of this title.

§ 314. Status of corporation.

Any corporation desiring to renew, extend and continue its corporate existence shall, upon complying with applicable constitutional provisions of this State, continue as provided in its certificate effecting the foregoing as a corporation and shall, in addition to the rights, privileges and immunities conferred by its charter, possess and enjoy all the benefits of this chapter, which are applicable to the nature of its business, and shall be subject to the restrictions and liabilities by this chapter imposed on such corporations.

Subchapter XIII. Suits Against Corporations, Directors, Officers or Stockholders

§ 321. Service of process on corporations.

(a) Service of legal process upon any corporation of this State shall be made **(**by delivering a copy personally to any officer or director of the corporation in this State, or the registered agent of the corporation in this State**)**, or **(**by leaving it at the dwelling house or usual place of abode in this State of any officer, director or registered agent (if the registered agent be an individual), or at the registered office or other place of business of the corporation in this State**)**. ■ **If** the registered agent be a corporation, [then] service of process upon it as such agent may be made by serving, in this State, a copy thereof on the president, vice-president, secretary, assistant secretary or any director of the corporate registered agent. ■ Service by copy left at the dwelling house or usual place of abode of any officer, director or registered agent, or at the registered office or other place of business of the corporation in this State, to be effective must be delivered thereat at least 6 days before the return date of the process, and in the presence of an adult person, and the officer serving the process shall distinctly state the manner of service in such person's return thereto. ■ Process returnable forthwith must be delivered personally to the officer, director or registered agent.

(b) In case the officer whose duty it is to serve legal process cannot by due diligence serve the process in any manner provided for by subsection (a) of this section, [then] it shall be lawful to serve the process against the corporation upon the Secretary of State, and such service shall be as effectual for all intents and purposes as if made in any of the ways provided for in subsection (a) of this section. ■ Process may be served upon the Secretary of State under this subsection by means of electronic transmission but only as prescribed by the Secretary of State. ■ The Secretary of State is authorized to issue such rules and regulations with respect to such service as the Secretary of State deems necessary or appropriate. ■ **In the event that** service is effected through the Secretary of State in accordance with this subsection, **[then]** the Secretary of State shall forthwith notify the corporation by letter, directed to the corporation at its principal place of business as it appears on the records relating to such corporation on file with the Secretary of State or, if no such address appears, at its last registered office. ■ Such letter shall be sent by a mail or courier service that includes a record of mailing or deposit with the courier and a record of delivery evidenced by the signature of the recipient. ■ Such letter shall enclose a copy of the process and any other papers served on the Secretary of State pursuant to this subsection. ■ It shall be the duty of the plaintiff in the event of such service **(**to serve process and any other papers in duplicate**)**, **(**to notify the Secretary of State that service is being effected pursuant to this subsection**)**, and **(**to pay the Secretary of State the sum of $50 for the use of the State, which sum shall be taxed as part of the costs in the proceeding if the plaintiff shall prevail therein**)**. ■ The Secretary of State shall maintain an alphabetical record of any such service setting forth (the name of the plaintiff and defendant), (the title, docket number and nature of the proceeding in which process has been served upon the Secretary of State), (the fact that service has been effected pursuant to this subsection), (the return date thereof), and (the day and hour when the service was made). ■ The Secretary of State shall not be required to retain such information for a period longer than 5 years from receipt of the service of process.

(c) Service upon corporations may also be made in accordance with § 3111 of Title 10 or any other statute or rule of court.

§ 322. Failure of corporation to obey order of court; appointment of receiver.

Whenever any corporation shall refuse, fail or neglect to obey any order or decree of any court of this State within the time fixed by the court for its observance, [then] such refusal, failure or neglect shall be a sufficient ground for the appointment of a receiver of the corporation by the Court of Chancery. ■ If the corporation be a foreign corporation, [then] such refusal, failure or neglect shall be a sufficient ground for the appointment of a receiver of the assets of the corporation within this State.

§ 323. Failure of corporation to obey writ of mandamus; quo warranto proceedings for forfeiture of charter.

If any corporation fails to obey the mandate of any peremptory writ of mandamus issued by a court of competent jurisdiction of this State for a period of 30 days after the serving of the writ upon the corporation in any manner as provided by the laws of this State for the service of writs, [then] any party in interest in the proceeding in which the writ of mandamus issued may file a statement of such fact prepared by such party or such party's attorney with the Attorney General of this State, and it shall thereupon be the duty of the Attorney General to forthwith commence proceedings of quo warranto against the corporation in a court of competent jurisdiction, and the court, upon competent proof of such state of facts and proper proceedings had in such proceeding in quo warranto, shall decree the charter of the corporation forfeited.

§ 324. Attachment of shares of stock or any option, right or interest therein; procedure; sale; title upon sale; proceeds.

(a) The shares of any person in any corporation with all the rights thereto belonging, or any person's option to acquire the shares, or such person's right or interest in the shares, may be attached under this section for debt, or other demands, if such person appears on the books of the corporation to hold or own such shares, option, right or interest. ■ So many of the shares, or so much of the option, right or interest therein may be sold at public sale to the highest bidder, as shall be sufficient to satisfy the debt, or other demand, interest and costs, (upon an order issued therefor by the court from which the attachment process issued), and (after such notice as is required for sales upon execution process). ■ ◄Except as to an uncertificated security as defined in § 8-102 of Title 6►, the attachment is not laid and no order of sale shall issue unless § 8-112 of Title 6 has been satisfied. ■ [Then] No order of sale shall be issued until after final judgment shall have been rendered in any case. ■ If the debtor lives out of the county, [then] a copy of the order shall be sent by registered or certified mail, return receipt requested, to such debtor's last known address, and shall

Subchapter XIII. Suits Against Corporations, Directors, Officers or Stockholders   § 325

also be published in a newspaper published in the county of such debtor's last known residence, if there be any, 10 days before the sale; [and] if the debtor be a nonresident of this State [then] shall be mailed as aforesaid and published (at least twice for 2 successive weeks, the last publication to be at least 10 days before the sale), (in a newspaper published in the county where the attachment process issued). ■ If the shares of stock [or] any of them [or] the option to acquire shares [or] any such right or interest in shares, [or] any part of them, be so sold, [then] any assignment, [or] transfer thereof, by the debtor, after attachment, shall be void.

(b) When attachment process issues for shares of stock, or any option to acquire such or any right or interest in such, [then] a certified copy of the process shall be left in this State with any officer or director, or with the registered agent of the corporation. ■ Within 20 days after service of the process, the corporation shall serve upon the plaintiff a certificate of the number of shares held or owned by the debtor in the corporation, with the number or other marks distinguishing the same, [or] in the case the debtor appears on the books of the corporation to have an option to acquire shares of stock or any right or interest in any shares of stock of the corporation, [then] there shall be served upon the plaintiff within 20 days after service of the process a certificate setting forth any such option, right or interest in the shares of the corporation in the language and form in which the option, right or interest appears on the books of the corporation, (anything in the certificate of incorporation or bylaws of the corporation to the contrary notwithstanding). ■ Service upon a corporate registered agent may be made in the manner provided in § 321 of this title.

(c) If, after sale made and confirmed, a certified copy of the order of sale and return and the stock certificate, if any, be left with any officer or director or with the registered agent of the corporation, [then] the purchaser shall be thereby entitled to the shares [or] any option to acquire shares [or] any right or interest in shares so purchased, [and] all income, or dividends which may have been declared, or become payable thereon since the attachment laid. ■ Such sale, returned and confirmed, shall transfer the shares [or] the option to acquire shares [or] any right or interest in shares sold to the purchaser, (as fully as if the debtor, or defendant, had transferred the same to such purchaser according to the certificate of incorporation or bylaws of the corporation), (anything in the certificate of incorporation or bylaws to the contrary notwithstanding). ■ The court which issued the levy and confirmed the sale shall have the power (to make an order compelling the corporation, the shares of which were sold, to issue new certificates or uncertificated shares to the purchaser at the sale) and (to cancel the registration of the shares attached on the books of the corporation) upon the giving of an open end bond by such purchaser adequate to protect such corporation.

(d) The money arising (from the sale of the shares) or (from the sale of the option or right or interest) shall be applied and paid, by the public official receiving the same, as by law is directed as to the sale of personal property in cases of attachment.

§ 325. Actions against officers, directors or stockholders to enforce liability of corporation; unsatisfied judgment against corporation.

(a) When the officers, directors or stockholders of any corporation shall be liable by the provisions of this chapter to pay the debts of the corporation, or any part thereof, [then] any person to whom they are liable may have an action, at law or in equity, against any 1 or more of them, and the complaint shall state the claim against the corporation, and the ground on which the plaintiff expects to charge the defendants personally.

(b) [Then] No suit shall be brought against any officer, director or stockholder for any debt of a corporation of which such person is an officer, director or stockholder, **until** judgment be obtained therefor against the corporation and execution thereon returned unsatisfied.

§ 326. Action by officer, director or stockholder against corporation for corporate debt paid.

When any officer, director or stockholder shall pay any debt of a corporation for which such person is made liable by the provisions of this chapter, **[then]** such person may recover the amount so paid in an action against the corporation for money paid for its use, and in such action only the property of the corporation shall be liable to be taken, and not the property of any stockholder.

§ 327. Stockholder's derivative action; allegation of stock ownership.

In any derivative suit instituted by a stockholder of a corporation, it shall be averred in the complaint **(**that the plaintiff was a stockholder of the corporation at the time of the transaction of which such stockholder complains**)** or **(**that such stockholder's stock thereafter devolved upon such stockholder by operation of law**)**.

§ 328. Effect of liability of corporation on impairment of certain transactions.

The liability of a corporation of this State, or the stockholders, directors or officers thereof, or the rights or remedies of the creditors thereof, or of persons doing or transacting business with the corporation, shall not in any way be lessened or impaired **(**by the sale of its assets**)**, or **(**by the increase or decrease in the capital stock of the corporation**)**, or **(**by its merger or consolidation with 1 or more corporations**)** or **(**by any change or amendment in its certificate of incorporation**)**.

§ 329. Defective organization of corporation as defense.

(a) No corporation of this State and no person sued by any such corporation shall be permitted to assert the want of legal organization as a defense to any claim.

(b) [Then] This section shall not be construed to prevent judicial inquiry into the regularity or validity of the organization of a corporation, or its lawful possession of any corporate power it may assert in any other suit or proceeding **where** its corporate existence or the power to exercise the corporate rights it asserts is challenged, and evidence tending to sustain the challenge shall be admissible in any such suit or proceeding.

§ 330. Usury; pleading by corporation.

No corporation shall plead any statute against usury in any court of law or equity **(**in any suit instituted to enforce the payment of any bond, note or other evidence of indebtedness issued or assumed by it**)**.

Subchapter XIV. Close Corporations; Special Provisions

§ 341. Law applicable to close corporation.

(a) This subchapter applies to all close corporations, as defined in § 342 of this title. ■ Unless a corporation elects to become a close corporation under this subchapter in the manner prescribed in this subchapter, [then] it shall be subject in all respects to this chapter, ◀except this subchapter▶.

(b) This chapter shall be applicable to all close corporations, as defined in § 342 of this title, ◀except insofar as this subchapter otherwise provides▶.

§ 342. Close corporation defined; contents of certificate of incorporation.

(a) A close corporation is a corporation organized under this chapter whose certificate of incorporation contains the provisions required by § 102 of this title and, in addition, provides that:

(1) All of the corporation's issued stock of all classes, exclusive of treasury shares, shall be represented by certificates and shall be held of record by not more than a specified number of persons, not exceeding 30; and

(2) All of the issued stock of all classes shall be subject to 1 or more of the restrictions on transfer permitted by § 202 of this title; and

(3) The corporation shall make no offering of any of its stock of any class which would constitute a "public offering" within the meaning of the United States Securities Act of 1933 [15 U.S.C. § 77a et seq.] as it may be amended from time to time.

(b) The certificate of incorporation of a close corporation may set forth the qualifications of stockholders, either (by specifying classes of persons who shall be entitled to be holders of record of stock of any class), or (by specifying classes of persons who shall not be entitled to be holders of stock of any class or both).

(c) For purposes of determining the number of holders of record of the stock of a close corporation, stock which is held in joint or common tenancy or by the entireties shall be treated as held by 1 stockholder.

§ 343. Formation of a close corporation.

A close corporation shall be formed in accordance with §§ 101, 102 and 103 of this title, except that:

(1) Its certificate of incorporation shall contain a heading stating (the name of the corporation) and (that it is a close corporation); and

(2) Its certificate of incorporation shall contain the provisions required by § 342 of this title.

§ 344. Election of existing corporation to become a close corporation.

Any corporation organized under this chapter may become a close corporation under this subchapter by executing, acknowledging and filing, in accordance with § 103 of this title, a certificate of amendment of its certificate of incorporation which shall contain (a statement that it elects to become a close corporation), (the provisions required by § 342 of this title to appear in the certificate of incorporation of a close corporation), and (a heading stating the name of the corporation and that it is a close corporation). ■ Such amendment shall be adopted in accordance with the requirements of § 241 or 242 of this title, ◄except that it must be approved by a vote of the holders of record of at least 2/3 of the shares of each class of stock of the corporation which are outstanding►.

§ 345. Limitations on continuation of close corporation status.

[Then] A close corporation continues to be such and to be subject to this subchapter **until**:

(1) It files with the Secretary of State a certificate of amendment deleting from its certificate of incorporation the provisions required or permitted by § 342 of this title to be stated in the certificate of incorporation to qualify it as a close corporation; or

(2) Any 1 of the provisions or conditions required or permitted by § 342 of this title to be stated in a certificate of incorporation to qualify a corporation as a close corporation has in fact been breached and neither the corporation nor any of its stockholders takes the steps required by § 348 of this title to prevent such loss of status or to remedy such breach.

§ 346. Voluntary termination of close corporation status by amendment of certificate of incorporation; vote required.

(a) A corporation may voluntarily terminate its status as a close corporation and cease to be subject to this subchapter (by amending its certificate of incorporation to delete therefrom the additional provisions required or permitted by § 342 of this title to be stated in the certificate of incorporation of a close corporation). ■ Any such amendment shall be adopted and shall become effective in accordance with § 242 of this title, except that it must be approved by a vote of the holders of record of at least 2/3 of the shares of each class of stock of the corporation which are outstanding.

(b) The certificate of incorporation of a close corporation may provide that on any amendment to terminate its status as a close corporation, a vote greater than 2/3 or a vote of all shares of any class shall be required; and if the certificate of incorporation contains such a provision, [then] that provision shall not be amended, repealed or modified by any vote less than that required to terminate the corporation's status as a close corporation.

§ 347. Issuance or transfer of stock of a close corporation in breach of qualifying conditions.

(a) If stock of a close corporation is issued or transferred to any person who is not entitled under any provision of the certificate of incorporation permitted by § 342(b) of this title to be a holder of record of stock of such corporation, and if the certificate for such stock conspicuously notes the qualifications of the persons entitled to be holders of record thereof, [then] such person is conclusively presumed to have notice of the fact of such person's ineligibility to be a stockholder.

(b) If the certificate of incorporation of a close corporation states the number of persons, not in excess of 30, who are entitled to be holders of record of its stock, and if the certificate for such stock conspicuously states such number, and if the issuance or transfer of stock to any person would cause the stock to be held by more than such number of persons,

[then] the person to whom such stock is issued or transferred is conclusively presumed to have notice of this fact.

(c) If a stock certificate of any close corporation conspicuously notes the fact of a restriction on transfer of stock of the corporation, and the restriction is one which is permitted by § 202 of this title, [then] the transferee of the stock is conclusively presumed to have notice of the fact that such person has acquired stock in violation of the restriction, if such acquisition violates the restriction.

(d) Whenever any person to whom stock of a close corporation has been issued or transferred has, or is conclusively presumed under this section to have, notice either:

> (1) That such person is a person not eligible to be a holder of stock of the corporation, or
>
> (2) That transfer of stock to such person would cause the stock of the corporation to be held by more than the number of persons permitted by its certificate of incorporation to hold stock of the corporation, or
>
> (3) That the transfer of stock is in violation of a restriction on transfer of stock,

[then] the corporation may, at its option, refuse to register transfer of the stock into the name of the transferee.

(e) Subsection (d) of this section shall not be applicable if the transfer of stock, even though otherwise contrary to subsection (a), (b) or (c) of this section has been consented to by all the stockholders of the close corporation, or if the close corporation has amended its certificate of incorporation in accordance with § 346 of this title.

(f) The term "transfer," as used in this section, is not limited to a transfer for value.

(g) The provisions of this section do not in any way impair any rights of a transferee regarding any right to rescind the transaction or to recover under any applicable warranty express or implied.

§ 348. Involuntary termination of close corporation status; proceeding to prevent loss of status.

(a) If any event occurs as a result of which 1 or more of the provisions or conditions included in a close corporation's certificate of incorporation pursuant to § 342 of this title to qualify it as a close corporation has been breached, [then] the corporation's status as a close corporation under this subchapter shall terminate **unless**:

> (1) Within 30 days after the occurrence of the event, or within 30 days after the event has been discovered, whichever is later, the corporation files with the Secretary of State a certificate, executed and acknowledged in accordance with § 103 of this title, stating that a specified provision or condition included in its certificate of incorporation pursuant to § 342 of this title to qualify it as a close corporation has ceased to be applicable, and furnishes a copy of such certificate to each stockholder; and
>
> (2) The corporation concurrently with the filing of such certificate takes such steps as are necessary to correct the situation which threatens its status as a close corporation, including, without limitation, (the refusal to register the transfer of stock which has been wrongfully transferred as provided by § 347 of this title), or (a proceeding under subsection (b) of this section).

(b) The Court of Chancery, upon the suit of the corporation or any stockholder, shall have jurisdiction to issue all orders necessary (to prevent the corporation from losing its status as a close corporation), or (to restore its status as a close corporation by enjoining or setting aside any act or threatened act on the part of the corporation or a stockholder which would be inconsistent with any of the provisions or conditions required or permitted by § 342 of this title to be stated in the certificate of incorporation of a close corporation, unless it is an act approved in accordance with § 346 of this title). ■ The Court of Chancery may enjoin or set aside any transfer or threatened transfer of stock of a close corporation which is contrary to the terms (of its certificate of incorporation) or (of any transfer restriction permitted by § 202 of this title), and may enjoin any public offering, as defined in § 342 of this title, or threatened public offering of stock of the close corporation.

§ 349. Corporate option where a restriction on transfer of a security is held invalid.

If a restriction on transfer of a security of a close corporation is held not to be authorized by § 202 of this title, [then] the corporation shall nevertheless have an option, for a period of 30 days after the judgment setting aside the restriction becomes final, to acquire the restricted security (at a price which is agreed upon by the parties), or (if no agreement is reached as to price, then at the fair value as determined by the Court of Chancery). ■ In order to determine fair value, the Court may appoint an appraiser to receive evidence and report to the Court such appraiser's findings and recommendation as to fair value.

§ 350. Agreements restricting discretion of directors.

A written agreement among the stockholders of a close corporation holding a majority of the outstanding stock entitled to vote, whether solely among themselves or with a party not a stockholder, is not invalid, as between the parties to the agreement, on the ground that (it so relates to the conduct of the business and affairs of the corporation as to restrict or interfere with the discretion or powers of the board of directors). ■ The effect of any such agreement shall be to relieve the directors and impose upon the stockholders who are parties to the agreement (the liability for managerial acts or omissions which is imposed on directors) to the extent and so long as the discretion or powers of the board in its management of corporate affairs is controlled by such agreement.

§ 351. Management by stockholders.

The certificate of incorporation of a close corporation may provide that (the business of the corporation shall be managed by the stockholders of the corporation rather than by a board of directors). ■ So long as this provision continues in effect [then]:

(1) No meeting of stockholders need be called to elect directors;

(2) Unless the context clearly requires otherwise, [then] the stockholders of the corporation shall be deemed to be directors for purposes of applying provisions of this chapter; and

(3) The stockholders of the corporation shall be subject to all liabilities of directors.

Such a provision may be inserted in the certificate of incorporation by amendment if all incorporators and subscribers or all holders of record of all of the outstanding stock, whether or not having voting power, authorize such a provision. ■ An amendment to the certificate of incorporation to delete such a provision shall be adopted by a vote of the holders of a majority of all outstanding stock of the corporation, whether or not otherwise entitled to vote. ■ If the certificate of incorporation contains a provision authorized by this section, [then] the existence of such provision shall be noted conspicuously on the face or back of every stock certificate issued by such corporation.

§ 352. Appointment of custodian for close corporation.

(a) [Then] In addition to § 226 of this title respecting the appointment of a custodian for any corporation, the Court of Chancery, upon application of any stockholder, may appoint 1 or more persons to be custodians, and, if the corporation is insolvent, to be receivers, of any close corporation **when**:

> **(1)** Pursuant to § 351 of this title the business and affairs of the corporation are managed by the stockholders and they are so divided that the business of the corporation is suffering or is threatened with irreparable injury and any remedy with respect to such deadlock provided in the certificate of incorporation or bylaws or in any written agreement of the stockholders has failed; or

> **(2)** The petitioning stockholder has the right to the dissolution of the corporation under a provision of the certificate of incorporation permitted by § 355 of this title.

(b) In lieu of appointing a custodian for a close corporation under this section or § 226 of this title the Court of Chancery may appoint a provisional director, whose powers and status shall be as provided in § 353 of this title **if** the Court determines that it would be in the best interest of the corporation. ■ Such appointment shall not preclude any subsequent order of the Court appointing a custodian for such corporation.

§ 353. Appointment of a provisional director in certain cases.

(a) Notwithstanding any contrary provision of the certificate of incorporation or the bylaws or agreement of the stockholders, the Court of Chancery may appoint a provisional director for a close corporation **if** the directors are so divided respecting the management of the corporation's business and affairs that the votes required for action by the board of directors cannot be obtained with the consequence **(**that the business and affairs of the corporation can no longer be conducted to the advantage of the stockholders generally**)**.

(b) An application for relief under this section must be filed **(1)** by at least one half of the number of directors then in office, **(2)** by the holders of at least one third of all stock then entitled to elect directors, or, **(3)** if there be more than 1 class of stock then entitled to elect 1 or more directors, [then] by the holders of two thirds of the stock of any such class; but the certificate of incorporation of a close corporation may provide that a lesser proportion of the directors or of the stockholders or of a class of stockholders may apply for relief under this section.

(c) A provisional director shall be an impartial person who is neither a stockholder nor a creditor of the corporation or of any subsidiary or affiliate of the corporation, and whose further qualifications, if any, may be determined by the Court of Chancery. ■ A provisional director is not a receiver of the corporation and does not have the title and powers of a custodian or receiver appointed under §§ 226 and 291 of this title. ■ [Then] A provisional director shall have all the rights and powers of a duly elected director of the corporation, including the right to notice of and to vote at meetings of directors, **until** such time as such person shall be removed (by order of the Court of Chancery or by the holders of a majority of all shares then entitled to vote to elect directors) or (by the holders of two thirds of the shares of that class of voting shares which filed the application for appointment of a provisional director). ■ A provisional director's compensation shall be determined (by agreement between such person and the corporation) (subject to approval of the Court of Chancery), which may fix such person's compensation (in the absence of agreement) or (in the event of disagreement) between the provisional director and the corporation.

(d) Even though the requirements of subsection (b) of this section relating to the number of directors or stockholders who may petition for appointment of a provisional director are not satisfied, the Court of Chancery may nevertheless appoint a provisional director if permitted by § 352(b) of this title.

§ 354. Operating corporation as partnership.

No written agreement among stockholders of a close corporation, nor any provision of the certificate of incorporation or of the bylaws of the corporation, which agreement or provision relates to any phase of the affairs of such corporation, including but not limited to the management of its business or declaration and payment of dividends or other division of profits or the election of directors or officers or the employment of stockholders by the corporation or the arbitration of disputes, shall be invalid on the ground that it is an attempt by the parties to the agreement or by the stockholders of the corporation (to treat the corporation as if it were a partnership) or (to arrange relations among the stockholders or between the stockholders and the corporation in a manner that would be appropriate only among partners).

§ 355. Stockholders' option to dissolve corporation.

(a) The certificate of incorporation of any close corporation may include a provision granting to any stockholder, or to the holders of any specified number or percentage of shares of any class of stock, an option to have the corporation dissolved at will or upon the occurrence of any specified event or contingency. ■ **Whenever** any such option to dissolve is exercised, **[then]** the stockholders exercising such option shall give written notice thereof to all other stockholders. ■ After the expiration of 30 days following the sending of such notice, the dissolution of the corporation shall proceed as if the required number of stockholders having voting power had consented in writing to dissolution of the corporation as provided by § 228 of this title.

(b) If the certificate of incorporation as originally filed does not contain a provision authorized by subsection (a) of this section, **[then]** the certificate may be amended to include such provision if adopted by the affirmative vote of the holders of all the outstanding stock, whether or not entitled to vote, **unless** the certificate of incorporation specifically authorizes such an amendment by a vote which shall be not less than 2/3 of all the outstanding stock whether or not entitled to vote.

(c) Each stock certificate in any corporation whose certificate of incorporation authorizes dissolution as permitted by this section shall conspicuously note on the face thereof the existence of the provision. ■ Unless noted conspicuously on the face of the stock certificate, the provision is ineffective.

§ 356. Effect of this subchapter on other laws.

This subchapter shall not be deemed to repeal any statute or rule of law which is or would be applicable to any corporation which is organized under this chapter but is not a close corporation.

Subchapter XV. Public Benefit Corporations

§ 361. Law applicable to public benefit corporations; how formed.

This subchapter applies to all public benefit corporations, as defined in §362 of this title. ■ If a corporation elects to become a public benefit corporation under this subchapter in the manner prescribed in this subchapter, [then] it shall be subject in all respects to the provisions of this chapter, ◂except to the extent this subchapter imposes additional or different requirements, in which case such requirements shall apply.▸

§ 362. Public benefit corporation defined; contents of certificate of incorporation.

(a) A "public benefit corporation" is a for-profit corporation organized under and subject to the requirements of this chapter that is intended to produce a public benefit or public benefits and to operate in a responsible and sustainable manner. ■ To that end, a public benefit corporation shall be managed in a manner that balances the stockholders' pecuniary interests, the best interests of those materially affected by the corporation's conduct, and the public benefit or public benefits identified in its certificate of incorporation. ■ In the certificate of incorporation, a public benefit corporation shall:

(1) Identify within its statement of business or purpose pursuant to §102(a)(3) of this title 1 or more specific public benefits to be promoted by the corporation; and

(2) State within its heading that it is a public benefit corporation.

(b) "Public benefit" means a positive effect (or reduction of negative effects) on 1 or more categories of persons, entities, communities or interests (other than stockholders in their capacities as stockholders) including, but not limited to, effects of an artistic, charitable, cultural, economic, educational, environmental, literary, medical, religious, scientific or technological nature. ■ "Public benefit provisions" means the provisions of a certificate of incorporation contemplated by this subchapter.

(c) The name of the public benefit corporation may contain the words "public benefit corporation," or the abbreviation "P.B.C.," or the designation "PBC," which shall be deemed to satisfy the requirements of §102(a)(1)(i) of this title. ■ If the name does not contain such language, [then] the corporation shall, prior to issuing unissued shares of stock or disposing of treasury shares, provide notice to any person to whom such stock is issued or who acquires such treasury shares that it is a public benefit corporation; provided that [then] such notice need not be provided if the issuance or disposal is pursuant to an offering registered under the Securities Act of 1933 [15 U.S.C. § 77r et seq.] or if, at the time of issuance or disposal, the corporation has a class of securities that is registered under the Securities Exchange Act of 1934 [15 U.S.C. § 78a et seq.].

§ 363. Nonprofit nonstock corporations.

A nonprofit nonstock corporation may not be a constituent corporation to any merger or consolidation with a public benefit corporation or in which the certificate of incorporation of the surviving corporation is amended to include a provision authorized by § 362(a)(1) of this title.

§ 364. Stock certificates; notices regarding uncertificated stock.

Any stock certificate issued by a public benefit corporation shall note conspicuously that the corporation is a public benefit corporation formed pursuant to this subchapter. ■ Any notice given by a public benefit corporation pursuant to §151(f) of this title shall state conspicuously that the corporation is a public benefit corporation formed pursuant to this subchapter.

§ 365. Duties of directors.

(a) The board of directors shall manage or direct the business and affairs of the public benefit corporation in a manner that balances the pecuniary interests of the stockholders, the best interests of those materially affected by the corporation's conduct, and the specific public benefit or public benefits identified in its certificate of incorporation.

(b) A director of a public benefit corporation shall not, by virtue of the public benefit provisions or §362(a) of this title, have any duty to any person on account of any interest of such person in the public benefit or public benefits identified in the certificate of incorporation or on account of any interest materially affected by the corporation's conduct and, [then] with respect to a decision implicating the balance requirement in subsection (a) of this section, will be deemed to satisfy such director's fiduciary duties to stockholders and the corporation if such director's decision is both informed and disinterested and not such that no person of ordinary, sound judgment would approve.

(c) A director's ownership of or other interest in the stock of the public benefit corporation shall not alone, for the purposes of this section, create a conflict of interest on the part of the director with respect to the director's decision implicating the balancing requirement in subsection (a) of this section, ◀except to the extent that such ownership or interest would create a conflict of interest if the corporation were not a public benefit corporation.▶ ■ In the absence of a conflict of interest, no failure to satisfy that balancing requirement shall, for the purposes of §102(b)(7) or § 145 of this title, constitute an act or omission not in good faith, or a breach of the duty of loyalty, unless the certificate of incorporation so provides.

§ 366. Periodic statements and third-party certification.

(a) A public benefit corporation shall include in every notice of a meeting of stockholders a statement to the effect that it is a public benefit corporation formed pursuant to this subchapter.

(b) A public benefit corporation shall no less than biennially provide its stockholders with a statement as to the corporation's promotion (of the public benefit or public benefits identified in the certificate of incorporation) and (of the best interests of those materially affected by the corporation's conduct). ■ The statement shall include:

(1) The objectives the board of directors has established to promote such public benefit or public benefits and interests;

(2) The standards the board of directors has adopted to measure the corporation's progress in promoting such public benefit or public benefits and interests;

(3) Objective factual information based on those standards regarding the corporation's success in meeting the objectives for promoting such public benefit or public benefits and interests; and

(4) An assessment of the corporation's success in meeting the objectives and promoting such public benefit or public benefits and interests.

(c) The certificate of incorporation or bylaws of a public benefit corporation may require that the corporation:

(1) Provide the statement described in subsection (b) of this section more frequently than biennially;

(2) Make the statement described in subsection (b) of this section available to the public; and/or

(3) Use a third-party standard in connection with and/or attain a periodic third-party certification addressing the corporation's promotion of the public benefit or public benefits identified in the certificate of incorporation and/or the best interests of those materially affected by the corporation's conduct.

§ 367. Suits to enforce the requirements of §365(a).

Any action to enforce the balancing requirement of § 365(a) of this title, including any individual, derivative or any other type of action, may not be brought unless the plaintiffs in such action own individually or collectively, (as of the date of instituting such action, at least 2% of the corporation's outstanding shares) or, (in the case of a corporation with shares listed on a national securities exchange, the lesser of such percentage or shares of the corporation with a market value of at least $2,000,000 as of the date the action is instituted). ■ This section shall not relieve the plaintiffs from complying with any other conditions applicable to filing a derivative action including § 327 of this title and any rules of the court in which the action is filed.

§ 368. No effect on other corporations.

This subchapter shall not affect a statute or rule of law that is applicable to a corporation that is not a public benefit corporation, (except as provided in § 363 of this title.)

Subchapter XVI. Foreign Corporations

§ 371. Definition; qualification to do business in State; procedure.

(a) As used in this chapter, the words "foreign corporation" mean a corporation organized under the laws of any jurisdiction other than this State.

(b) [Then] No foreign corporation shall do any business in this State, through or by branch offices, agents or representatives located in this State, **until** it shall have paid to the Secretary of State of this State for the use of this State, $80, and shall have filed in the office of the Secretary of State:

  (1) A certificate, as of a date not earlier than 6 months prior to the filing date, issued by an authorized officer of the jurisdiction of its incorporation evidencing its corporate existence. ■ **If** such certificate is in a foreign language, **[then]** a translation thereof, under oath of the translator, shall be attached thereto;

  (2) A statement executed by an authorized officer of each corporation setting forth **(i)** the name and address of its registered agent in this State, which agent may be any of the foreign corporation itself, an individual resident in this State, a domestic corporation, a domestic partnership (whether general (including a limited liability partnership) or limited (including a limited liability limited partnership)), a domestic limited liability company, a domestic statutory trust, a foreign corporation (other than the foreign corporation itself), a foreign partnership (whether general (including a limited liability partnership) or limited (including a limited liability limited partnership)), a foreign limited liability company or a foreign statutory trust, **(ii)** a statement, as of a date not earlier than 6 months prior to the filing date, of the assets and liabilities of the corporation, and **(iii)** the business it proposes to do in this State, and a statement that it is authorized to do that business in the jurisdiction of its incorporation. ■ The statement shall be acknowledged in accordance with § 103 of this title.

(c) The certificate of the Secretary of State, under seal of office, of the filing of the certificates required by subsection (b) of this section, shall be delivered to the registered agent upon the payment to the Secretary of State of the fee prescribed for such certificates, and the certificate shall be prima facie evidence of the right of the corporation to do business in this State; `provided, that` the Secretary of State shall not issue such certificate **unless** the name of the corporation is such as to distinguish it upon the records in the office of the Division of Corporations in the Department of State from the names that are reserved on such records and from the names on such records of each other corporation, partnership, limited partnership, limited liability company or statutory trust organized or registered as a domestic or foreign corporation, partnership, limited partnership, limited liability company or statutory trust under the laws of this State, (except with the written consent of the person who has reserved such name or such other corporation, partnership, limited partnership, limited liability company or statutory trust, executed, acknowledged and filed with the Secretary of State in accordance with § 103 of this title). ■ **If** the name of the foreign corporation conflicts with (the name of a corporation, partnership, limited partnership, limited liability company or statutory trust organized under the laws of this State), or (a name reserved for a corporation, partnership, limited partnership, limited liability company or statutory trust to be organized under the laws of this State), or (a name reserved or registered as that of a foreign corporation, partnership, limited partnership, limited liability company or statutory trust under the laws of this State), **[then]** the foreign corporation may qualify to do business **if** it adopts an assumed name which shall be used when doing business in this State as long as the assumed name is authorized for use by this section.

§ 372. Additional requirements in case of change of name, change of business purpose or merger or consolidation.

(a) Every foreign corporation admitted to do business in this State which shall change its corporate name, or enlarge, limit or otherwise change the business which it proposes to do in this State, shall, within 30 days after the time said change becomes effective, file with the Secretary of State a certificate, which shall set forth:

(1) The name of the foreign corporation as it appears on the records of the Secretary of State of this State;

(2) The jurisdiction of its incorporation;

(3) The date it was authorized to do business in this State;

(4) If the name of the foreign corporation has been changed, [then] (a statement of the name relinquished), (a statement of the new name) and (a statement that the change of name has been effected under the laws of the jurisdiction of its incorporation) and (the date the change was effected);

(5) If the business it proposes to do in this State is to be enlarged, limited or otherwise changed, [then] a statement reflecting such change and a statement that it is authorized to do in the jurisdiction of its incorporation (the business which it proposes to do in this State).

(b) Whenever a foreign corporation authorized to transact business in this State shall be the survivor of a merger permitted by the laws of the state or country in which it is incorporated, [then] it shall, within 30 days after the merger becomes effective, file a certificate, issued by the proper officer of the state or country of its incorporation, attesting to the occurrence of such event. ■ If the merger has changed the corporate name of such foreign corporation [or] has enlarged, limited or otherwise changed the business it proposes to do in this State, [then] it shall also comply with subsection (a) of this section.

(c) Whenever a foreign corporation authorized to transact business in this State ceases to exist because of a statutory merger or consolidation, [then] it shall comply with § 381 of this title.

(d) The Secretary of State shall be paid, for the use of the State, $50 for filing and indexing each certificate required by subsection (a) or (b) of this section, [and] in the event of a change of name an additional $50 shall be paid for a certificate to be issued as evidence of filing the change of name.

§ 373. Exceptions to requirements.

(a) [Then] No foreign corporation shall be required to comply with §§ 371 and 372 of this title, under any of the following conditions:

(1) If it is in the mail order or a similar business, merely (receiving orders by mail or otherwise in pursuance of letters, circulars, catalogs or other forms of advertising, or solicitation), (accepting the orders outside this State), and (filling them with goods shipped into this State);

(2) If it employs salespersons, either resident or traveling, to solicit orders in this State, either by display of samples or otherwise (whether or not maintaining sales offices in this State), (all orders being subject to approval at the offices of the corporation without

this State), and (all goods applicable to the orders being shipped in pursuance thereof from without this State to the vendee or to the seller or such seller's agent for delivery to the vendee), and if any samples kept within this State are for display or advertising purposes only, and [if] no sales, repairs or replacements are made from stock on hand in this State;

(3) If it sells, by contract consummated outside this State, and agrees, by the contract, to deliver into this State, machinery, plants or equipment, (the construction, erection or installation of which within this State requires the supervision of technical engineers or skilled employees performing services not generally available), and as a part of the contract of sale agrees to furnish such services, and such services only, to the vendee at the time of construction, erection or installation;

(4) If its business operations within this State, although not falling within the terms of paragraphs (a)(1), (2) and (3) of this section or any of them, are nevertheless wholly interstate in character;

(5) If it is an insurance company doing business in this State;

(6) If it creates, as borrower or lender, or acquires, evidences of debt, mortgages or liens on real or personal property;

(7) If it secures or collects debts or enforces any rights in property securing the same.

(b) This section shall have no application to the question of (whether any foreign corporation is subject to service of process and suit in this State under § 382 of this title or any other law of this State).

§ 374. Annual report.

Annually on or before June 30, a foreign corporation doing business in this State shall file a report with the Secretary of State. ■ The report shall be made on a form designated by the Secretary of State and shall be signed by the corporation's president, secretary, treasurer or other proper officer duly authorized so to act, or by any of its directors, or if filing an initial report by any incorporator in the event its board of directors shall not have been elected. ■ The fact that an individual's name is signed on a certification attached to a corporate report shall be prima facie evidence that such individual is authorized to certify the report on behalf of the corporation; however the official title or position of the individual signing the corporate report shall be designated. ■ The report shall contain the following information:

(1) The location of its registered office in this State, which shall include the street, number, city and postal code;

(2) The name of the agent upon whom service of process against the corporation may be served;

(3) The location of the principal place of business of the corporation, which shall include the street, number, city, state, or foreign country; and

(4) The names and addresses of all the directors as of the filing date of the report and the name and address of the officer who signs the report.

Subchapter XVI. Foreign Corporations § 375

If any officer or director of a foreign corporation required to file an annual report with the Secretary of State shall knowingly make any false statement in the report, **[then]** such officer or director shall be guilty of perjury.

§ 375. Failure to file report.

Upon the failure, neglect or refusal of any foreign corporation to file an annual report as required by § 374 of this title, the Secretary of State may, in the Secretary of State's discretion, investigate the reasons therefor and shall terminate the right of the foreign corporation to do business within this State upon failure of the corporation to file an annual report within any 2-year period.

§ 376. Service of process upon qualified foreign corporations.

(a) All process issued out of any court of this State, all orders made by any court of this State, [and] all rules and notices of any kind required to be served on any foreign corporation which has qualified to do business in this State may be served (on the registered agent of the corporation designated in accordance with § 371 of this title), or, if there be no such agent, then (on any officer, director or other agent of the corporation then in this State).

(b) **In case** the officer whose duty it is to serve legal process cannot by due diligence serve the process in any manner provided for by subsection (a) of this section, **[then]** it shall be lawful to serve the process against the corporation upon the Secretary of State, and such service shall be as effectual for all intents and purposes as if made in any of the ways provided for in subsection (a) of this section. ■ Process may be served upon the Secretary of State under this subsection by means of electronic transmission but only as prescribed by the Secretary of State. ■ The Secretary of State is authorized to issue such rules and regulations with respect to such service as the Secretary of State deems necessary or appropriate. ■ **In the event that** service is effected through the Secretary of State in accordance with this subsection, **[then]** the Secretary of State shall forthwith notify the corporation by letter, directed to the corporation (at its principal place of business as it appears on the last annual report filed pursuant to § 374 of this title) or, if no such address appears, (at its last registered office). ■ Such letter shall be sent by a mail or courier service that includes (a record of mailing or deposit with the courier) and (a record of delivery evidenced by the signature of the recipient). ■ Such letter shall enclose a copy of the process and any other papers served upon the Secretary of State pursuant to this subsection. ■ It shall be the duty of the plaintiff in the event of such service (to serve process and any other papers in duplicate), (to notify the Secretary of State that service is being effected pursuant to this subsection), and (to pay the Secretary of State the sum of $50 for the use of the State, which sum shall be taxed as a part of the costs in the proceeding if the plaintiff shall prevail therein). ■ The Secretary of State shall maintain an alphabetical record of any such service setting forth the name of the plaintiff and the defendant, the title, docket number and nature of the proceeding in which process has been served upon the Secretary of State, the fact that service has been effected pursuant to this subsection, the return date thereof, and the day and hour when the service was made. ■ The Secretary of State shall not be required to retain such information for a period longer than 5 years from receipt of such service.

§ 377. Change of registered agent

(a) Any foreign corporation, which has qualified to do business in this State, may change its registered agent and substitute another registered agent by filing a certificate with the Secretary of State, acknowledged in accordance with § 103 of this title, setting forth:

(1) The name and address of its registered agent designated in this State upon whom process directed to said corporation may be served; and

(2) A revocation of all previous appointments of agent for such purposes.

Such registered agent shall comply with § 371(b)(2)(i) of this title.

(b) Any individual or entity designated by a foreign corporation as its registered agent for service of process may resign in the same manner as provided in § 136(a) of this title.

(c) If any agent designated and certified as required by § 371 of this title shall die or remove from this State, or resign, **then** the foreign corporation for which the agent had been so designated and certified shall, within 10 days after the death, removal or resignation of its agent, substitute, designate and certify to the Secretary of State, the name of another registered agent for the purposes of this subchapter, and all process, orders, rules and notices mentioned in § 376 of this title may be served on or given to the substituted agent with like effect as is prescribed in that section.

(d) A foreign corporation whose qualification to do business in this State has been forfeited pursuant to § 132(f)(4) or § 136(b) of this title may be reinstated by filing a certificate of reinstatement with the Secretary of State, acknowledged in accordance with § 103 of this title, setting forth:

(1) The name of the foreign corporation;

(2) The effective date of the forfeiture; and

(3) The name and address of the foreign corporation's registered agent required to be maintained by § 132 of this title.

(e) Upon the filing of a certificate of reinstatement in accordance with subsection (d) of this section, the qualification of the foreign corporation to do business in this State shall be reinstated with the same force and effect as if it had not been forfeited pursuant to this title.

§ 378. Penalties for noncompliance.

Any foreign corporation doing business of any kind in this State without first having complied with any section of this subchapter applicable to it, shall be fined not less than $200 nor more than $500 for each such offense. ■ Any agent of any foreign corporation that shall do any business in this State for any foreign corporation before the foreign corporation has complied with any section of this subchapter applicable to it, shall be fined not less than $100 nor more than $500 for each such offense.

§ 379. Banking powers denied.

(a) No foreign corporation shall, within the limits of this State, by any implication or construction, be deemed to possess the power **(**of discounting bills, notes or other evidence of debt**)**, **(**of receiving deposits**)**, **(**of buying and selling bills of exchange**)**, or **(**of issuing bills, notes or other evidences of debt upon loan for circulation as money**)**, anything in its charter or articles of incorporation to the contrary notwithstanding, (except as otherwise provided in subchapter VII of Chapter 7 or in Chapter 14 of Title 5).

(b) All certificates issued by the Secretary of State under § 371 of this title shall expressly set forth the limitations and restrictions contained in this section.

§ 380. Foreign corporation as fiduciary in this State.

[Then] A corporation organized and doing business under the laws of the District of Columbia or of any state of the United States other than Delaware, duly authorized by its certificate of incorporation or bylaws so to act, may be appointed by any last will and testament or other testamentary writing, probated within this State, or by a deed of trust, mortgage or other agreement, as executor, guardian, trustee or other fiduciary, and may act as such within this State, **when and to the extent that** the laws of the District of Columbia or of the state in which the foreign corporation is organized confer like powers upon corporations organized and doing business under the laws of this State.

§ 381. Withdrawal of foreign corporation from State; procedure; service of process on Secretary of State.

(a) Any foreign corporation which shall have qualified to do business in this State under § 371 of this title, may surrender its authority to do business in this State and may withdraw therefrom by filing with the Secretary of State:

(1) A certificate executed in accordance with § 103 of this title, (stating that it surrenders its authority to transact business in the state and withdraws therefrom); and (stating the address to which the Secretary of State may mail any process against the corporation that may be served upon the Secretary of State), or

(2) A copy of an order or decree of dissolution made by any court of competent jurisdiction or other competent authority of the State or other jurisdiction of its incorporation, (certified to be a true copy under the hand of the clerk of the court or other official body), and the official seal of the court or official body or clerk thereof, together with a certificate executed in accordance with paragraph (a)(1) of this section, (stating the address to which the Secretary of State may mail any process against the corporation that may be served upon the Secretary of State).

(b) The Secretary of State shall, upon payment to the Secretary of State of the fees prescribed in § 391 of this title, issue a sufficient number of certificates, under the Secretary of State's hand and official seal, evidencing the surrender of the authority of the corporation to do business in this State and its withdrawal therefrom. ■ One of the certificates shall be furnished to the corporation withdrawing and surrendering its right to do business in this State.

(c) Upon the issuance of the certificates by the Secretary of State, the appointment of the registered agent of the corporation in this State, upon whom process against the corporation may be served, shall be revoked, and the corporation shall be deemed to have consented that service of process in any action, suit or proceeding based upon any cause of action arising in this State, during the time the corporation was authorized to transact business in this State, may thereafter be made by service upon the Secretary of State. ■ Process may be served upon the Secretary of State under this subsection by means of electronic transmission but only as prescribed by the Secretary of State. ■ The Secretary of State is authorized to issue such rules and regulations with respect to such service as the Secretary of State deems necessary or appropriate.

(d) In the event of service upon the Secretary of State in accordance with subsection (c) of this section, the Secretary of State shall forthwith notify the corporation by letter, directed to the corporation at the address stated in the certificate which was filed by the corporation with the Secretary of State pursuant to subsection (a) of this section. ■ Such letter shall be sent by a mail or courier service that includes (a record of mailing or deposit with the courier) and (a record of delivery evidenced by the signature of the recipient). ■ Such letter shall enclose a copy of the process and any other papers served upon the Secretary of State. ■ It shall be the duty of the plaintiff in the event of such service to serve process and any other papers in duplicate, (to notify the Secretary of State that service is being made pursuant to this subsection), and (to pay the Secretary of State the sum of $50 for the use of the State, which sum shall be taxed as part of the cost of the action, suit or proceeding if the plaintiff shall prevail therein). ■ The Secretary of State shall maintain an alphabetical record of such service setting forth the name of the plaintiff and defendant, the title, docket number and nature of the proceeding in which the process has been served upon the Secretary of State, the fact that service has been effected pursuant to this subsection, the return date thereof, and the day and hour when the service was made. ■ The Secretary of State shall not be required to retain such information for a period longer than 5 years from receipt of the service of process.

§ 382. Service of process on nonqualifying foreign corporations.

(a) Any foreign corporation which shall transact business in this State without having qualified to do business under § 371 of this title shall be deemed to have thereby appointed and constituted the Secretary of State of this State its agent for the acceptance of legal process in any civil action, suit or proceeding against it (in any state or federal court in this State) (arising or growing out of any business transacted by it within this State). ■ **If** any foreign corporation consents in writing to be subject to the jurisdiction of any state or federal court in this State for any civil action, suit or proceeding against it arising or growing out of any business or matter, and **if** the agreement or instrument setting forth such consent does not otherwise provide a manner of service of legal process in any such civil action, suit or proceeding against it, [then] such foreign corporation shall be deemed to have thereby appointed and constituted the Secretary of State of this State its agent for the acceptance of legal process in any such civil action, suit or proceeding against it. ■ The transaction of business in this State by such corporation and/or such consent by such corporation to the jurisdiction of any state or federal court in this State without provision for a manner of service of legal process shall be a signification of the agreement of such corporation that (any process served upon the Secretary of State when so served shall be of the same legal force and validity as if served upon an authorized officer or agent personally within this State). ■ Process may be served upon the Secretary of State under this subsection by means of electronic transmission but only as prescribed by the Secretary of State. ■ The Secretary of State is authorized to issue such rules and regulations with respect to such service as the Secretary of State deems necessary or appropriate.

(b) Section 373 of this title shall not apply in determining whether any foreign corporation is transacting business in this State within the meaning of this section; and "the transaction of business" or "business transacted in this State," by any such foreign corporation, whenever those words are used in this section, shall mean the course or practice of carrying on any business activities in this State, including, without limiting the generality of the foregoing, the solicitation of business or orders in this State. ■ This section shall not apply to any insurance company doing business in this State.

(c) In the event of service upon the Secretary of State in accordance with subsection (a) of this section, the Secretary of State shall forthwith notify the corporation thereof by letter, directed to the corporation at the address furnished to the Secretary of State by the plaintiff in such action, suit or proceeding. ■ Such letter shall be sent by a mail or courier service that includes (a record of mailing or deposit with the courier) and (a record of delivery evidenced by the signature of the recipient). ■ Such letter shall enclose a copy of the process and any other papers served upon the Secretary of State. ■ It shall be the duty of the plaintiff in the event of such service (to serve process and any other papers in duplicate), (to notify the Secretary of State that service is being made pursuant to this subsection), and (to pay the Secretary of State the sum of $50 for the use of the State, which sum shall be taxed as a part of the costs in the proceeding if the plaintiff shall prevail therein). ■ The Secretary of State shall maintain an alphabetical record of any such process setting forth the name of the plaintiff and defendant, the title, docket number and nature of the proceeding in which process has been served upon the Secretary of State, the fact that service has been effected pursuant to this subsection, the return date thereof, and the day and hour when the service was made. ■ The Secretary of State shall not be required to retain such information for a period longer than 5 years from receipt of the service of process.

§ 383. Actions by and against unqualified foreign corporations.

(a) A foreign corporation which is required to comply with §§ 371 and 372 of this title and which has done business in this State without authority shall not maintain any action or special proceeding in this State **unless and until** such corporation has been authorized to do business in this State and has paid to the State all fees, penalties and franchise taxes for the years or parts thereof during which it did business in this State without authority. ■ This prohibition shall not apply to any successor in interest of such foreign corporation.

(b) The failure of a foreign corporation to obtain authority to do business in this State shall not impair the validity of any contract or act of the foreign corporation or the right of any other party to the contract to maintain any action or special proceeding thereon, and shall not prevent the foreign corporation from defending any action or special proceeding in this State.

§ 384. Foreign corporations doing business without having qualified; injunctions.

[Then] The Court of Chancery shall have jurisdiction to enjoin any foreign corporation, or any agent thereof, from transacting any business in this State **if** such corporation has failed to comply with any section of this subchapter applicable to it or **if** such corporation has secured a certificate of the Secretary of State under § 371 of this title on the basis of false or misleading representations. ■ The Attorney General shall, upon the Attorney General's own motion or upon the relation of proper parties, proceed for this purpose by complaint in any county in which such corporation is doing business.

§ 385. Filing of certain instruments with recorder of deeds not required.

No instrument that is required to be filed with the Secretary of State of this State by this subchapter need be filed with the recorder of deeds of any county of this State in order to comply with this subchapter.

Subchapter XVII. Domestication and Transfer

§ 388. Domestication of non-United States entities.

(a) As used in this section, the term:

(1) "Foreign jurisdiction" means any foreign country or other foreign jurisdiction (other than the United States, any state, the District of Columbia, or any possession or territory of the United States); and

(2) "Non-United States entity" means a corporation, a limited liability company, a statutory trust, a business trust or association, a real estate investment trust, a common-law trust, or any other unincorporated business or entity, including a partnership (whether general (including a limited liability partnership) or limited (including a limited liability limited partnership)), formed, incorporated, created or that otherwise came into being under the laws of any foreign jurisdiction.

(b) Any non-United States entity may become domesticated as a corporation in this State by (complying with subsection (h) of this section) and (filing with the Secretary of State:

(1) A certificate of corporate domestication which shall be executed in accordance with subsection (g) of this section and filed in accordance with § 103 of this title; and

(2) A certificate of incorporation, which shall be executed, acknowledged and filed in accordance with § 103 of this title).

Each of the certificates required by this subsection (b) shall be filed simultaneously with the Secretary of State and, if such certificates are not to become effective upon their filing as permitted by § 103(d) of this title, then each such certificate shall provide for the same effective date or time in accordance with § 103(d) of this title.

(c) The certificate of corporate domestication shall certify:

(1) The date on which and jurisdiction where the non-United States entity was first formed, incorporated, created or otherwise came into being;

(2) The name of the non-United States entity immediately prior to the filing of the certificate of corporate domestication;

(3) The name of the corporation as set forth in its certificate of incorporation filed in accordance with subsection (b) of this section; and

(4) The jurisdiction that constituted (the seat, siege social, or principal place of business or central administration of the non-United States entity) or (any other equivalent thereto) under applicable law, immediately prior to the filing of the certificate of corporate domestication; and

(5) That the domestication has been approved in the manner provided for (by the document, instrument, agreement or other writing, as the case may be, governing the internal affairs of the non-United States entity and the conduct of its business) or (by applicable non-Delaware law), as appropriate.

(d) Upon the certificate of corporate domestication and the certificate of incorporation becoming effective in accordance with § 103 of this title, <u>the non-United States entity shall be domesticated</u> as a corporation in this State and <u>the corporation shall thereafter be subject to all</u> of the provisions of this title, ◀except that notwithstanding § 106 of this title, the existence of the corporation shall be deemed to have commenced on the date the non-United States entity commenced its existence in the jurisdiction in which the non-United States entity was first formed, incorporated, created or otherwise came into being.▶

(e) <u>The domestication</u> of any non-United States entity as a corporation in this State <u>shall not be deemed to affect any obligations</u> or liabilities of the non-United States entity incurred prior to its domestication as a corporation in this State, or <u>the personal liability</u> of any person therefor.

(f) <u>The filing</u> of a certificate of corporate domestication <u>shall not affect the choice of law applicable</u> to the non-United States entity, ◀except that, from the effective time of the domestication, the law of the State of Delaware, including this title, shall apply to the non-United States entity to the same extent as if the non-United States entity had been incorporated as a corporation of this State on that date.▶

(g) <u>The certificate</u> of corporate domestication <u>shall be signed</u> by any person who is authorized to sign the certificate of corporate domestication on behalf of the non-United States entity.

(h) Prior to the filing of a certificate of corporate domestication with the Secretary of State, <u>the domestication shall be approved</u> in the manner provided for (by the document, instrument, agreement or other writing, as the case may be, governing the internal affairs of the non-United States entity and the conduct of its business) or (by applicable non-Delaware law), as appropriate, and <u>the certificate of incorporation shall be approved</u> by the same authorization required to approve the domestication.

(i) <u>When</u> <u>a non-United States entity has become domesticated</u> as a corporation pursuant to this section, [then] for all purposes of the laws of the State of Delaware, <u>the corporation shall be deemed to be the same entity</u> as the domesticating non-United States entity and <u>the domestication shall constitute a continuation</u> of the existence of the domesticating non-United States entity in the form of a corporation of this State. ■ <u>When</u> <u>any domestication shall have become effective</u> under this section, [then] for all purposes of the laws of the State of Delaware, <u>all</u> of the rights, <u>privileges and powers</u> of the non-United States entity that has been domesticated, and <u>all property</u>, real, personal and mixed, and all debts due to such non-United States entity, as well as all other things and causes of action belonging to such non-United States entity, <u>shall remain vested</u> in the corporation to which such non-United States entity has been domesticated (and also in the non-United States entity, if and for so long as the non-United States entity continues its existence in the foreign jurisdiction in which it was existing immediately prior to the domestication) and <u>shall be the property</u>

of such corporation (and also of the non-United States entity, if and for so long as the non-United States entity continues its existence in the foreign jurisdiction in which it was existing immediately prior to the domestication), and the title to any real property vested by deed or otherwise in such non-United States entity shall not revert or be in any way impaired by reason of this title; but all rights of creditors and all liens upon any property of such non-United States entity shall be preserved unimpaired, and all debts, liabilities and duties of the non-United States entity that has been domesticated shall remain attached to the corporation to which such non-United States entity has been domesticated (and also to the non-United States entity, if and for so long as the non-United States entity continues its existence in the foreign jurisdiction in which it was existing immediately prior to the domestication), and may be enforced against it to the same extent as if said debts, liabilities and duties had originally been incurred or contracted by it in its capacity as such corporation. ■ The rights, privileges, powers and interests in property of the non-United States entity, as well as the debts, liabilities and duties of the non-United States entity, shall not be deemed, as a consequence of the domestication, to have been transferred to the corporation to which such non-United States entity has domesticated for any purpose of the laws of the State of Delaware.

(j) Unless otherwise agreed or otherwise required under applicable non-Delaware law, the domesticating non-United States entity shall not be required to wind up its affairs or pay its liabilities and distribute its assets, and the domestication shall not be deemed to constitute a dissolution of such non-United States entity. ■ If, following domestication, a non-United States entity that has become domesticated as a corporation of this State continues its existence in the foreign jurisdiction in which it was existing immediately prior to domestication, [then] the corporation and such non-United States entity shall, for all purposes of the laws of the State of Delaware, constitute a single entity formed, incorporated, created or otherwise having come into being, as applicable, and existing under the laws of the State of Delaware and the laws of such foreign jurisdiction.

(k) In connection with a domestication under this section, shares of stock, rights or securities of, or interests in, the non-United States entity that is to be domesticated as a corporation of this State may be exchanged for or converted into cash, property, or shares of stock, rights or securities of such corporation or, in addition to or in lieu thereof, may be exchanged for or converted into cash, property, or shares of stock, rights or securities of, or interests in, another corporation or other entity or may be cancelled.

§ 389. Temporary transfer of domicile into this State.

(a) As used in this section:

    (1) The term "emergency condition" shall be deemed to include but not be limited to any of the following:

        a. War or other armed conflict;

        b. Revolution or insurrection;

        c. Invasion or occupation by foreign military forces;

        d. Rioting or civil commotion of an extended nature;

        e. Domination by a foreign power;

f. Expropriation, nationalization or confiscation of a material part of the assets or property of the non-United States entity;

g. Impairment of the institution of private property (including private property held abroad);

h. The taking of any action under the laws of the United States whereby **(**persons resident in the jurisdiction, the law of which governs the internal affairs of the non-United States entity, might be treated as "enemies" or otherwise restricted under laws of the United States relating to trading with enemies of the United States**)**;

i. The immediate threat of any of the foregoing; and

j. Such other event which, under the law of the jurisdiction governing the internal affairs of the non-United States entity, permits the non-United States entity to transfer its domicile.

(2) The term "foreign jurisdiction" and the term "non-United States entity" shall have the same meanings as set forth in § 388(a) of this title.

(3) The terms "officers" and "directors" include, in addition to such persons, trustees, managers, partners and all other persons performing functions equivalent to those of officers and directors, however named or described in any relevant instrument.

(b) [Then] Any non-United States entity may, subject to and upon compliance with this section, transfer its domicile (which term, as used in this section, shall be deemed to refer in addition to the seat, siege social or principal place of business or central administration of such entity, or any other equivalent thereto under applicable law) into this State, and may perform the acts described in this section, **so long as** the law by which the internal affairs of such entity are governed does not expressly prohibit such transfer.

(c) Any non-United States entity that shall propose to transfer its domicile into this State shall submit to the Secretary of State for the Secretary of State's review, at least 30 days prior to the proposed transfer of domicile, the following:

(1) A copy of its certificate of incorporation and bylaws (or the equivalent thereof under applicable law), certified as true and correct by the appropriate director, officer or government official;

(2) A certificate issued by an authorized official of the jurisdiction the law of which governs the internal affairs of the non-United States entity evidencing its existence;

(3) A list indicating the person or persons who, in the event of a transfer pursuant to this section, shall be the authorized officers and directors of the non-United States entity, together with evidence of their authority to act and their respective executed agreements in writing regarding service of process as set out in subsection (j) of this section;

(4) A certificate executed by the appropriate officer or director of the non-United States entity, setting forth:

a. The name and address of its registered agent in this State;

b. A general description of the business in which it is engaged;

c. That the filing of such certificate has been duly authorized by any necessary action and does not violate the certificate of incorporation or bylaws (or equivalent thereof under applicable law) or any material agreement or instrument binding on such entity;

d. A list indicating the person or persons authorized to sign the written communications required by subsection (e) of this section;

e. An affirmance that such transfer is not expressly prohibited under the law by which the internal affairs of the non-United States entity are governed; `and`

f. An undertaking that any transfer of domicile into this State will take place only in the event of an emergency condition in the jurisdiction the law of which governs the internal affairs of the non-United States entity and that such transfer shall continue only so long as such emergency condition, in the judgment of the non-United States entity's management, so requires; and

(5) The examination fee prescribed under § 391 of this title.

If any of the documents referred to in paragraphs (c)(1)-(5) of this section are not in English, [then] a translation thereof, under oath of the translator, shall be attached thereto. ■ If such documents satisfy the requirements of this section, `and` if the name of the non-United States entity meets the requirements of § 102(a)(1) of this title, [then] the Secretary of State shall notify the non-United States entity that such documents have been accepted for filing, `and` the records of the Secretary of State shall reflect such acceptance and such notification. ■ In addition, the Secretary of State shall enter the name of the non-United States entity on the Secretary of State's reserved list to remain there so long as the non-United States entity is in compliance with this section. ■ [Then] No document submitted under this subsection shall be available for public inspection pursuant to Chapter 100 of Title 29 **until, and unless**, such entity effects a transfer of its domicile as provided in this section. ■ The Secretary of State may waive the 30-day period `and` translation requirement provided for in this subsection upon request by such entity, supported by facts (including, without limitation, the existence of an emergency condition) justifying such waiver.

(d) On or before March 1 in each year, **(**prior to the transfer of its domicile as provided for in subsection (e) of this section**)**, **(**during any such transfer**)** and, in the event that it desires to continue to be subject to a transfer of domicile under this section, **(**after its domicile has ceased to be in this State**)**, the non-United States entity shall file a certificate executed by an appropriate officer or director of the non-United States entity, certifying that the documents submitted pursuant to this section remain in full force and effect or attaching any amendments or supplements thereto `and` translated as required in subsection (c) of this section, together with the filing fee prescribed under § 391 of this title. ■ **In the event that** any non-United States entity fails to file the required certificate on or before March 1 in each year, [then] all certificates and filings made pursuant to this section shall become null and void on March 2 in such year, `and` any proposed transfer thereafter shall be subject to all of the required submissions `and` the examination fee set forth in subsection (c) of this section.

(e) If the Secretary of State accepts the documents submitted pursuant to subsection (c) of this section for filing, [then] such entity may transfer its domicile to this State at any time by means of a written communication to such effect **(**addressed to the Secretary of State**)**, **(**signed by 1 of the persons named on the list filed pursuant to paragraph (c)(4)d. of this section**)**, and **(**confirming that the statements made pursuant to paragraph (c)(4) of this section remain true and correct**)**; `provided, that` if emergency conditions have affected ordinary means of communication, [then] such notification may be made by telegram, telex, telecopy or other form of writing **so long as** a duly signed duplicate is received by the Secretary of State within 30 days thereafter. ■ The records of the Secretary of State shall reflect the fact of such transfer. ■ Upon the payment to the Secretary of State of the fee prescribed under § 391 of this title, the Secretary of State shall certify that the non-United States entity has filed all documents and paid all fees required by this title. ■ Such certificate of the Secretary of State shall be prima facie evidence of transfer by such non-United States entity of its domicile into this State.

(f) ❰Except to the extent expressly prohibited by the laws of this State❱, from and after the time that a non-United States entity transfers its domicile to this State pursuant to this section, the non-United States entity shall have all of the powers which it had immediately prior to such transfer under the law of the jurisdiction governing its internal affairs and the directors and officers designated pursuant to paragraph (c)(3) of this section, and their successors, may manage the business and affairs of the non-United States entity in accordance with the laws of such jurisdiction. ■ Any such activity conducted pursuant to this section shall not be deemed to be doing business within this State for purposes of § 371 of this title. ■ Any reference in this section to the law of the jurisdiction governing the internal affairs of a non-United States entity which has transferred its domicile into this State shall be deemed to be a reference to such law as in effect immediately prior to the transfer of domicile.

(g) For purposes of any action in the courts of this State, no non-United States entity which has obtained the certificate of the Secretary of State referred to in subsection (e) of this section shall be deemed to be an "enemy" person or entity for any purpose, including, without limitation, in relation ❰to any claim of title to its assets❱, wherever located, or ❰to its ability to institute suit in said courts❱.

(h) The transfer by any non-United States entity of its domicile into this State shall not be deemed to affect any obligations or liabilities of such non-United States entity incurred prior to such transfer.

(i) [Then] The directors of any non-United States entity which has transferred its domicile into this State may withhold from any holder of equity interests in such entity any amounts payable to such holder on account of dividends or other distributions, **if** the directors shall determine that such holder will not have the full benefit of such payment, **so long as** the directors shall make provision for the retention of such withheld payment in escrow or under some similar arrangement for the benefit of such holder.

(j) All process issued out of any court of this State, all orders made by any court of this State and all rules and notices of any kind required to be served on any non-United States entity which has transferred its domicile into this State may be served on the non-United States entity pursuant to § 321 of this title ❰in the same manner as if such entity were a corporation of this State❱. ■ The directors of a non-United States entity which has transferred its domicile into this State shall agree in writing that they will be ❰amenable to service of process by the same means as❱, and ❰subject to the jurisdiction of the courts of this State to the same extent as❱ are directors of corporations of this State, and such agreements shall be submitted to the Secretary of State for filing before the respective directors take office.

(k) Any non-United States entity which has transferred its domicile into this State may voluntarily return to the jurisdiction the law of which governs its internal affairs by filing with the Secretary of State an application to withdraw from this State. ■ Such application shall be accompanied (by a resolution of the directors of the non-United States entity authorizing such withdrawal) and (by a certificate of the highest diplomatic or consular official of such jurisdiction accredited to the United States indicating the consent of such jurisdiction to such withdrawal). ■ The application shall also contain, or be accompanied by, the agreement of the non-United States entity that it may be served with process in this State in any proceeding for enforcement of any obligation of the non-United States entity arising prior to its withdrawal from this State, which agreement (shall include the appointment of the Secretary of State as the agent of the non-United States entity to accept service of process in any such proceeding) and (shall specify the address to which a copy of process served upon the Secretary of State shall be mailed). ■ Upon the payment of any fees and taxes owed to this State, the Secretary of State shall file the application and the non-United States entity's domicile shall, as of the time of filing, cease to be in this State.

§ 390. Transfer, domestication or continuance of domestic corporations.

(a) Upon compliance with the provisions of this section, any corporation existing under the laws of this State may transfer to or domesticate or continue in any foreign jurisdiction and, in connection therewith, may elect to continue its existence as a corporation of this State. ■ As used in this section, the term:

(1) "Foreign jurisdiction" means any foreign country, or other foreign jurisdiction (other than the United States, any state, the District of Columbia, or any possession or territory of the United States); and

(2) "Resulting entity" means the entity formed, incorporated, created or otherwise coming into being as a consequence of the transfer of the corporation to, or its domestication or continuance in, a foreign jurisdiction pursuant to this section.

(b) The board of directors of the corporation which desires to transfer to or domesticate or continue in a foreign jurisdiction shall adopt a resolution approving such transfer, domestication or continuance specifying the foreign jurisdiction to which the corporation shall be transferred or in which the corporation shall be domesticated or continued and, if applicable, that in connection with such transfer, domestication or continuance the corporation's existence as a corporation of this State is to continue and recommending the approval of such transfer or domestication or continuance by the stockholders of the corporation. ■ Such resolution shall be submitted to the stockholders of the corporation at an annual or special meeting. ■ Due notice of the time, place and purpose of the meeting shall be given to each holder of stock, whether voting or nonvoting, of the corporation (at the address of the stockholder as it appears on the records of the corporation), (at least 20 days prior to the date of the meeting). ■ At the meeting, the resolution shall be considered and a vote taken for its adoption or rejection. ■ If all outstanding shares of stock of the corporation, whether voting or nonvoting, shall be voted for the adoption of the resolution, [then] the corporation shall file with the Secretary of State (a certificate of transfer if its existence as a corporation of this State is to cease) or (a certificate of transfer and domestic continuance if its existence as a corporation of this State is to continue), executed in accordance with § 103 of this title, which certifies:

(1) The name of the corporation, and if it has been changed, [then] the name under which it was originally incorporated.

(2) The date of filing of its original certificate of incorporation with the Secretary of State.

(3) The foreign jurisdiction to which the corporation shall be transferred or in which it shall be domesticated or continued and the name of the resulting entity.

(4) That the transfer, domestication or continuance of the corporation has been approved in accordance with the provisions of this section.

(5) In the case of a certificate of transfer, **(i)** that the existence of the corporation as a corporation of this State shall cease when the certificate of transfer becomes effective, and **(ii)** the agreement of the corporation that it may be served with process in this State in any proceeding for enforcement of any obligation of the corporation arising while it was a corporation of this State which shall also (irrevocably appoint the Secretary of State as its agent to accept service of process in any such proceeding) and (specify the address (which may not be that of the corporation's registered agent without the written consent of the corporation's registered agent, such consent to be filed along with the certificate of transfer) to which a copy of such process shall be mailed by the Secretary of State). ■ Process may be served upon the Secretary of State under this subsection by means of electronic transmission but only as prescribed by the Secretary of State. ■ The Secretary of State is authorized to issue such rules and regulations with respect to such service as the Secretary of State deems necessary or appropriate. ■ In the event of service upon the Secretary of State in accordance with this subsection, the Secretary of State shall forthwith notify such corporation that has transferred out of the State of Delaware by letter, [then] directed to such corporation that has transferred out of the State of Delaware at the address so specified, unless such corporation shall have designated in writing to the Secretary of State a different address for such purpose, in which case it shall be mailed to the last address designated. ■ Such letter shall be sent by a mail or courier service that includes (a record of mailing or deposit with the courier) and (a record of delivery evidenced by the signature of the recipient). ■ Such letter shall enclose a copy of the process and any other papers served on the Secretary of State pursuant to this subsection. ■ It shall be the duty of the plaintiff in the event of such service to serve process and any other papers in duplicate, (to notify the Secretary of State that service is being effected pursuant to this subsection) and (to pay the Secretary of State the sum of $50 for the use of the State, which sum shall be taxed as part of the costs in the proceeding, if the plaintiff shall prevail therein). ■ The Secretary of State shall maintain an alphabetical record of any such service setting forth the name of the plaintiff and the defendant, the title, docket number and nature of the proceeding in which process has been served, the fact that service has been effected pursuant to this subsection, the return date thereof, and the day and hour service was made. ■ The Secretary of State shall not be required to retain such information longer than 5 years from receipt of the service of process.

(6) In the case of a certificate of transfer and domestic continuance, [then] that the corporation will continue to exist as a corporation of this State after the certificate of transfer and domestic continuance becomes effective.

(c) Upon (the filing of a certificate of transfer in accordance with subsection (b) of this section) and (payment to the Secretary of State of all fees prescribed under this title), the Secretary of State shall certify that the corporation has filed all documents and paid all fees required by this title, and thereupon the corporation shall cease to exist as a corporation of this State at the time the certificate of transfer becomes effective in accordance with § 103 of this title. ■ Such certificate of the Secretary of State shall be prima facie evidence of the transfer, domestication or continuance by such corporation out of this State.

(d) The transfer, domestication or continuance of a corporation out of this State in accordance with this section and the resulting cessation of its existence as a corporation of this State pursuant to a certificate of transfer shall not be deemed to affect any obligations or liabilities of the corporation incurred prior to such transfer, domestication or continuance, the personal liability of any person incurred prior to such transfer, domestication or continuance, or the choice of law applicable to the corporation with respect to matters arising prior to such transfer, domestication or continuance. ■ Unless otherwise agreed or otherwise provided in the certificate of incorporation, the transfer, domestication or continuance of a corporation out of the State of Delaware in accordance with this section shall not require such corporation to wind up its affairs or pay its liabilities and distribute its assets under this title and shall not be deemed to constitute a dissolution of such corporation.

(e) **If** a corporation files a certificate of transfer and domestic continuance, [then] after the time the certificate of transfer and domestic continuance becomes effective, the corporation shall continue to exist as a corporation of this State, and the law of the State of Delaware, including this title, shall apply to the corporation to the same extent as prior to such time. ■ **So long as** a corporation continues to exist as a corporation of the State of Delaware following the filing of a certificate of transfer and domestic continuance, [then] the continuing corporation and the resulting entity shall, for all purposes of the laws of the State of Delaware, constitute a single entity formed, incorporated, created or otherwise having come into being, as applicable, and existing under (the laws of the State of Delaware) and (the laws of the foreign jurisdiction).

(f) **When** a corporation has transferred, domesticated or continued pursuant to this section, for all purposes of the laws of the State of Delaware, [then] the resulting entity shall be deemed to be the same entity as the transferring, domesticating or continuing corporation and shall constitute a continuation of the existence of such corporation in the form of the resulting entity. ■ **When** any transfer, domestication or continuance shall have become effective under this section, [then] for all purposes of the laws of the State of Delaware, all of the rights, privileges and powers of the corporation that has transferred, domesticated or continued, and all property, real, personal and mixed, and all debts due to such corporation, as well as all other things and causes of action belonging to such corporation, shall remain vested in the resulting entity (and also in the corporation that has transferred, domesticated or continued, if and for so long as such corporation continues its existence as a corporation of this State) and shall be the property of such resulting entity (and also of the corporation that has transferred, domesticated or continued, if and for so long as such corporation continues its existence as a corporation of this State), and the title to any real property vested by deed or otherwise in such corporation shall not revert or be in any way impaired by reason of this title; but all rights of creditors and all liens upon any property of such corporation shall be preserved unimpaired, and all debts, liabilities and duties of such corporation shall remain attached to the resulting entity (and also to the corporation that has transferred, domesticated or continued, if and for so long as such corporation continues its existence as a corporation of this State), and may be enforced against it (to the same extent as if said debts, liabilities and duties had originally been incurred or contracted by it in its capacity as such resulting entity). ■ The rights, privileges, powers and interests in property of the corporation, as well as the debts, liabilities and duties of the corporation, shall not be deemed, as a consequence of the transfer, domestication or continuance, to have been transferred to the resulting entity for any purpose of the laws of the State of Delaware.

(g) In connection with a transfer, domestication or continuance under this section, shares of stock of the transferring, domesticating or continuing corporation may be exchanged for or converted into cash, property, or shares of stock, rights or securities of, or interests in, the resulting entity or, in addition to or in lieu thereof, may be exchanged for or converted into cash, property, or shares of stock, rights or securities of, or interests in, another corporation or other entity or may be cancelled.

(h) [Then] No vote of the stockholders of a corporation shall be necessary to authorize a transfer, domestication or continuance if no shares of the stock of such corporation shall have been issued prior to the adoption by the board of directors of the resolution approving the transfer, domestication or continuance.

(i) Whenever it shall be desired to transfer to or domesticate or continue in any foreign jurisdiction any nonstock corporation, [then] the governing body shall perform all the acts necessary to effect a transfer, domestication or continuance (which are required by this section to be performed by the board of directors of a corporation having capital stock). ■ If the members of a nonstock corporation are entitled to vote for the election of members of its governing body or are entitled under the certificate of incorporation or the bylaws of such corporation to vote on such transfer, domestication or continuance or on a merger, consolidation, or dissolution of the corporation, [then] they, and any other holder of any membership interest in the corporation, shall perform all the acts necessary to effect a transfer, domestication or continuance (which are required by this section to be performed by the stockholders of a corporation having capital stock). ■ If there is no member entitled to vote thereon, nor any other holder of any membership interest in the corporation, [then] the transfer, domestication or continuance of the corporation shall be authorized (at a meeting of the governing body), (upon the adoption of a resolution to transfer or domesticate or continue) (by the vote of a majority of members of its governing body then in office). ■ In all other respects, the method and proceedings for the transfer, domestication or continuance of a nonstock corporation shall conform as nearly as may be (to the proceedings prescribed by this section for the transfer, domestication or continuance of corporations having capital stock). ■ In the case of a charitable nonstock corporation, due notice of the corporation's intent to effect a transfer, domestication or continuance shall be mailed to the Attorney General of the State of Delaware 10 days prior to the date of the proposed transfer, domestication or continuance.

Subchapter XVIII. Miscellaneous Provisions

§ 391. Amounts payable to Secretary of State upon filing certificate or other paper.

(a) The following fees and penalties shall be collected by and paid to the Secretary of State, for the use of the State:

(1) Upon the receipt for filing of an original certificate of incorporation, the fee shall be computed on the basis of ($0.02 for each share of authorized capital stock having par value up to and including 20,000 shares), ($0.01 for each share in excess of 20,000 shares up to and including 200,000 shares), and (2/5 of a $0.01 for each share in excess of 200,000 shares); ($0.01 for each share of authorized capital stock without par value up to and including 20,000 shares), (1/2 of $0.01 for each share in excess of 20,000 shares up to and including 2,000,000 shares), and (2/5 of $0.01 for each share in excess of 2,000,000 shares). ■ In no case shall the amount paid be less than $15. ■ For the purpose of computing the fee on par value stock each $100 unit of the authorized capital stock shall be counted as 1 assessable share.

(2) Upon the receipt for filing of (a certificate of amendment of certificate of incorporation), or (a certificate of amendment of certificate of incorporation before payment of capital), or a restated certificate of incorporation, increasing the authorized capital stock of a corporation, the fee shall be an amount equal to the difference between (the fee computed at the foregoing rates upon the total authorized capital stock of the corporation including the proposed increase), and (the fee computed at the foregoing rates upon the total authorized capital stock excluding the proposed increase). ■ In no case shall the amount paid be less than $30.

(3) Upon the receipt for filing of (a certificate of amendment of certificate of incorporation before payment of capital and not involving an increase of authorized capital stock), or (an amendment to the certificate of incorporation not involving an increase of authorized capital stock), or (a restated certificate of incorporation not involving an increase of authorized capital stock), or (a certificate of retirement of stock), the fee to be paid shall be $30. ■ For (all other certificates relating to corporations, not otherwise provided for), the fee to be paid shall be $5.00. ■ In the case of exempt corporations no fee shall be paid under this paragraph.

(4) Upon the receipt for filing of (a certificate of merger or consolidation of 2 or more corporations), the fee shall be an amount equal to the difference between (the fee computed at the foregoing rates upon the total authorized capital stock of the corporation created by the merger or consolidation), and (the fee so computed upon the aggregate amount of the total authorized capital stock of the constituent corporations). ■ In no case shall the amount paid be less than $75. ■ The foregoing fee shall be in addition to (any tax or fee required under any other law of this State to be paid by any constituent entity that is not a corporation in connection with the filing of the certificate of merger or consolidation).

(5) Upon the receipt for filing of (a certificate of dissolution), there shall be paid to and collected by the Secretary of State a fee of:

   a. Forty dollars; or
   b. Ten dollars in the case of a certificate of dissolution which certifies that:

1. The corporation has no assets and has ceased transacting business; and

2. The corporation, for each year since its incorporation in this State, has been required to pay only the minimum franchise tax then prescribed by § 503 of this title; and

3. The corporation has paid all franchise taxes and fees due to or assessable by this State through the end of the year in which said certificate of dissolution is filed.

(6) Upon the receipt for filing of (a certificate of reinstatement of a foreign corporation) or (a certificate of surrender and withdrawal from the State by a foreign corporation), there shall be collected by and paid to the Secretary of State a fee of $10.

(7) For receiving and filing and/or indexing (any certificate, affidavit, agreement or any other paper provided for by this chapter, for which no different fee is specifically prescribed), a fee of $115 in each case shall be paid to the Secretary of State. ■ The fee in the case of (a certificate of incorporation filed as required by § 102 of this title) shall be $25. ■ For (entering information from each instrument into the Delaware Corporation Information System in accordance with § 103(c)(8) of this title), the fee shall be $5.00.

a. A certificate of dissolution which meets the criteria stated in paragraph (a)(5)b. of this section shall not be subject to such fee; and

b. A certificate of incorporation filed in accordance with § 102 of this title shall be subject to a fee of $25.

(8) For receiving and filing and/or indexing (the annual report of a foreign corporation doing business in this State), a fee of $125 shall be paid. ■ In the event of (neglect, refusal or failure on the part of any foreign corporation to file the annual report with the Secretary of State on or before June 30 each year), the corporation shall pay a penalty of $125.

(9) For recording and indexing (articles of association and other papers required by this chapter to be recorded by the Secretary of State), a fee computed on the basis of $0.01 a line shall be paid.

(10) For (certifying copies of any paper on file provided by this chapter), a fee of $50 shall be paid for each copy certified. ■ In addition, a fee of $2.00 per page shall be paid in each instance where (the Secretary of State provides the copies of the document to be certified).

(11) For issuing (any certificate of the Secretary of State other than a certification of a copy under paragraph (a)(10) of this section, or a certificate that recites all of a corporation's filings with the Secretary of State), a fee of $50 shall be paid for each certificate. ■ For issuing (any certificate of the Secretary of State that recites all of a corporation's filings with the Secretary of State), a fee of $175 shall be paid for each certificate. ■ For issuing any certificate via the Division's online services, a fee of up to $175 shall be paid for each certificate.

(12) For filing in the office of the Secretary of State (any certificate of change of location or change of registered agent, as provided in § 133 of this title), there shall be collected by and paid to the Secretary of State a fee of $50, provided that no fee shall be charged pursuant to § 103(c)(6) and (c)(7) of this title.

(13) For filing in the office of the Secretary of State (any certificate of change of address or change of name of registered agent, as provided in § 134 of this title), there shall be collected by and paid to the Secretary of State a fee of $50, plus (the same fees for receiving, filing, indexing, copying and certifying the same as are charged in the case of filing a certificate of incorporation).

(14) For filing in the office of the Secretary of State (any certificate of resignation of a registered agent and appointment of a successor, as provided in § 135 of this title), there shall be collected by and paid to the Secretary of State a fee of $50.

(15) For filing in the office of the Secretary of State, (any certificate of resignation of a registered agent without appointment of a successor, as provided in §§ 136 and 377 of this title), there shall be collected by and paid to the Secretary of State a fee of $2.00 for each corporation whose registered agent has resigned by such certificate.

(16) For preparing and providing (a written report of a record search), a fee of up to $100 shall be paid.

(17) For (preclearance of any document for filing), a fee of $250 shall be paid.

(18) For receiving and filing and/or indexing (an annual franchise tax report of a corporation provided for by § 502 of this title), a fee of $25 shall be paid by exempt corporations and a fee of $50 shall be paid by all other corporations.

(19) For receiving and filing and/or indexing by the Secretary of State of (a certificate of domestication and certificate of incorporation prescribed in § 388(d) of this title), a fee of $165, plus the fee payable upon the receipt for filing of an original certificate of incorporation, shall be paid.

(20) For receiving, reviewing and filing and/or indexing by the Secretary of State of (the documents prescribed in § 389(c) of this title), a fee of $10,000 shall be paid.

(21) For receiving, reviewing and filing and/or indexing by the Secretary of State of (the documents prescribed in § 389(d) of this title), an annual fee of $2,500 shall be paid.

(22) (Except as provided in this section), the fees of the Secretary of State shall be as provided for in § 2315 of Title 29.

(23) In the case of exempt corporations, the total fees payable to the Secretary of State upon the filing of a Certificate of Change of Registered Agent and/or Registered Office or a Certificate of Revival shall be $5.00 and such filings shall be exempt from any fees or assessments pursuant to the requirements of § 103(c)(6) and (c)(7) of this title.

(24) For accepting (a corporate name reservation application), (an application for renewal of a corporate name reservation), or (a notice of transfer or cancellation of a corporate name reservation), there shall be collected by and paid to the Secretary of State a fee of up to $75.

(25) For receiving and filing and/or indexing by the Secretary of State of (a certificate of transfer or a certificate of continuance prescribed in § 390 of this title), a fee of $1,000 shall be paid.

(26) For receiving and filing and/or indexing by the Secretary of State of (a certificate of conversion and certificate of incorporation prescribed in § 265 of this title), a fee of

$115, plus the fee payable upon the receipt for filing of an original certificate of incorporation, shall be paid.

(27) For receiving and filing and/or indexing by the Secretary of State of (a certificate of conversion prescribed in § 266 of this title), a fee of $165 shall be paid.

(28) For receiving and filing and/or indexing by the Secretary of State of (a certificate of validation prescribed in § 204 of this title), a fee of $2,500 shall be paid; provided, that if the certificate of validation has the effect of increasing the authorized capital stock of a corporation, [then] an additional fee, calculated in accordance with paragraph (a)(2) of this section, shall also be paid.

(b)(1) For the purpose of computing the fee prescribed in paragraphs (a)(1), (2), (4) and (28) of this section the authorized capital stock of a corporation shall be considered to be the total number of shares which the corporation is authorized to issue, (whether or not the total number of shares that may be outstanding at any 1 time be limited to a less number).

(2) For the purpose of computing the fee prescribed in paragraphs (a)(2), (3) and (28) of this section, a certificate of amendment of certificate of incorporation, or an amended certificate of incorporation before payment of capital, or a restated certificate of incorporation, or a certificate of validation, shall be considered as increasing the authorized capital stock of a corporation provided it involves an increase in the number of shares, or an increase in the par value of shares, or a change of shares with par value into shares without par value, or a change of shares without par value into shares with par value, or any combination of 2 or more of the above changes, and provided further that the fee computed at the rates set forth in paragraph (a)(1) of this section upon the total authorized capital stock of the corporation (including the proposed change or changes) exceeds the fee so computed upon the total authorized stock of the corporation (excluding such change or changes).

(c) The Secretary of State may issue photocopies or electronic image copies of (instruments on file), as well as (instruments, documents and other papers not on file), and for all such photocopies or electronic image copies which are not certified by the Secretary of State, a fee of $10 shall be paid for the first page and $2.00 for each additional page. ■ Notwithstanding Delaware's Freedom of Information Act (Chapter 100 of Title 29) or any other provision of law granting access to public records, the Secretary of State upon request shall issue only photocopies or electronic image copies of public records in exchange for the fees described in this section, and in no case shall the Secretary of State be required to provide copies (or access to copies) of such public records (including without limitation bulk data, digital copies of instruments, documents and other papers, databases or other information) in an electronic medium or in any form (other than photocopies or electronic image copies of such public records in exchange, as applicable, for the fees described in this section or § 2318 of Title 29 for each such record associated with a file number).

(d) No fees for the use of the State shall be charged or collected (from any corporation incorporated for the drainage and reclamation of lowlands) or (for the amendment or renewal of the charter of such corporation).

(e) The Secretary of State may in the Secretary of State's discretion permit the extension of credit for the fees required by this section upon such terms as the Secretary of State shall deem to be appropriate.

(f) The Secretary of State shall retain from the revenue collected from the fees required by this section a sum sufficient to provide at all times a fund of at least $500, but not more than $1,500, from which [then] the Secretary of State may refund any payment made pursuant to this section to the extent that it exceeds the fees required by this section. ∎ The fund shall be deposited in the financial institution which is the legal depository of state moneys to the credit of the Secretary of State and shall be disbursable on order of the Secretary of State.

(g) The Secretary of State may in the Secretary of State's discretion charge a fee of $60 for each (check received for payment of any fee or tax under Chapter 1 or Chapter 6 of this title) (that is returned due to insufficient funds or as the result of a stop payment order).

(h) In addition to those fees charged under subsections (a) and (c) of this section, there shall be collected by and paid to the Secretary of State the following:

(1) (For all services described in subsection (a) of this section that are requested to be completed within 30 minutes on the same day as the day of the request, an additional sum of up to $7,500) and (for all services described in subsections (a) and (c) of this section that are requested to be completed within 1 hour on the same day as the day of the request, an additional sum of up to $1,000) and (for all services described in subsections (a) and (c) of this section that are requested to be completed within 2 hours on the same day as the day of the request, an additional sum of up to $500); and

(2) (For all services described in subsections (a) and (c) of this section that are requested to be completed within the same day as the day of the request, an additional sum of up to $300); and

(3) (For all services described in subsections (a) and (c) of this section that are requested to be completed within a 24-hour period from the time of the request, an additional sum of up to $150).

The Secretary of State shall establish (and may from time to time alter or amend) a schedule of specific fees payable pursuant to this subsection.

(i) [Then] A domestic corporation or a foreign corporation registered to do business in this State that files with the Secretary of State any instrument or certificate, and in connection therewith, neglects, refuses or fails to pay any fee or tax under Chapter 1 or Chapter 6 of this title shall, after written demand therefor by the Secretary of State by mail addressed to such domestic corporation or foreign corporation in care of its registered agent in this State, cease to be (in good standing as a domestic corporation) or (registered as a foreign corporation) in this State on the ninetieth day following the date of mailing of such demand, **unless** such fee or tax and, if applicable, the fee provided for in subsection (g) of this section are paid in full prior to the ninetieth day following the date of mailing of such demand. ∎ A domestic corporation that has ceased to be in good standing or a foreign corporation that has ceased to be registered by reason of the neglect, refusal or failure to pay any such fee or tax shall be restored to and have the status of a domestic corporation in good standing or a foreign corporation that is registered in this State upon the payment of (the fee or tax which such domestic corporation or foreign corporation neglected, refused or failed to pay) together with (the fee provided for in subsection (g) of this section, if applicable). ■ [Then] The Secretary of State shall not accept for filing any instrument authorized to be filed with the Secretary of State under this title in respect of any domestic corporation that is not in good standing or any foreign corporation that has ceased to be registered by reason of the neglect, refusal or failure to pay any such fee or tax, and shall not issue any certificate of good standing with respect to such domestic corporation or foreign corporation, **unless and until** such domestic corporation or foreign corporation shall have been restored to and have the status of a domestic corporation in good standing or a foreign corporation duly registered in this State.

(j) As used in this section, the term "exempt corporation" shall have the meaning given to it in § 501(b) of this title.

§ 392. [Reserved.]

§ 393. Rights, liabilities and duties under prior statutes.

All rights, privileges and immunities vested or accrued by and under any laws enacted prior to the adoption or amendment of this chapter, all suits pending, all rights of action conferred, and all duties, restrictions, liabilities and penalties imposed or required by and under laws enacted prior to the adoption or amendment of this chapter, shall not be impaired, diminished or affected by this chapter.

§ 394. Reserved power of State to amend or repeal chapter; chapter part of corporation's charter or certificate of incorporation.

This chapter may be amended or repealed, at the pleasure of the General Assembly, but any amendment or repeal shall not take away or impair any remedy under this chapter against any corporation or its officers for any liability which shall have been previously incurred. ■ This chapter and all amendments thereof shall be a part of the charter or certificate of incorporation of every corporation ◂except so far as the same are inapplicable and inappropriate to the objects of the corporation.▸

§ 395. Corporations using "trust" in name, advertisements and otherwise; restrictions; violations and penalties; exceptions.

(a) ◂Except as provided below in subsection (d) of this section▸, every corporation of this State using the word "trust" as part of its name, ◂except a corporation regulated under the Bank Holding Company Act of 1956, 12 U.S.C. § 1841 et seq., or § 10 of the Home Owners' Loan Act, 12 U.S.C. § 1467a et seq., as those statutes shall from time to time be amended▸, shall be under the supervision of the State Bank Commissioner of this State and shall make not less than 2 reports during each year to the Commissioner, (according to the form which shall be prescribed by the Commissioner), (verified by the oaths or affirmations of the president or vice-president, and the treasurer or secretary of the corporation), and (attested by the signatures of at least 3 directors).

(b) ◂Except as provided below in subsection (d) of this section▸, no corporation of this State shall use the word "trust" as part of its name, ◂except a corporation reporting to and under the supervision of the State Bank Commissioner of this State or a corporation regulated under the Bank Holding Company Act of 1956, 12 U.S.C. § 1841 et seq., or § 10 of the Home Owners' Loan Act, 12 U.S.C. § 1467a et seq., as those statutes shall from time to time be amended▶. ■ [Then] ◀Except as provided below in subsection (d) of this section▶, the name of any such corporation shall not be amended so as to include the word "trust" unless such corporation shall report to and be under the supervision of the Commissioner, or unless it is regulated under the Bank Holding Company Act of 1956 or the Savings and Loan Holding Company Act.

(c) No corporation of this State, ◀except corporations reporting to and under the supervision of the State Bank Commissioner of this State or corporations regulated under the Bank Holding Company Act of 1956, 12 U.S.C. § 1841 et seq., or § 10 of the Home Owners' Loan Act, 12 U.S.C. § 1467a et seq., as those statutes shall from time to time be amended▶, shall advertise or put forth any sign as a trust company, or in any way solicit or receive deposits or transact business as a trust company.

(d) The requirements and restrictions set forth above in subsections (a) and (b) of this section shall not apply to, and shall not be construed to prevent the use of the word "trust" as part of the name of, a corporation ◀that is not subject to the supervision of the State Bank Commissioner of this State▶ and ◀that is not regulated under the Bank Holding Company Act of 1956, 12 U.S.C. § 1841 et seq., or § 10 of the Home Owners' Loan Act, 12 U.S.C. § 1467a et seq.▶, where use of the word "trust" as part of such corporation's name clearly:

(1) Does not refer to a trust business;

(2) Is not likely to mislead the public into believing that the nature of the business of the corporation includes activities ◀that fall under the supervision of the State Bank Commissioner of this State▶ or ◀that are regulated under the Bank Holding Company Act of 1956, 12 U.S.C. § 1841 et seq., or § 10 of the Home Owners' Loan Act, 12 U.S.C. § 1467a et seq.▶; and

(3) Will not otherwise lead to a pattern and practice of abuse that might cause harm to the interests of the public or the State, as determined by the Director of the Division of Corporations and the State Bank Commissioner.

§ 396. Publication of chapter by Secretary of State; distribution.

The Secretary of State may have printed, from time to time as the Secretary of State deems necessary, pamphlet copies of this chapter, and the Secretary of State shall dispose of the copies to persons and corporations desiring the same for a sum not exceeding the cost of printing. ■ The money received from the sale of the copies shall be disposed of as are other fees of the office of the Secretary of State. ■ Nothing in this section shall prevent the free distribution of single pamphlet copies of this chapter by the Secretary of State, for the printing of which provision is made from time to time by joint resolution of the General Assembly.

§ 397. Penalty for unauthorized publication of chapter.

Whoever prints or publishes this chapter without the authority of the Secretary of State of this State, shall be fined not more than $500 or imprisoned not more than 3 months, or both.

§ 398. Short title.

This chapter shall be known and may be identified and referred to as the "General Corporation Law of the State of Delaware."

◆

Made in the USA
San Bernardino, CA
11 July 2020